# A CHRONICLE OF
# OLD MUSKEGO

*The Diary of Søren Bache, 1839–1847*

*Translated and Edited by*
CLARENCE A. CLAUSEN
*and* ANDREAS ELVIKEN

NORWEGIAN-AMERICAN HISTORICAL ASSOCIATION
NORTHFIELD, MINNESOTA
1951

# *Preface*

FEW IMMIGRANT settlements — and none in Norwegian-American annals — have provoked more historical interest than "Old Muskego" in southeastern Wisconsin, yet the basic record of that germinal colony has not been available hitherto in translation. This record — the diary of Søren Bache, 1839–1847 — is now published for the first time in English.

Here is a contemporary document, with dated entries, by a man who not only was on the scene but occupied a leading role in the Muskego community. His diary is, in the main, a faithful record of first-hand observation and experience — a genuine "historical source."

By no stretch of the imagination can this source be called a work of art. Bache's writing is not distinguished by wit or urbanity — it is not marked by any particular depth of reflection. Many of the entries are humdrum, a mirroring of everyday interests and everyday affairs. Like Everyman, Bache finds the weather a subject of perennial interest. And, good weather or bad, he is a wanderer who enjoys packing up and starting off on journeys, here, there, and everywhere. These travels he details with insistence and patience, if not with searching perception of the meanings of the country and culture he observes.

An alert reader will have no difficulty in indicting Bache for sins both of omission and of commission. Many of the details of immigrant transition which he was in an excellent position to observe go unnoticed; and on not a few subjects that are noted, he fails to give much specific illumination — in part perhaps because he could be a trifle pompous and opinionated, in part because he naturally took for granted many things the modern reader would be glad to see discussed. But historians can neither remake the persons nor rewrite the records of the past, and it is vain to waste tears on what Bache did not do or did inadequately from our point of view. The important thing is that this is Bache's diary. This is his own record. And it has value for the reader. After going through it — more than a century after Bache wrote it — he will have fresh impressions of what the second discovery of America meant to millions of everyday Europeans. He will have a sharper realization of the human factors in pioneering and of the actualities of frontier life. And he will have added something to his understanding of the shaping of midwestern America in its foundation period.

Old Muskego, famous as a "mother colony" in the story of Norwegian immigrant settlement, lives in Bache's pages, not as a spot of romance and legend, but as a real place — a farming region — where real people worked, suffered from want and disease, organized their social and religious life, and seemingly enjoyed clashes of stubborn wills, ideas, and purposes.

Søren Bache himself is revealed as a genuine person. He profoundly distrusted the pioneer pastors who attempted to bring "order" into a somewhat confused religious situation. He was a man of comparative wealth who handled his money with shrewd care. He was an enthusiastic promoter who, though he ultimately returned to his native country, was impressed by American opportunity and democratic promise. He was a traveler and observer who realized that Muskego was not all America, though his own American world was definitely centered in Muskego.

Bache was endlessly curious about the pageant of America in the 1840s. He crossed and re-crossed the Atlantic, visited New York and Washington, climbed the Bunker Hill Monument, built a home in an ancient Indian mound, wandered about in the pioneer Wisconsin settlements, celebrated a Fourth of July in the infant city of Madison, took an interest in politics and in the War with Mexico, helped to launch the pioneer Norwegian newspaper in America, quarreled with and grumbled about the "papistry" of pioneer Lutheran clergymen, thumbed over almanacs and gazeteers for information about the many states he visited, walked rough country roads, had a look at Niagara Falls, set forth theories about disease in the frontier communities, took note of Joseph Smith and the Mormons, and in general tossed into his diary, or "Memorandum," as he calls it, odd bits of information that he picked up from whatever source. Thus his record is both a diary and a collection of miscellaneous memoranda.

The chronicle, written in fine script, was difficult both to transcribe and to translate, and much time has elapsed since the initial transcription was made. The Association owes a debt of gratitude to Professor Clarence A. Clausen and the late Professor Andreas Elviken, who labored long and hard to reduce the mass of Bache's "Memorandum" to coherent and understandable form. In the later stages of the work Professor Clausen reworked the transcription and the translation and also penned the historical introduction. He divided the text into chapters and supplied titles for them, and he prepared the detailed annotations. The Association owes much also to the late Professor M. O. Wee of Luther Theological Seminary, St. Paul, Minnesota, who was instrumental in bringing the diary to public attention by publishing the Norwegian text in the magazine *Norsk Ungdom*. Similarly the Association is indebted to Marie Bache, a daughter of the diarist, who supplied Professor Wee with very informing biographical sketches of Tollef Bache and his son Søren and a copy of the diary.

In preparing the present English text, Dr. Clausen has not felt it advisable to include certain materials that Bache obviously copied from manuals and other sources that fell into his hands. Wherever material is omitted, its nature is explained in a footnote or a brief summary in the text itself. Readers who wish to consult the complete text in Norwegian may communicate with the Norwegian-American Historical Association in Northfield, Minnesota, where both the original and a transcription are deposited. Some ninety pages of the original — an old bound notebook — have been torn out, but the missing pages are from the section

vii

postdating Bache's American experiences. The fine handwriting of the notebook is uniform script, and the entries, in ink, evidently have been copied from the original notes and records of Bache, but we do not know definitely when this was done.

University of Minnesota                    Theodore C. Blegen
Minneapolis

# Introduction

NORWEGIANS were tremendously interested in the United States in the 1840s and 50s, for the "America fever" was spreading its contagion into practically every valley, hamlet, and city in the country. To satisfy this interest and curiosity a remarkable number of articles, pamphlets, and "America books" poured from the presses. "In the early fifties a newspaper asserted that the 'North American Free States' were that part of the world the geographical and statistical conditions of which were most investigated and studied by Norwegians – both by prospective emigrants and by those remaining at home." [1]

It is possible that Søren Bache, who spent the years 1839–47 on the Wisconsin frontier, also intended to publish a book about America and his experiences there. Several indications to this effect are found in his diary, which was discovered some years ago by Professor M. O. Wee, of Luther Theological Seminary, St. Paul, during a visit to Norway. But if Bache had any such dreams, they were not fulfilled. Aside from a somewhat abridged version of the original that appeared in a Norwegian-American periodical,[2] Søren Bache's "Memorandum" – as he called it – has not previously been made available to the public.

Søren Bache was born in Drammen, Norway, on March 22, 1814. His father, Tollef Bache, was a gifted man who early in life came under the influence of the famous religious leader, Hans

[1] Theodore C. Blegen, *Norwegian Migration to America, 1825–1860*, 239 (Northfield, 1931). Interesting analyses of the "America books" which appeared in Norway during this period can be found in Blegen's volume just cited, Chapter XI, and in Ingrid Semmingsen, *Veien Mot Vest, Utvandringen Fra Norge Til Amerika, 1825–1865*, 179–215 (Oslo, 1942).

[2] "Søren Bache's dagboksoptegnelser under sit ophold i Amerika," *Norsk Ungdom* (Minneapolis) beginning with the December 1927 issue. The diary was presented to St. Olaf College and is now in the archives of the Norwegian-American Historical Association in the St. Olaf College library at Northfield, Minnesota.

Nielsen Hauge,[3] and in time became one of the leading Haugeans in that part of the country. But Hauge's influence on Bache was not confined to religion. Hauge was a very practical man who reasoned that his opponents, "the worldly-minded," had secured power in society by applying themselves to "the most useful or most profitable activities, such as trade, factories, or other large establishments." [4] Part of his plan was to make his followers independent by increasing their economic strength; and it was upon his advice that Tollef Bache in 1803 moved to Drammen to found a flourishing lumber company and eventually engage in various other business enterprises, such as banking and shipping.

Tollef Bache's private life, however, flowed less smoothly. His

[3] Hans Nielsen Hauge, 1771–1824, was of peasant stock and had little formal education. As a youth he was deeply influenced by mystical and pietistic writings. In 1796 he opened a vigorous campaign against the "dead orthodoxy and nerveless rationalism" of the Norwegian State Church, but he never seceded from that institution. During the next eight years he visited practically every part of the country, preaching primarily to rural audiences. To them he became not only a religious leader but also a champion who gave voice to the latent opposition to Norwegian officialdom, with which he was practically always in conflict. In 1804 he was imprisoned, and when released ten years later he was broken in health and fortune. He resumed his religious work but in a much quieter spirit. He had numerous energetic followers, however. Through them and his writings he exerted profound influence upon the religious life of Norway and the Norwegian settlements in America. There is a rich literature about Hauge in Norwegian. English accounts of his life and work are found in M. O. Wee, *Haugeanism: A Brief Sketch of the Movement and Some of Its Chief Exponents* (St. Paul, 1919); Wilhelm Pettersen, *The Light in the Prison Window: The Life Story of Hans Nielsen Hauge* (Minneapolis, 1921); Knut Gjerset, *A History of the Norwegian People*, 2:403 (New York, 1915); J. M. Rohne, *Norwegian-American Lutheranism up to 1872*, 9–17 (New York, 1926). Rohne's work discusses fully the impact of Haugeanism upon Norwegian-American religious life up to 1872. The influence of Haugeanism upon the emigration movement is discussed in Blegen, *Norwegian Migration, 1825–1860*, 160–63.

[4] Brief biographical sketches of Tollef Bache and Søren Bache are given by Marie Bache in the December 1927 issue of *Norsk Ungdom*. These sketches are reprinted in *Numedalslagets Aarbok*, no. 14, 92–97, (1928). A sketch of Tollef Bache's life by Andreas Brandrud is found in *Norsk Biografisk Leksikon*, 1:338 (Kristiania, 1923). An autobiographical sketch of Tollef Bache, *En del av T. O. Baches levnetslöp*, was published in Drammen in 1849, the year after his death.

wife did not share his Haugean interests and is said to have resented the many religious meetings he held in their home. Because of this incompatibility they were divorced; and some time later he entered into a second marriage. These developments shocked the Haugean circles, and a bitter "Bache strife" ensued, as a result of which he was read out of the society. Probably because of this break with his former companions Bache left Drammen in 1828 and moved to his near-by farm, Store Walle. He continued to take an interest in his business, however, and also remained loyal to the memory of Hans Nielsen Hauge. He even published a life of the great leader to defend him and his teachings against unjust criticism.

By his first wife Tollef Bache had five children, four sons and one daughter. The latter married Erik Olsen, a merchant in Drammen. The two oldest sons, Nils and Tollef, were educated in England and later engaged in business in their home town. The third son, Ole, was also sent to England, but while there he developed a mental disease from which he never quite recovered. His father established him on a farm. The fourth son, Søren, left for America in 1839.

The question why the son of a wealthy family should embark upon such a problematic venture as emigration to America has aroused some speculation. It has been suggested that Tollef Bache, who supplied the funds for his son's travels and land purchases, had hopes of establishing a colony of Haugeans in the New World where they would be free from state-church interference. Many Haugeans from the Drammen district did, indeed, follow Søren Bache to America in the next few years, but there is no evidence either in the diary or any other contemporary source to indicate that the elder Bache planned to found an American refuge for his fellow believers. It has also been stated that Søren Bache was "an impractical dreamer, so full of all sorts of whims and notions that many believed there was something wrong with his head." His father therefore — so runs the account — decided to send him to America, hoping that "the new circumstances over there would awaken his faculties and desire for work. He provided him liberally with money and sent a shrewd, reliable old office worker named Johannes Johannesen [Johansen] along as companion."[5] While it may be unjust to characterize Søren Bache as an "impractical dreamer," it nevertheless is true that he emerges from his own diary as a man who was more interested in travel and unusual experiences than in the practical, everyday aspects of life. And when he returned to Norway he evidently had a tendency to live beyond his income. It is therefore possible that the shrewd father detected an element of weakness in Søren's make-up and hence encouraged him to go to America, hoping that contact with the hard facts of pioneer life would endow him with the necessary realism. If the father had any such schemes, we are safe in assuming that the son did not need much urging, because he had obviously been touched by the "America fever." He says himself that he had read various reports which aroused his desire to emigrate, and years later his daughter wrote that "he could not think of settling down without first having been around in the world. The object of his dreams was America, about which he had read so many romantic accounts. But he did not get his father's permission to leave until he had become a full-grown man of twenty-five years."

The Muskego settlement some twenty miles from Milwaukee, where Søren Bache bought land and began his experiences as a frontier farmer in 1840, had been founded the previous year by a group of immigrants from Telemark and Stavanger.[6] It is one of the most famous settlements in Norwegian immigrant history, but its repute does not rest upon size and prosperity. In these

[5] H. R. Holand, "Muskego," *Symra*, 3:190 (Decorah, 1907).

[6] Earlier than Muskego the following Norwegian settlements had been founded: (1) Kendall, Orleans County, New York, 1825. (2) Fox River, La Salle County, Illinois, 1834. (3) Beaver Creek, Iroquois County, Illinois, 1836. (4) Shelby County, Missouri, 1837. (5) Jefferson Prairie, Rock County, Wisconsin, 1838. (6) Rock Prairie (Luther Valley), Rock County, Wisconsin, 1838. Beginning with 1836 Norwegians had also settled in Chicago.

respects it was outstripped by many settlements in the Middle West. In fact, most prospectors warned against it as a region difficult to clear because of dense forests and unhealthful because of its many lakes and large swamps. Truly Muskego did suffer more than its share of malaria during the first dozen years of its history. The settlement earned its distinction largely because of the outstanding leadership of a few men who lived there during the 1840s — men like Even Heg, Johansen, Pastor C. L. Clausen, Pastor J. W. C. Dietrichson, and Bache himself, who all appear in the diary. As a result of the initiative of these men, Muskego can boast a number of "firsts" in Norwegian-American history: there was organized the first Norwegian Lutheran congregation in America, there was built the first Norwegian church in the United States, and there was unleashed the first fury of those disputes which rent Norwegian-American Lutheranism through following generations; there was published the first strictly Norwegian newspaper in America, there appeared the progenitor of all Norwegian-American politicians, and there, it is claimed, the Norwegian-Americans made their first fumbling attempts to meet the educational needs of their new surroundings; finally it may be mentioned that Muskego fostered Hans C. Heg, one of the first Norwegian-Americans to win fame in American military annals. During the formative years of the Middle West, Muskego also became well known because it served as a mother colony of other settlements springing up on new frontiers. We learn from the diary, for instance, that (in heavy immigrant years like 1843) wagonload after wagonload of newcomers who had landed in Milwaukee arrived for longer or shorter stops in Muskego. Many of these immigrants were too ill or too poor to proceed farther for the time being. As best they could, the people of the settlement therefore had to give of their hospitality. These overcrowded conditions naturally increased the ravages of the dread malaria, and many an immigrant who had set his face hopefully toward the West reached his journey's end in "Old Muskego."

Søren Bache was an enthusiastic promoter of the Muskego settlement. "I believe time will show that this region is equal to, if not better than, the other places where Norwegians have settled," he says. "Here we have woods and good well water almost everywhere while our meadows yield an abundance of hay, advantages which are usually lacking in other regions." He bristled at the unfavorable comments made by many observers and dismissed them with the opinion that they had little knowledge of soils. In 1845 he was happy to remark that other settlements had been ravaged more severely by malaria than his own district, and by 1846 he believed that Muskego had regained the favorable reputation it had earlier enjoyed. Bache took a lively interest in the affairs of the settlement. He fought fiercely against the alleged papistry of the clergymen, Clausen and Dietrichson. He has been variously described as the banker and the philanthropist of the settlement. As the son of a wealthy father, he commanded the wherewithal to lend helping sums on occasion to neighbors in need. But judging by the transactions of this nature recorded in the diary, he must be numbered among those who "lend to them of whom ye hope to receive" rather than among those who lend, "hoping for nothing again." Indeed, he speaks rather harshly of men who are tender-hearted enough to lend unto others until they fall into difficulties themselves.

We do not know how Bache's material fortunes fared at Muskego. He gives us few details about business affairs or the work-a-day life of the settlement—and here we touch on the main weakness of the diary as a historical document. He dismisses practically the whole year of 1841 with the remark that he stayed at home "and helped with such improvements as are necessary to put new land under cultivation. Nothing remarkable or worthy of recording happened during this long period." The present-day reader would gladly exchange some of his travel accounts for information about "such improvements as are necessary to put new lands under cultivation." Information of this nature is not entirely

SØREN BACHE

[Original photograph in the possession of the Norwegian-American
Historical Association, Northfield, Minnesota]

lacking, but it is too meager to give a full picture of the life, the work, and the progress of the pioneer community. After Johansen's death, Bache says that the accounts covering their joint undertakings will soon be settled. "At last we shall learn how our affairs have prospered in this land which for decades has been a haven for Europeans seeking refuge from their harsh lot in the Old World," but he does not confide any of this information to his diary. In the early years he bought a considerable amount of land, some of which was subdivided and sold to later comers. According to reports, he left an investment of six thousand dollars in Muskego land, most of which he never regained, presumably because of mismanagement on the part of his friend J. D. Reymert, who was entrusted with the care of his American property.[7]

Bache believed in America as a land of freedom and opportunity, but he was by no means an unrestrained booster, as we see both from his diary and letters.[8] He urged no one to emigrate. This was a question, he said, which every man had to settle for himself, and he warned that people with overly rosy dreams about America were doomed to disappointment if they emigrated. On one occasion, at least, he asked specifically that his letter should not be used as propaganda material. But he did assure those who asked him that America offered far better opportunities for winning a good livelihood than Norway, provided one were willing to put his brains and brawn to the task. Bache emphasized the need of mastering the language of the country in order to get ahead in America and himself acted on this conviction. He resolutely set about learning English and soon was able to carry on both friendly chats and more serious business negotiations with the native Americans. He got along well with the "Yankees," it

[7] R. B. Anderson, *The First Chapter of Norwegian Immigration (1820–1840), its Causes and Results*, 294 (Madison, 1896).

[8] Several letters by Bache, written in reply to prospective emigrants, were affixed to the original diary. They have been translated and edited by C. A. Clausen, *Norwegian-American Studies and Records*, 15:77–84 (Northfield, 1949).

seems, and admired them for their friendliness, democratic ways, and industry. Bache promptly entered into the spirit of American politics, both local and national. In the party conflicts of the day he favored the Whigs and attacked the Democrats for diverting funds — as he claimed — from internal improvement in the Middle West to the extension of territory for the southern slaveocracy. In short, he seems to have acclimated himself readily to the American atmosphere. Apparently he escaped almost entirely those deep emotional crises which many immigrants passed through in the course of adapting themselves to the ways and scenes of their new surroundings. He spoke sarcastically of those who could not find rest until they had returned to their native land: "Such people had better return to the old country and when they have nothing else to do they can sit and twiddle their fingers and take comfort in the fact that they have at least been across the Atlantic and seen the land of the immigrants."

Why, then, did Bache himself join the renegades and return to the old country? One explanation frequently given is stated as follows by Anderson.[9] "He and his friend Rev. C. L. Clausen were out hunting one day and stopped at the house of a Norwegian settler. While Søren Bache was making some examination of the trigger his gun accidentally discharged and killed the housewife. . . . It made the husband almost distracted and Søren Bache was in danger of losing his reason. . . . It is believed that this accident was the main reason why Bache returned to Norway in 1845. He wanted to get away from the scene of his great misfortune." H. R. Holand[10] adds that this mishap occurred some time before Johansen's death early in February 1846. Several factors make this explanation untenable. In the first place, it will be noticed that Anderson places Bache's return to Norway in 1845, but actually he did not leave until in September 1847. Hence he must have endured the scene of his misfortune for at least a year or two. Furthermore, there is nothing in the diary to indicate that

[9] Anderson, *Norwegian Immigration*, 281.
[10] Holand, "Muskego," *Symra*, 193.

Bache was practically "out of his mind with sorrow and tribulation," to quote Holand, during this period. He does not appear to have been waging a Jacob's battle. His life shows all the signs of normality: he managed his farm, carried on business transactions, helped organize a newspaper, visited his friends as formerly, chatted cheerfully with acquaintances, took a cup of cheer when offered, and continued to shoot critical arrows at "his friend Rev. Clausen" at every opportunity. A more plausible reason is offered by his daughter. According to her, Søren Bache returned to Norway because of his father's serious illness. A reader of the diary gets the impression that Bache was more closely attached to his father than to any other person, for he showed frequent concern about the latter's welfare. It was natural that he should return when he learned that his father, then seventy-seven years old, had little chance of surviving. Søren Bache reached home in November, and his father died the following January. The daughter states that it was undoubtedly his intention to return to America, since he sold neither his land nor his other property in Wisconsin.[11] On the deathbed, however, his father prevailed on him to remain permanently in Norway.

It is natural to assume that, as one inducement to remain in Norway, Søren would have been named master of Store Walle since his brothers were already established in business. This did not happen; Tollef Bache had already deeded the farm to a son-in-law of his second wife, "a stern and imperious woman." Søren had his heart set on farming, however, and enrolled, the following fall, as a student in the well-known Norwegian agricultural school conducted by Jan Adolph Budde. It must have delighted Budde to have a recaptured "American" in his classes, because he fought emigration as vigorously as he championed agricultural reform.[12]

---

[11] The diary recounts that Søren Bache paid a long visit to his home in Norway during part of the years 1842 and 1843.

[12] Both at the school and in writing Budde urged the adoption of modern farming methods. In a pamphlet *Af et Brev om Amerika* (Stavanger,

In spite of his agricultural schooling, Søren Bache evidently did not make a success of farming. From his daughter's account it would appear that his fortunes declined gradually. She indicates that frugality was not one of his virtues. In the spring of 1850 he bought Korsvalle, a large farm with good buildings, near Store Walle. "Since the inheritance left him by his father gave him a good income besides the proceeds from the farm, he entertained very freely at Korsvalle." We are given no further details about his life there, but in 1879 "he found it advisable to sell Korsvalle, the management of which became too expensive for him, and he felt that he would get along better with a smaller farm." He then bought Tokerud in Bärum, a place noted for its beautiful location. As the buildings there were not satisfactory, he immediately built a new house — probably too large and costly a house, because we are told that he now had "more space than necessary" and that his wife opened a summer hotel "to help along with the finances." But this venture did not succeed either. Hence he sold Tokerud in 1889 and moved temporarily to the capital. There his robust health broke down, and he also lost his eyesight. He nevertheless bought a new place, Marienborg in Botne near Holmestrand, a beautiful place he remembered from earlier years. There he no doubt hoped to live quietly in retirement, but he died in October 1890, shortly after he had taken possession of his new home.

The spring he bought Korsvalle, Søren Bache married Gunhild Marie Andersdatter, a girl who had grown up in his childhood home. They had many children, most of whom died young.

1850), Budde gave expression to his views on emigration. He painted a gloomy picture of health conditions in America and not too bright a one of the economic possibilities there. He maintained that Norway offered ample opportunities to the rural classes if they would only apply themselves more industriously and adopt scientific agricultural methods. Budde's pamphlet has been translated by Miss Sophie Böe and published with an introduction by Theodore C. Blegen under the title "Emigration as Viewed by a Norwegian Student of Agriculture in 1850," *Studies and Records,* 3:43–57. An analysis of the pamphlet is found in Blegen, *Norwegian Migration, 1825–1860,* 261–65.

His daughter gives the following interesting characterization of Søren Bache, one which agrees with the impression we get from his diary. "He was always in good humor, though he might become a bit sharp when things did not move as quickly as he wished. He took long walks and spent as much time as possible in the open. He would sit for long periods and dream, presumably about the journeys he had desired to make. Travel interested him greatly, and travel accounts, both from the East and from the West, were his favorite reading. America he loved and admired to the day of his death and he never wearied of discussing news from there whenever he had listeners. . . ."

\* \* \*

The translation of the Bache Diary was undertaken at the suggestion of Dean Theodore C. Blegen. He has followed our work with much interest and has given valuable advice out of his wide experience as translator, editor, and author. Besides preparing the index, Mrs. Zephyra Shepherd has gone through the manuscript and helped make the way smoother for the prospective readers. My wife, Marian Baker Clausen, has shared in our labor from the first page to the last and in countless ways made our task easier. I am certain that Professor Elviken would have joined me in acknowledging our deep indebtedness to these persons.

Clarence A. Clausen

# Table of Contents

A *Chronicle of Old Muskego*

# 1. To the Promised Land

In RECENT YEARS emigrants from various parts of Norway have gone to America, far in the West, seeking to improve their station in life. They have sent accounts back to friends and relatives telling of their fortunes and of conditions in the new land; but since opinions vary widely and people frequently write to further their own interests, it is natural that many conflicting reports have appeared. Furthermore, most of the emigrants belong to the least educated classes, and consequently no thorough and reliable accounts have been received from them. The most satisfactory one so far is that written by a student, Ole Rynning, which aroused the desire of numerous people to seek the promised land.[1] Indeed it was this report, together with many others, that induced me to emigrate — and in the pages following is an account of my experiences.

On Friday afternoon about six o'clock on the twenty-eighth of June 1839, I parted from my parents at Store Walle in Lier and left for Drammen with Johannes Johansen, who was to share my travels. Though the distance was not more than a half mile [2] and the town — no less than my father's farm — might be called my home, I must begin at the beginning, since minor happenings play their part in everything. Now I was to leave my parents for the first time, and it was uncertain whether I should ever see them again, both of them being well advanced in years.

[1] Ole Rynning is one of the outstanding figures in Norwegian immigrant history. He came to America in 1837, and the following year his *Sandfærdig Beretning om Amerika*, referred to above, was published in Oslo. It gave clear, succinct answers to the questions which most commonly puzzled the prospective immigrants. This pamphlet has been translated and edited by Theodore C. Blegen under the title *Ole Rynning's True Account of America* (Northfield, 1926). A full account of Ole Rynning's activities is in Blegen, *Norwegian Migration, 1825–1860*, 81–110.

[2] This refers to a Norwegian mile, which is equal to about seven English miles.

3

*June 20* [*1839*]. This morning at eight o'clock we left my brother's farm on Landfaldøren and went down the river in a boat accompanied by my brother Niels and my brother-in-law E. Olsen (who with his family has lived there since the great fire last fall). When we were just off Hauvestul farm, my other brother rowed alongside us and followed us down to the customhouse where the steamship *Collett* of Drammen was anchored. We went on board the ship, and after a short while it moved up the river to the bridge where it stopped and took on more passengers. Here my two brothers and brother-in-law left us; indeed, it was here that I saw them for the last time, not knowing whether we should ever meet again. Toward noon we arrived at Moss after a pleasant little voyage with the weather clear and calm. After we had taken our luggage ashore and stored it in the customhouse, we took lodgings at the home of a dyer named Smaaland, where we stayed until the next morning.

*June 30*. Today, Sunday morning, Smaaland did us the courtesy of getting us a carriage in which, accompanied by him and his wife, we went out to Rygge to see Søren Roen before we left Norway. Smaaland went home in the evening, while we stayed until Monday afternoon.

*July 2*. Today, Tuesday, the steamship from Christiania, by which we were to leave the country, was expected, and after we had made ready and got our tickets, we remained at the dock waiting for it. About twelve o'clock the ship arrived, and we had to hurry aboard with Smaaland, who, on taking leave, extended his good wishes for the voyage. Some fifteen minutes later we left Moss and, after a stop of about an hour at the saltworks, sailed for Gothenburg at four in the afternoon, reaching our destination at eight the next morning.[3] The weather was favorable, and no one was seasick during the trip.

*July 3*. When our luggage had been inspected by the customs

[3] The reference here is undoubtedly to the large saltworks which at that time were located at Vallø (present Valløy), a short distance southeast of Tønsberg.

officials, we took it ashore and were allowed to store it at the place where emigrants to America usually have their quarters. On landing we learned that we could not leave for some time, and I decided to go to Copenhagen with the boat on which we had arrived. At two o'clock in the afternoon we began the voyage along the Swedish coast and continued on our way, still enjoying beautiful weather.

*July 4.* We passed between Helsingborg on the Swedish and Helsingör on the Danish shore. Here the sound is at its narrowest, and the scenery is beautiful, particularly as you look out over Zealand. We arrived at Copenhagen about noon. Since I could not stay here very long, I roamed about the city seeing as many of the sights as the short time would allow.

*July 5.* I used this day also as fully as possible in sight-seeing. It was very windy with a strong breeze from the north. In order to be back in Gothenburg on time, I left at four o'clock in the afternoon, taking the same boat that I had come down on. After we passed Helsingör the wind was stronger than it was when we came up the sound.

*July 6.* The wind howled all last night. It was unpleasant to travel in such weather, and many were queasy. Although I was unaccustomed to the sea I was not sick and felt as well as if the weather had been fine. I ate and drank as usual and believed that I would be able to stand the sea very well, a guess that later was confirmed. We were due at Gothenburg at eight in the morning but did not dock until two in the afternoon. When I reached my lodgings, near the landing place, I learned from my companion that we had to remain there about eight days more before we could start for America, so we had a good opportunity to become acquainted with things of interest in the city. The people struck me as being rather extravagantly polite, which I suppose is a national characteristic of the Swedes. During our stay here, I often took short trips into the country that were most enjoyable since we generally had beautiful weather.

*July 7.* As this was Sunday we went to church both in the morning and in the afternoon but did not understand the Swedish sermons very well.

*July 15.* Finally the day came when we were to start on a strange, long voyage, bound for a remote country approachable only by sea. On the thirteenth we had taken all our luggage on board, and yesterday, the fourteenth, we were to have weighed anchor, but as there was no wind we had to lie at our moorings. For that reason we were ashore most of the time yesterday. At two o'clock this morning we left the harbor with a light breeze. The ship on which we traveled was of fine American construction, two years old, the *Skogmand*, under Captain E. Rundberg, of Gothenburg. At eleven o'clock we passed Skagen in North Jutland.

*July 16.* At eight o'clock in the morning we saw Oxe Light near Christiansand. We followed the coast some distance out beyond Lindesnes where the fatherland at last vanished from sight and we saw nothing but sea and sky.

*July 19.* Friday evening we passed the Orkney Islands.

*August 14.* We reached Newfoundland.

*August 29.* This afternoon at four o'clock we ran into a hurricane from the northeast which lasted until four the next morning. The mate then sighted land. Only slight damage had been done.

*September 2.* Yesterday, Sunday, after seven weeks at sea we caught our first view of the New World. The weather was fine both yesterday and today. About noon we cast anchor in the harbor of Newport in the state of Rhode Island. Here the captain was to learn whether the ship should be unloaded in this port or in Boston farther to the north. When we went ashore he found that it was to be at the latter place. We passengers, fifteen in all, decided to go ashore and not continue on to Boston, because the trip would then be longer and more expensive, as we intended to go inland from New York. We tidied ourselves and got our luggage ashore. Meanwhile, a steamship had arrived from Providence bound for New York, and we took our luggage aboard and at eight o'clock in the evening continued the voyage down Long Island Sound. When we left, the captain bade us a friendly good-by. Since everything here happened in such a hurry, we had no opportunity to look the place over except what little we could see from the harbor. While we passed through Long Island Sound, two steamships kept side by side during the whole night. In the starlit dusk, the sound lay beautiful before us, and on each side, as we sailed along, we saw lighthouses on the islands or reefs jutting out into the water.

*September 3.* In the morning, at some distance, we sighted America's greatest commercial city, which has a beautiful location on a tongue of land between Long Island Sound and the Hudson River. On the left shore of the sound, right across from New York lay Brooklyn. We disembarked at the southern end of the city near the Castle and found lodgings close by with a German.[4] Then we took care of a little business affair which was not particularly serious since it was merely a matter of cashing a London draft drawn on a New York merchant. Now for the first time in my life I saw streets lit with gas in the evening. We spent our short stay in the city looking about as best we could.

*September 4.* After a morning of sight-seeing, we left the city about five o'clock in the afternoon by steamer for Albany, about one hundred and sixty English miles from New York.

*September 5.* In the evening we arrived at Albany. The trip took us up the Hudson River, whose shores resembled the country up the Drammen River to Hougsund, although the soil, as far as we could judge, seemed poorer. It was clearly more fertile, however, than that kind of sandy soil usually is in Norway, because we saw fields of Indian corn in luxuriant growth. The reason this kind of soil yields more in America than in Norway must be that the summers are warmer and longer here.

[4] Doubtless Bache here refers to Castle Garden.

*September 6.* We left Albany in the morning, without having had a chance to go sight-seeing, and went by train to a city called Schenectady, about sixteen miles away. This part of the journey passed rapidly and was not unpleasant. The land was of the very poorest kind known in our country. It consisted mostly of small marshes and sandy plains covered with copsewood and only such things as thrive in the poorest soil. Nevertheless, here and there we could see tilled fields and good crops of grain. In Schenectady, which was well built-up with small houses, almost all of which seemed to be new, we remained until evening and then went aboard a canal boat to continue the trip to Buffalo, about three hundred and forty miles away. We left about nine o'clock and, because of the darkness, could not see what the country was like. But whenever we were on deck we heard the ceaseless chirping of innumerable swarms of insects in the long grass on the shores of the canal. We traveled both day and night.

*September 14.* We arrived at Buffalo this morning, Saturday. The Erie Canal, which runs through New York, the most advanced of all the states, passes many large and beautiful cities. The oldest of these, although founded only fourteen or fifteen years ago, are quite as large as Drammen or Christiania. It is quite natural, therefore, that here and there were some fine and well-cultivated farms. The cleared area, however, appeared small compared with the amount of land which lay untilled on both sides of the canal and which was covered with woods containing trees, some familiar to us, some, like the cedar, unfamiliar.

At the beginning of our journey, the land along the canal was high and hilly as in many parts of Norway. The soil, however, nowhere seemed to surpass in quality that usually found in the southern part of our country. But as we went inland the country grew flatter and flatter and the soil richer but also more marshy and more densely wooded. As yet we saw none of that very good soil which we had so often heard was to be found in America. In several places near the canal we saw farmers plowing for winter

8

wheat, and this gave us an opportunity to form some idea of the quality of the soil. Everywhere lay beautiful orchards with apple, pear, and other fruit trees, all now loaded with fruit.

Because of the high and hilly nature of the country, we had to pass many locks. The town of Lockport has five double ones through which boats going up the canal pass on one side and those going down pass on the other. The height of these five locks is, I believe, approximately one hundred and fifty feet, thus giving ample opportunity for the development of water power. There were several flour mills and saw mills here, and we had a chance to inspect a couple. One of these was set up in the same manner as our gang saws, but it was larger and more strongly built. The water wheel, for instance, which was of the overshot type, was quite large and made of cast iron. This mill sawed huge oak logs which I estimated to be from sixty to seventy feet long and so thick that each log, cut simultaneously by ten blades, produced eight or nine three-inch planks.

The section of the canal through which we had to pass beyond Lockport has been blasted through solid rock for about three English miles. The height from the edge of the cliff to the water is between twenty and thirty feet. Since we had to pass through there at night we missed the pleasure of inspecting the country any further before we arrived at Buffalo this morning, from where our journey was to continue by steamboat on the lakes. Buffalo is situated at the edge of Lake Erie, the outlet of which, the Niagara River, forms the greatest waterfall in the world — Niagara Falls — about twenty-two miles from the city. On our arrival here, we found a steamer ready to leave for Chicago and so had to take our luggage on board immediately. It sailed the same morning at eleven o'clock. We traveled on this boat across Lakes Erie, St. Clair, Huron, and Michigan, a total distance of about one thousand and twenty-eight miles from Buffalo to Chicago. When we reached Milwaukee, a city founded recently on Lake Michigan in Wisconsin Territory about seventy miles north of Chicago, a Danish carpenter named Johnsen came on board our boat.[5]

*September 21.* By Saturday evening we were in Milwaukee. Johnsen told us that he had served as interpreter for some Norwegian emigrants with whom he had traveled from Gothenburg and who had arrived in Milwaukee about a fortnight earlier. Following his advice, they had bought land and had settled about twenty miles from the city. He sought to persuade us also to land here, for reasons which I shall explain in detail.

When we were about to start our journey from Schenectady, we were told by a Swede of that city that there was much sickness in Illinois and that the southern part of the state, particularly, was generally considered to have an unhealthful climate. Before leaving our home land, however, we had heard very favorable reports about the climate in Illinois from Norwegians living there, so we were not inclined to take the Swede's account too seriously. But when we came to Rochester, a man named Lars Larsen gave us much the same information and also told us that Ole Rynning and many other settlers in his district had died.[6] This depressed us greatly, especially the loss of Ole Rynning, for in him we had hoped to find a true friend possessed of much useful knowledge and helpful information about the country. I am sure that he would not have disappointed us if he had lived because he impressed all those who came in touch with him as a man of upright and unselfish character. It is related, among other things, that he sold some of his much-needed bedding to pay the fares for several of his poverty-stricken countrymen. But he was unfortunate

[5] *Author's note:* Later Johnsen died by accident on a boat which capsized as it was being rowed to a steamer. Four passengers lost their lives, Johnsen being one of them.

[6] Lars Larsen, a Quaker from Stavanger, was the leader of the first group of Norwegian immigrants to America, the "sloop folk" who arrived aboard the sloop *Restauration* in 1825. Larsen settled in Rochester, New York, where his home became a veritable immigrant station. He and his hospitable wife Martha kept open house for poor Norwegian immigrants pouring into the West. See Blegen, *Norwegian Migration, 1825–1860, passim*, and Anderson, *Norwegian Immigration (1821–1840), passim.*

in his choice of a site for a Norwegian settlement. The colony was located on a little brook called Beaver Creek,[7] about seventy miles south of Chicago and about the same distance from the Norwegian community at Fox River,[8] where most of the Norwegian immigrants had settled. The place had always been considered very unhealthful, as men of experience told him, but there had been a drought during the summer they arrived so the land appeared to be well drained and the grass was also more abundant than usual. They had more faith in what they saw than in what they were told by better-informed men, namely, that the lowness of the district made it damp and unhealthful, a statement which, to their own great misfortune, later proved true. When the rains came the next year, the land was so flooded that the only places which escaped inundation were the highest points where they had built their houses. Experience in this country is said to prove that low-lying areas, dry only in exceptional seasons, are unhealthful and partly responsible for epidemics which may become fatal. There is reason to believe that the Beaver Creek district is a

[7] The Beaver Creek settlement was founded in the late summer of 1837 by Rynning and his followers. It was practically wiped out by disease. The last Norwegian settler left in 1840.

[8] The first Norwegian settlement in the United States, the Kendall settlement in Orleans County, New York, did not attract many immigrants. The price of land was comparatively high, and the region was heavily wooded, making clearing difficult. In 1833, therefore, Cleng Peerson, the founder of the settlement, set out to explore newly opened areas in the West. He returned with enthusiastic reports about the attractions of lands which he had discovered in La Salle County, Illinois. The next year several families from Kendall accompanied him to the new region and laid the foundations of the first Norwegian settlement in the Middle West, the well-known Fox River settlement. In the following years most of the Norwegian families in Kendall moved to Fox River, and, more important, the fame of the new settlement soon spread to Norway, thus giving impetus to the real emigration movement from that country. Numerous settlers arrived in 1836, 1837, and 1838. Fox River became a "mother colony" of many new settlements springing up in neighboring regions. For accounts of this settlement see Anderson, *Norwegian Immigration, (1821–1840)*, 170–79, and Blegen, *Norwegian Migration, 1825–1860, passim.* For a discussion of the turbulent religious life of the Fox River settlement see Rohne, *Norwegian American Lutheranism up to 1872*, 34–39, 45–51.

case in point because about half of the forty settlers died before
Rynning passed away. With the exception of one family, the
survivors moved to the Norwegian settlement at Fox River last
spring, either abandoning their houses entirely or selling them for
less than the cost of construction. Likewise, the labor spent on
the land they had selected to give them a livelihood was wasted.
Rynning died about St. Michael's Day last year and is missed by
all who knew him.

These events had already been told us before we met Johnsen,
and it is natural enough that hearing them repeated by him made
us ponder which course we should take. He told us that he had
been in Chicago and had found it so unhealthful and disease-
ridden as to frighten anyone from going there. In fact the sad
state of affairs had given him good reason to persuade his companions to go back to Milwaukee and settle where the country
was considered more healthful. But as he gave us the impression
of painting dangers in rather too strong colors, we suspected that
he might have ulterior motives for trying to persuade us to stay
in Milwaukee. This opinion was subsequently confirmed when
we learned that he harvested a goodly profit by serving as interpreter for his Norwegian fellow passengers.[9] Since none of them

[9] The group mentioned in this entry as settling some twenty miles from
Milwaukee was undoubtedly the group from Telemark and Stavanger
which laid the foundations of the Muskego settlement. According to a
more colorful but less plausible story the group was induced to abandon
Illinois for Wisconsin by a clever "Yankee," not by a wily Dane. It runs
to the effect that when the group reached Milwaukee they were met by
some citizens of the aspiring town. One of them told the newcomers that
they were, of course, free to settle wherever they pleased but before choos-
ing Illinois he would advise them to take a good look at two of his companions, one of whom was in blooming health while the other was an
emaciated skeleton. "Look!" said he, "the robust man is from Wisconsin,
where there is a healthful climate and food in abundance. The sick man
is from Illinois, where people are destroyed by the burning summer heat
and die like flies from malarial fever!" This demonstration, so the story
goes, caused the immigrants to change their plans, with the result that
they settled near Lake Muskego where the lands at that time of year looked
their best. For full accounts see Anderson, *Norwegian Immigration (1821–
1840)*, 266–99, and Blegen, *Norwegian Migration, 1825–1860*, 115–18.

knew how to express themselves in English, Johnsen had become so invaluable to them that, according to reports, he refused to translate a single syllable for less than a Spanish dollar. Our conversation with him was brief, and he did not discover whether any one of us understood English, so I suppose he had hopes of making some money at our expense also. We did not quite trust his stories, and, as we had already paid our fare to Chicago and knew that Ansten Nattestad with his party had gone there before us without returning, we continued our voyage undaunted, according to the original plan.[10]

*September 22.* Sunday afternoon we arrived at Chicago where we still found most of those who had come with Nattestad, besides some forty other Norwegians who had arrived on another steamer about half an hour before us. Most of the latter came from Telemark and were the first party to leave from Gothenburg this spring; but they had the misfortune of sailing on such a poor ship that they were forced to return to England for repairs after having been far out on the Atlantic Ocean. The trip from Gothenburg to New York took them fifteen weeks, four of which spent at Falmouth repairing the ship. All these people, as well as those who came with Ansten Nattestad, were in good health. Another company, however, had arrived from Hardanger and Voss about six weeks earlier, during the most intense heat of the year. Many of them fell sick and were taken to

[10] Ansten Nattestad and his brother Ole migrated from Numedal to America in 1837, thus becoming the leaders of the great migration from the interior mountain regions of Norway. The Nattestad brothers went to the Beaver Creek settlement, but in the spring of 1838 Ansten returned to Norway for a year's visit. He brought with him the manuscripts of Rynning's book and a journal written by his brother Ole entitled *Beskrivelse over en Reise til Nord-america.* The latter was published in Drammen in 1839. An English translation by R. B. Anderson appeared in the *Wisconsin Magazine of History,* 1:178 (December 1917) under the title "Description of a Journey to North America." In the summer of 1838 Ole Nattestad moved to the Wisconsin Territory and, locating in what is now Clinton Township, Rock County, became the founder of the important Jefferson Prairie settlement.

the hospital in Chicago. Some of them died there, and with few exceptions the rest have died since — in all, fifteen or sixteen.

The sickness which caused their death was the so-called fever and ague, accompanied by a bilious fever which affects the abdomen, the back, and the head, and though often fatal, is not considered contagious. The reason this group was especially hard hit can probably be found in the fact that they left earlier than the rest of us, were thus exposed to greater cold during the voyage, and then landed during the most intense summer heat, which was worse this year than usual. Naturally this sudden change of temperature would have a bad effect upon their health. Furthermore, immediately after their arrival many of them started hard work, especially on the canals, work which in many regions is regarded as very unhealthful during the hot season.

On the morning of the day we landed, Ansten Nattestad, with a few of his company, had set off to visit his brother Ole, who last summer moved from Illinois to a district in Wisconsin Territory called Jefferson Prairie. With a few exceptions, the rest of his company followed him several days later. On our arrival in Chicago, we met a man by the name of Kristen Olsen who was one of the older Norwegian settlers in the Fox River area.[11] Partly because of this meeting we decided to call on our countrymen in that settlement and get an impression of the place.

*September 25.* Wednesday morning, accordingly, we left Chicago. This gave us our first view of the vast Illinois prairie. But we saw only a small part of it because this lap of our journey turned out to be merely a two days' drive with horses. Here in the western states oxen are also used for transport, perhaps more frequently than horses, since they are commonly used on the farm, two oxen costing no more than one horse.

*September 26.* This evening we arrived at Kristen Olsen's house

[11] This is probably Christian Olson, who "came from Norway in 1829 and settled in Kendall, New York. After living there eight years he moved to LaSalle County, Illinois, in 1837, and died there in 1858." Anderson, *Norwegian Immigration (1821–1840)*, 133.

in the Norwegian settlement at Fox River, about sixty or seventy miles southwest of Chicago. Besides most of those who had been in our company from Gothenburg, Knud Watnebrønd with his wife and children came with us. The prairies we crossed were still covered with green grass and many varieties of flowers in full bloom. The plains with their patches of woodland appearing in the distance after long hours of travel resembled the sea where, once the land has faded away, there is nothing but sky and water except for occasional islands upon the rim of the horizon, like groves upon the plains. According to our observation, the soil of this prairie really measures up to the high expectations raised by the accounts of Rynning and others. Without manure and with scarcely half the labor we would give to fields at home, it yields abundant crops of wheat, rye, barley, oats, melons, cabbage, kohlrabi, and other vegetables.

When we arrived at the Norwegian settlement, we found considerable sickness, particularly among those who had come during the last two or three years. There had been many deaths, and there were others after our arrival, so that about . . .[12] have died in the course of the summer. In proportion to the number of Norwegians who live here, however — between five and six hundred — the mortality does not appear to be excessive. Most of the sick have now recovered although a few still suffer from fever and ague, which has been the most common illness. On the other hand, none of the Norwegians who first came here has been ill during the last two years, the period when the maladies just mentioned have been the most widespread. The prevalence of these diseases is ascribed to the unusual drought of the last two summers, which dried up the sloughs, lowered the water levels of the rivers, and brought about an unhealthful miasma during the most intense heat of the summer. Although practically everyone who comes here from a foreign country suffers an attack, it is claimed by people of experience that these diseases are not as severe now

---

[12] The number is not given in the original.

as in previous summers and that upon recovery a person is actually healthier than before. In spite of these assurances, it was primarily the prevalence of sickness which would have made us hesitate to settle here even if land could have been had at government price, which was not the case.[13]

But before going elsewhere to look for land, we found it advisable to stay here for some time to rest after our travels. This seemed especially wise since prices of commodities were lower here than we had found them or hoped to find them anywhere else. A bushel of wheat costs fifty cents, a pound of pork about five Norwegian skillings, a pound of beef three skillings.[14] By boarding with the farmers, one can live well on $1.50 a week. A day laborer gets his board and half a dollar or one bushel of wheat a day; some get even more. A servant girl earns from $1.50 to $2.00 a week plus board, so that anyone who can keep his health has no difficulty in making a living. Unfortunately many have been unable to do so of late. During the summer not a few were ill from twelve to sixteen weeks. In spite of the sudden changes of temperature, which assuredly must have a bad effect on health, I cannot fail to note what others too believe, that the flimsy shacks which are ordinarily used for dwellings here contribute not a little to the high incidence of disease.[15] Such a shack is thrown together in one day — at least all but the roof. The walls are so open that in many places the logs are three or four inches apart. In the winter these spaces are chinked up with clay and bits of wood so as to make the walls fairly tight, but usually the caulking falls out, leaving holes almost wide enough for a cat to crawl through. There is seldom more than one room, which must serve as kitchen, dining room, and bedroom. Anyone

[13] The "government price" of public land at this time was $1.25 an acre.
[14] The skilling was a monetary unit in use in Norway until 1877. It was valued at three *øre* or a little less than an American cent.
[15] *Author's note:* When we arrived here toward the end of September, it was as cold as I have ever felt at home at that time of year. On the other hand, for a while in October it was as warm as it ever is in Norway at midsummer. This should be carefully noted.

will realize that these conditions must have a bad effect upon the
health of people who are used to warmer and more comfortable
houses because it must be remembered that the cold may at times
become just as intense here as at home. In fact, out on the prairie
where there is no protection against the north wind, the cold
seems more penetrating than in Norway.

During our stay here we had an opportunity to talk with most
of the Norwegians, some of whom are well off while many others
are in straitened circumstances because of sickness which has
made it impossible for them to work. Moreover, the fact that not
a few of them were supposed to pay for their land this fall but
had little prospect of being able to raise the money caused dejec-
tion and many expressions of discontent for a while. The worry
caused by this latter difficulty, however, has since disappeared for
most of the people concerned were able to raise the necessary
cash and have now paid for their land. Everyone we have met
agrees that it is far easier to make a living here than in Norway
if only one is fortunate enough to keep well. In this country we
never hear complaints of scarcity of food or find a lack of it in
anyone's house no matter how many other difficulties there may
be to face.

As has been said, we could not buy land at government price
in this region; in any event we should not have considered it wise
to settle here because everyone said that this part of the country
was regarded as especially unhealthful. We therefore had to consider which part of the country would be best for us. A number
of Norwegians have gone to Missouri, but the reports from there
are not favorable either.[16] They have other difficulties to wrestle
with which make it equally inadvisable to settle there. The water
is said to be impure, and since there is no opportunity of setting

[16] In 1837, on the advice of Cleng Peerson, a group of twelve or fourteen immigrants who were dissatisfied with the Fox River area settled
in Shelby County in northeastern Missouri. Largely because of Peerson's
efforts some more recruits arrived in 1838 and 1839, but the venture was
not a success. Disaffection set in almost at once, and in 1840 a number of
the settlers moved north into Lee County, Iowa, where a little earlier some

up a mill, the people are at times forced to bake bread out of cracked corn.

We had heard that Wisconsin Territory is supposed to have a better climate than the neighboring states. In general, however, such accounts are not trustworthy because everybody, for one selfish purpose or another, likes to attract people to his own settlement. For this reason strangers are assured that some certain region is the most healthful place in the world even though it may be quite the opposite. However, since it seemed reasonable to us that this part of the country, lying just north of Illinois, would have a climate more like what we were accustomed to, we decided to go there and look about. We were influenced also by the additional fact that one of our company had visited the settlers in Milwaukee and had found the land thereabouts good and more heavily wooded than here.

*October 31.* Having hired a horse and a small wagon, we started on our inspection tour but got no farther today than a village by the name of Yorktown, about eight miles from our starting point.

*November 1.* At this place we crossed Fox River and went almost straight north between Fox and Rock rivers, both of which have their sources in Wisconsin and run southwesterly through Illinois between forty and seventy miles distant from each other. The former empties into the Illinois River and the latter into the Mississippi. Before we reached Wisconsin we had to cover about ninety English miles through Illinois, and we had an opportunity to observe the land, which everywhere appeared to be quite as good as it was where we started from — indeed, in many places even more attractive, since it became more wooded the farther we traveled. Spruce, however, is rare, except along rivers and creeks where a poor variety is usually found. As we proceeded

immigrants from Fox River had founded the Sugar Creek settlement. The pull of the new lands in Wisconsin and Iowa as well as the Norwegian aversion to slavery were probably the prime reasons for the failure of the Shelby County settlement.

northward the country became higher and rougher as well as drier, with fewer of those marshes so often found on the prairies. There were several places which we liked, but since they were all taken and were not to be had except at a very high price, we did not stop to inspect them closely. We continued our journey until we arrived at Jefferson Prairie in Wisconsin, where Ansten Nattestad and his company had settled, about two miles beyond the Illinois boundary.

On Saturday evening, November 2, before we came to Jefferson Prairie, an amusing incident took place while we were crossing a little river. Johansen, who understood the language, had stopped at the house of an American near by to ask directions. After he had obtained the information, we had to cross the river at a place where there was a dam and a sawmill. When we came to the sawmill we stopped to have a look at it. Our eyes also followed the man who was driving the horse across the stream. He had apparently fallen into deep meditation and held the reins loosely. Just as he drove up the river bank, the front wheels separated from the wagon, and he was left sitting with the back wheels and the wagon box while the horse ran away with the front wheels. Every time the horse came to an oak tree along his way, he paid it special compliments by circling around it and cutting curious capers. After running about like this for a while he finally had to stop his crazy antics. We who stood by the sawmill laughed heartily at all this because it looked so funny. The driver was much offended but could only choke his wrath.

When we reached the horse, we found that the axle of the wagon was broken and that the horse had hurt his right foreleg. We tied him to a tree and put the bag of oats by him so that he could eat all he wanted. Then we got an axe and some other tools as well as an axle. After going to the nearest house to get live coals, I built a camp fire, and throughout the night I was busy tending the fire and doing the cooking since we drank coffee no less than four times. In the meanwhile one of my companions acted as wheelwright while the second served as blacksmith. The next morning our vehicle was in good condition, and we could continue our journey. After we had crossed one or two miles of prairie, the horse ran away again but was soon caught, and everything went well once more.

I have already mentioned that Ole Nattestad settled here last summer. We stayed with him for two days. He had built his house on the highest hill in the neighborhood, about a mile and a half from the nearest woods, and he had raised enough wheat and corn on the few acres he plowed this year to support a small family quite comfortably. Most of those who had come with his brother stayed with Americans in the neighborhood, some as boarders and others as farm hands. Two families had built houses for the winter, though without any intention of settling here, for all of the best and most desirable land had already been bought and occupied. They were all healthy and, so far as I could learn, quite well satisfied, because there was no lack of work and they usually earned a bushel of wheat plus board per day.

*November* 7. We left Nattestad's place and took the road toward Milwaukee since we intended to visit the Norwegian settlement some sixteen miles from that city and have a look at the land thereabouts. But when we had gone twenty miles or so and were about fifty miles from Milwaukee, we met a man whom we engaged in conversation and who seeemd to be acquainted with the country. He told us that there was some good land in the district we were going to that he believed could be bought at government price; but he added that if he were in our place, he would go straight west to Fort Atkinson on the Rock River and cross to the west bank where, it was said, we could find good land with sufficient timber.

Since it was late in the fall with occasional frosts at night, we doubted whether we should be able to get to Fort Atkinson if we carried out our original plan. We therefore turned about, following this man's advice, and after about a day's travel, arrived at Fort Atkinson. Along this route we traveled mostly through woodland, but from time to time we skirted small prairies. People had settled everywhere along the edge of the woods, and many also lived within the woods along the roadside. We did not meet anybody, however, who had lived there more than three years; most of them had been there only a year or two.

*November 9*. When Mr. Foretes [*Forster?*], the ferryman at Fort Atkinson, heard we were looking for land, he advised us to cross over to the other side of Rock River where he felt certain that within a distance of ten or twelve miles we would find desirable land still obtainable at government price. He also showed us the courtesy of offering us a map he had of a township where little or no land had been sold and directed us to a man who lived about nine miles away on the other side of the river from whom he thought we could obtain more information about the location of the land. As luck would have it, this man, whose name was Mr. Snell, arrived at the ferry just as we were ready to continue on our way. He offered not only to act as our guide but also to provide us with lodgings. About noon we left Mr. Snell, who could not join us at his house until late in the evening.

We left our wagon and borrowed a saddle in order to take turns on horseback, for the road on the other side of the river was so bad that we could use a vehicle only with great difficulty. At the outset the country we crossed was level and thinly wooded with oak, which is the most common kind of tree in the western states. After traveling about two miles, we passed the first house along our way. Now the country gradually became higher and rougher but with level stretches between the hills. When we arrived at what seemed to be the highest point on the road, we climbed a hill from which we thought we might get the finest view of the surrounding country. Before our eyes in every direction stretched small valleys covered with patches of woods, and some five miles away in the direction we were taking were beautiful little lakes with small islands and points of land on which grew dense oak forests. To us it seemed the most beautiful region we had seen in this country. The soil, too, appeared to be good for the grass stood as high as on the prairies. After feasting our eyes for a while, we continued on our way, thinking that here, perhaps, we had discovered the place where we would choose to settle. About eight o'clock we arrived at the home of Mr. Snell, who had promised us lodgings. It was situated about seven miles from the nearest settler, on the shores of the lake we had already seen from a distance.

We went in but found nobody at home. It was beginning to get cool, and we decided to remain inside where it was warm and pleasant until somebody arrived, thinking we should not have to wait long as it was late in the evening. About a quarter of an hour later the woman of the house came home. She hesitated a bit when she opened the door and found people there. But soon she collected herself and broke out laughing when we greeted her from her husband and told her that he had promised us lodgings. In reply to our question if she was not frightened to find strangers in the house, she answered that she would have been but for the fact that the Indians who were in the neighborhood during the summer had left long ago. Soon her husband also returned. We were well received by these people. They seemed very glad to have travelers in their house, evidently because so few ever came that way.

*November 10.* Today, Sunday morning, Mr. Snell went along with us to have a look at the country toward the west. It was rather level or gently rolling and well wooded until we reached a little stream about two miles away called Koshkonong Creek. Because the water was too cold for wading, our host, who had a horse, served as "ferryman." Our driver was to be taken across first. He mounted the horse behind Mr. Snell, and everything went well until he was about to step ashore on the opposite bank when — what did we see? — he slipped over the rump of the horse and went splash into the river. Johansen and I, who watched the whole performance, were greatly amused, as you might expect, and burst out laughing, while the poor wretch in the water bared his teeth like a snarling dog. I might tell you that this fellow is a Bergensian from Voss and that he is the very incarnation of Old Nick himself. Cursing like a madman he managed to clamber ashore, but for some time we could not restrain our laughter at this little comedy.[17] The rest of us were fortunate enough to get across without falling into the water. After that we had to climb a steep bank to reach a prairie which stretched beautifully before us.

Plans were afoot to establish a town, to be called Clinton, at the point where we crossed the river. Lots had already been bought, but building had not yet started. The prairie close by is also called Clinton. The river carries enough water throughout the year to run a mill, but the fall is slight. We judged, however, that sufficient power might be developed for productive use. The land on the side of the river from which we came was low, but on the opposite side, as already mentioned, the bank was high and steep, so that we had quite a climb before reaching the edge of the prairie we wished to inspect. Having reached the top, however, we saw an expanse of grasslands which in setting and luxuriance was much like the finest and best-kept meadows in Norway. But as there was a scarcity of woods in the neighborhood, we decided that this was not a good place in which to settle. We could not go far since there were no settlers in this region to give us lodging for the night. Accordingly, sooner than we wished, we

[17] According to E. O. Mörstad, *Elling Eielsen og den "Evangelisk-Lutherske Kirke" i Amerika*, 86 (Minneapolis, 1917), the well-known Haugean leader Elling Eielsen accompanied Bache and Johansen on their trip into Wisconsin in 1839. Eielsen had this in common with the "driver" that he could be described as a Bergensian from Voss, because he was born in Voss in 1804 but went to Bergen as an apprentice in blacksmithing and carpentry. But assuredly Eielsen would not have been guilty of "cursing like a madman" under the circumstances even though he was hot tempered and had unusual powers of expression. It is a major mystery that Bache makes no mention of Eielsen in the diary.

had to return with our host and spend another night at his house.

Going back, we again had to cross the river on horseback, and I was the first one to make the attempt. As I was stepping ashore, I fell into the water up to my knees and got quite wet. It was lucky that I could soon get into the house and dry my clothes instead of having to go about wet a whole day as the driver had done. By way of a little revenge, he started to laugh at my mishap, but I was not offended as he had been — though he did not admit it.

Last summer some Indians roamed over this region, but since none had been seen during the last six weeks, it was assumed that they had withdrawn to the woods farther west where they usually spend the winter. Our host regarded them as peaceful folk who wandered about only to hunt and fish. [*At this point eight lines of the diary are so obscure in meaning as to defy precise translation. The passage refers to land between Rock River and some region where government land could still be bought. There was uncertainty as to just what had been sold and what was still open. The matter was deferred, therefore, until information could be secured later at the land office in Milwaukee, something they could not attend to on this trip.*]

*November 11.* This morning we said good-by to our friendly host and hostess with hopes that we should meet again. We followed the same road back to Fort Atkinson where we stayed overnight.

*November 12.* We now took another road which at first followed the river and passed through several fine new towns. The land along our route was good and had been bought and settled wherever there was any timber. One day's journey brought us within seven miles of the Illinois boundary and took us over a fine dry prairie which, however, was not large.

*November 13.* This morning, as we continued our return trip, we decided to visit Ole Nattestad again at Jefferson Prairie, only seven miles distant. On our way we met Ansten Nattestad, but he was home again almost as soon as we reached his house. We stayed with him overnight.

*November 14.* Today we bade a final farewell to the Norwegians here and took the road toward Beloit to a little town on the Illinois-Wisconsin boundary near which a Norwegian lives who came over with us from Gothenburg. We spent the night with him.

*November 15.* Early in the morning we left this man who was from Numedal. By evening we passed through a beautiful town called Rockport, if my memory serves me right, which was said to be only two or three years old. We took lodgings for the night a few miles beyond the town.

*November 16.* Today we crossed a large plain called Grand Prairie, said to be about three hundred miles long. Where we crossed, the distance from the edge of the woods to the nearest grove was about twenty-two miles. We had to travel a long time before catching sight of it because it was small. When we arrived there we found that it was occupied by only one family. They had a good deal of land under cultivation but lived as hermits, without any neighbors. Though there was still some time before sundown, we decided to spend the night here because we were told that it was fourteen miles to the next patch of woodland where a human dwelling could be found.

*November 17.* A fire had already swept across that part of the prairie which we covered yesterday, leaving everything parched. After traveling a short distance today, we arrived at a spot where we found a little pond and a few trees around which the grass had not been burned. As I have always had a desire to burn things, I was eager to set this little patch of grass on fire, especially since there was nothing of value here which could be damaged. I chanced to have some matches in my vest pocket, and soon there was a great blaze going. My companions were well ahead of me and did not notice what I was up to. But when I rejoined them, they discovered what I had done and spoke sharply to me.

The distance from the nearest woods to Big Indian Creek was about ten miles. We arrived there in the evening and stayed with a man whose name I do not remember but who looked like a lawyer or a clergyman. According to my reckoning, we had traveled forty-six miles across this single stretch of prairie and had seen only two human dwellings.

*November 18.* Today we continued our journey to Little Indian Creek, a distance of only ten miles, and stopped with some orphaned girls from the western part of Norway. A number of Norwegians live in this vicinity, but the land is marshy and poor. We stayed here two nights and a day, visiting our countrymen, who were none too fortunately situated.

*November 20.* Now only ten miles remained between us and the Norwegian settlement at Fox River, where we would end this year's travels and settle down for the winter. Toward noon we arrived at the river, in the middle of which were two small islands. While looking about, we happened to see deer running across the river at full speed. It was a strange sight. They came from the bank where we stood and crossed by way of the islands. When they plunged in they looked like mackerel at play in the sea, for they splashed water so high that they were hidden until they reached the opposite shore. This was a steep bluff, and they paused at the top to look around, then streaked across the plain. It was good fun watching their agility and grace. Just as we turned about we saw another arresting sight. Our driver was careening along at a wild speed as his horse ran away with him.

We got across the river safely, however, and about four o'clock finally reached the place where we intended to remain quietly until next spring, when the roads would allow us to continue our investigations. We had the satisfaction of learning that health conditions in Wisconsin were generally good. For the first time in fourteen or fifteen years, a few cases of the sickness mentioned earlier occurred there last summer among people who lived down in the river valleys.

# 2. Settling at Muskego

WE SPENT the whole winter quietly here in the settlement with no recreation but wood chopping. Johansen, who understood English, tutored me for a few weeks to teach me the pronunciation, but after that I had to be satisfied without a teacher and get along as best I could by myself. As was to be expected, under these conditions my progress was very slow, but I still managed to learn a little.

We had hoped to be on our way again by the end of March, but our departure was delayed because the rather severe winter lasted much longer than usual and the spring was so rainy that the roads on the long and marshy prairies became impassable. The winter, properly speaking — that is, the snow and severe cold — did not last beyond the end of February. During the last days of that month the warmth caused the snow and the frost in the ground to thaw as quickly as during the warmest May days in Norway. But with the month of March cold north winds and heavy frosts at night set in again, and this condition prevailed generally until the end of April when there were frequent, brief rains. The coldest spell began in the middle of January and lasted well into February. We judged that the most intense cold was about fifteen degrees. Even though this was not nearly so severe as it sometimes is in Norway, we felt the cold quite as much on the prairie as if it had been twenty below. To give an example of how cold it was, I may mention that a thin layer of ice sometimes formed on fresh milk before we could get it from the barn to the house. We noticed, however, that the intense cold did not last as long as it usually does in Norway; otherwise it would have been almost impossible for us, accustomed as we were to better quarters, to spend the winter in such miserable houses as they have here. People who have observed the weather maintain that the cold spells run through three-day periods: if, for instance, no change comes after three days, the spell will last through six; and if it does not abate after six days, it will last nine; which, so far as anyone knows, is the longest the cold has ever lasted at any one time. When temperatures were lowest, people could not do much work outdoors but had to stay inside near the stove, which was always kept red-hot in order to give off enough heat to keep those who crowded around it from getting stiff with cold. Not all the people in the house could find a place around the stove at the same time, and the ones who got there first, whether master or servants, enjoyed rights of priority. Late comers had to wait for a place until someone left, which rarely happened unless it was absolutely necessary, although anyone seated near the stove ran the risk of being burned on one side while freezing on the other. Since our life here was so uncomfortable and monotonous, it was only natural that we eagerly awaited the day when we could resume our travels.

Meanwhile we had plenty of time to decide where we should go. Even though we rather liked some of the places we saw last fall and realized that they had many desirable points, we felt that it would be advantageous to locate nearer Lake Michigan where the principal markets for the interior of the country are situated. We therefore decided to go to Milwaukee, which is the chief port in Wisconsin, and having bought a team of oxen, a wagon, and two cows, we started out.

*June 3, 1840.* After spending about half a year in comfortable ease — I said "comfortable," but it would be truer to say "comfortless" since we almost perished from cold both indoors and out during the bitter winter days — we were glad to welcome summer when, like the hare, we could say that we had a home under every bush. No longer would we need to hug the stove, burning our shoes and trousers, as we did last winter when we were forced to hibernate like bears sucking their paws. Thank heavens, we could now escape like birds from their cages into the open.

We were now at liberty in this land of the free to roam about at will, without knowing exactly whither, in search of a better dwelling place for next winter. This, indeed, we succeeded in finding, although it was to be about a hundred miles nearer to the North Pole!

Today we started for Chicago with a little company of Norwegians bound for the same place. We had much trouble with one of our cows, a black, stupid beast which stubbornly refused to leave her home. One of our companions and I had to tie a rope about the animal's neck and lead her. Our host brought up the rear, beating her with a long whip whenever she became obstinate. In this manner we proceeded a couple of miles until we struck the main road we intended to follow. Here we said good-by to our host and some others who had accompanied us this far. The cow must have been glad to get rid of the man with the whip because welts left by the blows were soon visible all over her body. I did not envy her for she learned as others have that evil is repaid with evil.

Our departure had been delayed on account of bad roads, and many places were still so wet that further progress would have been impossible if we had not been lucky enough to fall in with two men who were going to Chicago with two span of oxen to fetch a couple of wagons. Thus we made a company of six altogether. Near a village about thirty miles from our starting point, we had to cross a little river, and as there was no bridge, I had to lead the cows across, half swimming. By way of compensation, however, in the middle of the stream I found a practically new tin pail which was of much use during the remainder of our journey. Since the two men had no vehicle for transporting their scanty stock of provisions, they offered to hitch up their oxen with ours, and we gladly accepted the offer. For a distance of about a mile the road was so soft in places that the wagon sank in to the hubs and the oxen practically swam in mud up to their bellies. Bridges over the rivers that we crossed had been washed out in places by the flood, and the water was often so deep that we had to float almost everything across. In spite of these difficulties, which were increased by the fact that we had occasional downpours and thunderstorms of a severity unknown in Norway, we did not find the going too hard because the air was mild and the green, fertile country through which we were passing was most pleasant. As we were equipped for camping we did not need to look for lodgings. We carried our own provisions, water, and even firewood which we collected wherever we could find it, since we might not be fortunate enough to strike a grove in the evening. When we could camp in the woods, of course, we found that more pleasant than spending the night on the open prairie. Our wagon was covered so that we could sleep in it as comfortably as in any house except during heavy rain.

After traveling three and a half days, we reached Chicago where we intended to stop a few days, partly because of business and partly to wait until the roads, which grew drier daily, had improved. This was the more important now, for henceforth we should have to travel alone with only one team of oxen along roads totally unfamiliar to us. As we were still entirely ignorant of a suitable place for settlement and it seemed unwise to travel about blindly, we agreed that Johansen should go to Milwaukee (leaving me and the hired man behind) in order to get information about available land and to have a look at the country thereabout.

*June 9.* Today was Whitsunday, and we all attended services in the Episcopal church for the first time in this country.[1]

Yesterday afternoon about two o'clock we arrived in the city of Chicago where we remained ten or twelve days before continuing our journey. While we were here I had a good opportunity to get acquainted with the city, which is situated at the mouth of a river flowing into Lake Michigan. It is a flourishing

---

[1] *Author's note:* That is to say, the first I heard in a foreign language in this country.

city, the largest commercial center on the lake, and the terminal of all the steamships that come down from Buffalo. For about nine miles to the west of Chicago, the country is low and swampy and becomes very wet during rainy summers. The canal which is to lead from here to the Illinois River has been under construction a long time, but there is still much work left before it will be completed. The streets are not paved yet and consequently are wet and muddy when it rains. Leading across the river are many bridges of simple construction. Although business is flourishing, there are but few factories — only one paper mill, one window factory, a brewery, and a few others. Otherwise commodities which are used in the interior of the country are brought from the East and some from the South. The city, surrounded by low, flat country, is exposed to all the winds that blow.

[*The following four paragraphs were presumably written not by Bache, but by Johansen.*]

I ran across another Norwegian who was on the same mission as I. First we went to the government office to get information about the land which we were interested in. Since it was my intention to locate as close to Milwaukee as possible, I was given a map of thirty-six sections, constituting a township six miles square. At its nearest point it was only six miles distant from the city, but this gave me little hope of finding what I desired because most of the sections in the township were already bought up, and I felt certain that there must be something wrong with the land that remained unsold. Nevertheless, I decided to look it over since this could easily be done, the land being such a short distance away. My companion took along maps of six or eight townships, none of which were less than sixty miles from Milwaukee.

Having finished this business, we left about twelve o'clock, taking a southwesterly direction. We did not eat before leaving because we had some provisions with us and hoped to be able to buy milk along the way. Soon we became hungry, and, as we could get no milk in any of the houses we came to, we sat down under a tree near the road some two miles from town and ate what we had. As we sat there we noticed a man coming our way whom we judged to be a Norwegian because of his clothes. He pretended not to notice us, and we left him to his own thoughts until he came directly opposite us. Then I called out, "Are you a Norwegian?" The man gave a start as if he had heard a ghost, so surprised he was to meet one of his countrymen. He was one of a company of Norwegians who had arrived here last autumn and lived about eighteen miles from Milwaukee.

For a while the three of us went along together. The heat made us very thirsty, and we frequently had to get a drink of water. About eight miles from Milwaukee we entered a tavern where, as it happened, the people of the neighborhood were holding a meeting to discuss the establishment of a school. It occurred to me that here I had occasion to learn something about the land I had come to see, for, judging by the distance we had covered, it must be in this neighborhood. I therefore inquired if anyone could direct me to the land I had marked on my map. One of the company asked to have a look at it and immediately indicated a section on the map which was next to his farm. As he said that the land was good, I left my companions and went with him to have a look at it. After waiting about an hour when he had finished his business, we started off for his home, about two miles from the tavern. We reached there so late that we had to leave our inspection until the next morning. I spent the night at his house, and in the morning we set out to look at the land. Only a quarter section was still unsold here. I was very favorably impressed, but since it was all woodland, thickly covered with trees such as oak and ash, I judged that the expense of clearing would be very great. I therefore decided to buy only half of it (eighty acres), which would at least give me a place to live. The country hereabouts is all wooded, most of it being covered by a vast forest that extends fifteen to thirty-five miles west of Milwaukee.

It was late when we got home. As I was not much used to

walking, I felt very tired from the exertions of the last two days and therefore accepted my host's kind invitation to stay another night at his house. I had intended to visit the Norwegians who live some ten miles farther out, but realizing that this would delay me too much and that we would be coming through there on our way from Chicago, I abandoned this scheme. I was afraid, too, that I might lose the land, for I was told that several other persons had examined it during the preceding few days. Accordingly, I hurried back to Milwaukee and was lucky enough to get there in time to finish my business before the office closed. I then went to a hotel and was told that a steamer for Chicago was expected in the evening. It did not come, however, until late at night, and we did not get off until five the next morning. Somewhat late that afternoon I arrived in Chicago where I once more met my traveling companions. They were in good health and were happy to learn that we had found a place where we could settle down and build our home.[2]

Some days, however, elapsed before we could leave Chicago. When we considered the difficulties of the journey we had to undertake accompanied only by our hired man, we decided that we must have a horse and accordingly bought a little Indian mare and a saddle for forty-five dollars.

While Johansen was in Milwaukee I had time to visit the Norwegians who live here. Most of them are common laborers who own nothing but wretched hovels of unplaned pine clapboarding that remind one of dog houses in Norway. We stayed with one of the settlers by the name of Halsteen . . . from the district of Stavanger, who was comparatively well off since he

[2] Since it is definitely stated that Johansen went to Milwaukee, leaving Bache and the hired man behind (p. 30), and since the account is given in the first person, it is probable that this section was written by him. The entries for July 5 and July 26, below, were apparently also written by Johansen because there, too, the first person is used in referring to him. We may probably assume that Bache had preserved some notes by Johansen among his own papers and that Marie Bache mistakenly entered them as her father's when she put his diary into final shape.

had a steady job with a rich merchant who paid well.[3] This man was the most prosperous of all the Norwegians in Chicago, and he also had a good reputation among the Americans as a decent, sober person who tried to stay clear of all dissipation.

Because of the low-lying situation of the city and the filthy state of the water in the river, which is polluted with all kinds of refuse, the inhabitants must take all the water they require for household purposes from Lake Michigan. This is a great inconvenience in so large a city, and no remedy is possible because water from springs or wells is unobtainable. Presumably the site is not healthful either as there is no runoff for the excessive summer rains. Nevertheless, the population increases considerably every year and will probably continue to do so, Chicago being the principal port for all shipping on the lake as well as the main market for the interior.

*June 17.* On Wednesday morning we left Chicago in fine weather, but the roads were still soft and muddy. Nevertheless everything went well the first eight or ten miles, better than we dared expect. When we had journeyed some twenty miles, it grew dark, and we decided to camp in the open as usual, although the air felt as if a storm were approaching. Thunder rumbled in the distance, and just as we had a fire started and were about to make coffee, rain began falling so heavily that we had to seek shelter in a little empty house close by. The storm increased, and soon rain fell with such force that water ran in streams across the floor of the wretched hut. We were afraid that our animals, which we

---

[3] The surname is omitted, but the reference doubtless is to Halstein Torrison, who, with his family, came from Fjeldberg, Norway, and settled in Chicago in October 1836. According to Anderson, he was the first Norwegian to make his home in that city. He remained there until 1848 when he removed to Calumet. *Norwegian Immigration (1821–1840)*, 194–95, 365. See also J. W. C. Dietrichson, *Reise blandt de norske Emigranter i De forenede nordamerikanske Fristater*, 89 (Stavanger, 1846; republished, Madison, 1896). In 1839 Halstein Torrison employed a number of his newly-arrived countrymen as laborers on a canal project thirteen miles from what was then Chicago. Knut A. Rene, *Historie om Udvandringen fra Voss og Vossingerne i Amerika*, 134 (Madison, 1930).

had put out to grass, would be frightened by the fearful thunder and lightning and run away. In about half an hour the storm began to abate; in an hour it was all over, the skies cleared, and we could return to camp. To our great surprise and satisfaction, we found that the animals were quite calm, as though nothing unusual had happened there. Furthermore, our campfire was still alive and we were able to cook supper. As usual, we slept in our wagon, which was well equipped for this purpose.

*June 18.* This morning the weather was fine again, and we covered about the same distance as yesterday, traveling mostly through thin woods interspersed with openings. The distance between settlers was not great, and the land everywhere seemed to be fertile. The night was clear and mild, undisturbed by any storm, and we slept as soundly and peacefully in our wagon as at an inn.

*June 19.* Still enjoying beautiful weather, we resumed our journey at seven o'clock this morning. Until we reached a little place called Pleasant Prairie, the terrain resembled that which we crossed yesterday. This prairie was very beautiful, dotted with attractive houses, and it had the loveliest setting we have yet seen. It had all the appearance of being well-fertilized and well-tilled, and there was plenty of timber near by for the settlers. We stayed here overnight — the first night of our present trip to be spent in this part of Wisconsin Territory. The first Norwegian settlement we planned to visit was only twenty miles distant, and we could have reached it in a day if we had only been acquainted hereabouts. But being strangers we often took the wrong road, and as we seldom met anyone who could put us straight before we had strayed many miles, we had to spend still another night in the wagon.

*June 21.*[4] Sunday afternoon we finally reached the Norwegian

[4] The date given in the manuscript is June 20, but the context of the paragraph above makes it plain that this is a mistake. Furthermore, Sunday fell on June 21 that year.

settlement and discovered that during the last two days we had traveled almost in a semicircle. We found our countrymen here all well and satisfied and decided to stay with them for some time to rest up after our journey.

Meanwhile we had a chance to examine the land in the neighborhood. Much of it was still unsold, but we had no thought of buying. It was unsatisfactory because there were many swamps which could not be turned into fields (though the grass here yielded excellent hay for cattle). Moreover, we regarded such soggy land as unhealthful.

At least this was invariably the case in Illinois. But the soil down there is much richer than in Wisconsin, and this may probably explain the unhealthful conditions. Practically everywhere in Illinois we found the humus to be from eighteen to thirty inches deep, exceedingly rich, as black as soot, and entirely free of sand. Experience has shown that this kind of soil is very rich, since the yields are greater after a half dozen crops than they are in the first years. Down there the grain does best during dry summers for the long, cool nights and the heavy dew afford sufficient moisture for growth. This year the poorer soil has yielded best, more rain than usual having fallen, although it has by no means been what we should call a wet summer. Winter grain is usually a failure in Illinois, for the uncertain winter weather frequently kills it off in the spring. In Wisconsin there is less risk in this respect, especially as far north as Milwaukee where the winters are steadily cold and snow covers the ground for three or four months. The soil here is more mixed with sand and not as rich as in Illinois, but it will produce grain without fertilizer. After several years of cultivation, however, the soil will probably need to be enriched. Presumably the easiest way to achieve this will be to sow clover and plow it under when in full bloom as they do in New York state.

*July 5.* Having spent a fortnight here, we set out on foot to take a closer look at the land we had bought some ten miles from here. (We were staying with Østen Olsen of Tind parish in Norway.) We had to walk because our mare ran away the night after our arrival in the settlement, and after a vain search throughout the neighborhood we had given her up for lost. When we got there we turned again to the man who had first called my attention to the land, and he kindly offered to take us around.[5] The whole tract is so densely wooded that it was impossible to get an over-all view of the land, but as far as we could see, it appeared to be very flat and dry enough for cultivation. Furthermore, the soil seems to be excellent, and since a little stream, which apparently never dries up, runs across our land, we will never lack water.

After the trip our guide said that he had always believed the land to be good but that he had never been so certain of it as now. If it belonged to him, he said, he would not take $300 for it even though it had cost only $100. Whether he said this in all seriousness or merely to flatter us we shall not try to decide. One thing is certain, however: everyone seems to agree that in a few years land around Milwaukee will bring a far higher price than prairie land in spite of the heavy costs involved in clearing it. Undoubtedly the timber can soon be sold at good profit to the steamboats, which annually consume such vast quantities of fuel that the woods closest to the lake can not satisfy the demand much longer.

Near our land was an enclosed plot of ground about half an acre in size on which there was a little house. It was planted to potatoes, vegetables, and some tobacco. Our guide thought that this property, including the crops, could be bought for $50, perhaps even less. This price did not seem unreasonable. We figured that with a few repairs the house could be made habitable for winter, and the crops would come in handy too. We therefore looked the place over and decided to keep it in mind. We also had to plan how to get winter fodder for our cattle, because

[5] This passage, also, seems to have been written by Johansen.

37

there was no extensive grassland in the neighborhood. Our guide suggested that we should get it from the Norwegian settlement, which markets a great amount of hay in Milwaukee. We spent the night with this man.

*July 6.* This morning we went to Milwaukee to meet some Norwegians who wanted us to help them with the language. Here we saw many Indians. The faces of most of the men were painted with designs of various colors. The following morning we recognized several of those whom we had seen on our arrival, and we noticed that the designs sometimes vary, as do the colors — red or blue or black. The Indians usually keep to the country hereabouts, living by hunting and fishing. Now and then bands of them come to the city partly to sell skins and partly to get drunk on whisky, to which they are much addicted. On such occasions they often fall to quarreling and fighting. We witnessed one fight which might have had serious consequences had not the person attacked been clever enough to disarm his opponent and trip him to the ground. Since some traders seemed very anxious to stop the quarrel, we believed at first that attacks from the savages were feared. To our comfort, however, we learned that this concern was caused by their having broken the law, for selling alcoholic drinks to the savages is strictly prohibited. Some of the sober Indians parted the combatants and ended the fight.

*July 7.* After spending the night in Milwaukee we returned to the Norwegian settlement and decided to harvest winter fodder, which was readily obtainable in this district. Almost everywhere the grass was so thick and high that a skilled man, without working too hard, could cut between ten and fifteen *skippund* a day.[6] We did not do so well, partly because we were inexperienced and partly because the intense heat made it impossible to work hard. Even so, in a fortnight we had cut enough, as we thought, for our livestock — five cows and one horse. This done, we took still another inspection trip because we had heard that about three

[6] A *skippund* equals about 350 pounds.

miles south of here there was some very good land not yet sold. Finding it even beyond our expectations, we decided at once to buy a piece which lay between two lakes well-stocked with fish. Since Johansen was best versed in the language, it fell to his lot to go to Milwaukee and close the deal. This had to be done quickly if we wished to be sure of getting the land, for we knew that many had already looked at it.

*July 25.* This decision was made yesterday, and the next day Johansen was to leave for Milwaukee. The heat has been intense and he was not used to walking that far — almost three Norwegian miles. The difficulty was further aggravated by the fact that he was not feeling well. He therefore wished very much that we still had our mare, as on horseback this would be merely a short, pleasant trip. So thinking he went to bed and fell asleep.

About one o'clock in the morning, a Norwegian living about a mile from here came and told us that the mare was grazing near his house, but she was so shy that all his efforts to catch her had been futile. At first we could not believe it was our mare, but he insisted that it must be; he had been close enough to see her color, and she had a halter around the neck just as ours had when she ran away. After this we could no longer doubt but went along with him and caught her. She had been away six weeks and presumably had neither seen nor been seen by any human being during that time. At least, to begin with, she was so frightened at meeting anyone on the road that we could scarcely get her to move.

*July 26.*[7] As the mare grew more accustomed to things, her fright disappeared, and Johansen arrived safely at the office where he purchased the desired piece of land, about one hundred and seventy-five acres. It was still our intention, however, to settle on the land we had bought first, because we thought it would be well to live as near the city as possible. It was agreed, therefore, that on his return trip Johansen should attempt to buy the house

[7] In the manuscript this entry is dated July 24, obviously an error, which has been corrected as above.

already mentioned. When he arrived there the owner was not at home, but the son told him that his father had changed his mind and did not intend to sell. Johansen was further informed that a piece of land, about fifty acres, lying close to ours, which previously was for sale and which he had thought of buying, was already sold.

After these miscalculations, we immediately decided to settle on the land we had bought most recently, which, incidentally, gave us the advantage of having to haul our hay only one third as far. Having determined to stay here, we became eager to get more land, for we wished to have as neighbors some Norwegian friends whom we were expecting this summer. With this in mind we again looked over the vicinity and bought seventy-five more acres of good land which lay next to ours and gave us access to still a third lake. After locating a convenient site, we erected a hut to serve as shelter until we could build a house.

*August 28.* Friday we moved into our hut, which is about three miles south of Østen Olsen's place, where we have been staying. Before continuing my story I shall have to tell something about these people who strike me as being — how shall I express it? — undoubtedly the meaning is clear, therefore I will not mince words but simply say that they are Indians in their filthiness. I have never seen anything to equal this woman. She always trudged about barefooted in the cow dung which covered the yard between the house and the barn. Especially when it rained this colorful mixture clung well to her legs, which were seldom or never washed. With legs painted in this fashion — how far up I do not know, but I think I can safely say above the knees — she would crawl into bed every evening. This ought to be enough about her, but I have another story which is equally revealing. One evening we were sitting by the window eating our supper of sweet milk and flat bread [8] while she and her husband were eating

[8] A thin, crisp type of bread common among Norwegians and Norwegian immigrants.

their bread and milk on another chest. She had a little baby in her lap, and once as I looked her way I chanced to spy a fine little jet arching from the baby into their bowl. But they continued eating with their usual gusto until she noticed that I had seen what had happened. Only then did she take the food and throw it to the pigs. If she had not realized that I had seen the mishap they would undoubtedly have eaten their food without any qualms. This is an example of genuine Norwegian mountaineer cleanliness, the equal of which I had never seen. According to my observations here in America, the mountaineers are generally so slovenly in their household ways that it is disgusting to associate with them.

There is only one American in our neighborhood, a widower who lives right next to us. At present a Norwegian family whom we visit occasionally is staying with him. In another direction an Irishman has bought the land adjoining ours.

*August 30.* Sunday morning after we had moved in, the Irishman came to our cottage before we were up and offered to sell us his property, about one hundred and forty acres with a fine location between Wind Lake and Waukesha Lake. The latter lake, which has an Indian name, is half a mile in diameter, while the former is two miles long by one and a half miles wide. In a way, we desired his land, but since we felt that we already had enough for ourselves, we hesitated to buy, especially as we could not be certain of getting more money from home this year. We had enough cash on hand to complete the deal but feared we might get into difficulty later on. However, we gave him the hope that there might be buyers for his land if our friends from Norway should arrive.

We spent most of the third day in our new environs at the home of the American widower, because the only Norwegian family we could visit was staying with him. In the evening I returned to our hut and stretched out on the bed. I had not been resting long before I heard voices outside and our hired man came running in to announce the arrival of Even Heg. I rushed out to meet him. The joy of seeing old friends in so distant a land can surely be appreciated by anyone. He had arrived in Milwaukee with his company this morning and was brought to our place by a Norwegian. Fortunately we were able to serve him a cup of tea and some fresh fish which our man had caught.

After eating, we retired because he was weary from his day's walk. The house was so small that we had to take out the bedstead and make a pallet on the floor. But in spite of his weariness there was no sleep all night long because of the ceaseless flow of questions and answers. Thus went the first night of our reunion.

*August 31.* Today, Monday, I went to town to meet the rest of the company, and our hired man followed with a wagon and oxen to fetch them home. They were just as happy to see us as we were to see them, and the prospect of having them as neighbors pleased us very much.

*September 2.* The Irishman sold his land to Johansen today at the price he originally paid for it. Since we had already bought the land next to him he could not expect to get a single one of his own countrymen as a neighbor. This was undoubtedly one reason he sold out.

Our first job now was to build a house. We had decided to make use of a mound out on a fine plot of ground with good drainage in all directions. Johansen and I had already started working, and with the aid of Heg and his companions the job was soon completed. The mound was so large that by excavating down to the level of the surrounding ground we got a room twenty-four feet long, eighteen feet wide, and seven feet high. This first story was entirely underground. Over it we built a loft five logs high which rested on six pillars about seven feet in height. The walls of our dugout were so firm that there was no danger of a cave-in, and we merely needed to provide it with a wainscot in order to get a good, warm dwelling. On one side of the main room we excavated a kitchen, which also was provided with boarded walls and a roof resting on pillars. Considering the circumstances, we now have a house which for comfort surpasses our expectations.

The mound proved to be an Indian grave. At the bottom we found twelve or fourteen skulls and some other bones which indicated that these had been tall people. By now these burial customs have doubtless been discarded. In the past, however, the Indians are supposed to have used this manner of burial for those killed in battle — an indication that they were formerly more enlightened in some ways than they are at present. Judging by these customs, they must have had a culture similar to that of pagan times in our own country, as is witnessed by the big mounds in Norway which can, in some ways, be compared to this one. There are many such mounds here, undoubtedly all burial places primarily for warriors. Many bodies were piled up on the ground and then covered with earth to the height already mentioned. It was evident that the earth had been brought some distance. This particular mound must have been built many years ago, because fair-sized oak trees, the largest twelve or fourteen inches in diameter, were growing on it.

There are not many Indians left in this neighborhood, and none of them are officially allowed to live here because they have sold their land to the American government. But since the number of those remaining is so small that no one fears an attack by them, they are left unmolested. They are usually found near streams or lakes. That is why they stay here. Even in the winter after the waters are frozen over, they go fishing in an unusual manner. When the ice is clear and strong enough to carry them, they go out to a place where the bottom can easily be seen and spy around until a fish is discovered swimming in the water below. They then start pursuing it, running on top of the ice in every direction until the fish stops, which seldom happens until it has found a hiding place in some grass, where it will remain absolutely quiet. With a sharp iron rod three yards long and as thick as a ramrod, they make a hole in the ice just above the fish and thrust the rod down with such accuracy that the fish is speared through the neck. There it is held until a larger hole is made with an axe through which the fish can be pulled up on the end of the rod. Even Heg recently had an opportunity to watch such a catch. The fisherman accompanied him home with three big pike he had caught in this manner. We bought them for twenty-five cents and found that all of them had been speared through the neck.

Until we came here and built our house we had been roaming around, not knowing where we would be next, with no definite place to stay. We were lucky enough to have fine, mild weather as long as the building went on. The little sod hut in which we first stayed was so small that there was no room in it for anything besides what we already had there. Consequently the people who helped us build the house in the mound had to sleep outdoors under a lean-to made of boards. Within the hut there was a bed along one wall and a chest along each of the remaining three walls. The small space remaining in the center was occupied by the cookstove and two hammocks which we hung there on the fourth day. Johansen and I slept in the bed, while Even Heg with his wife lay under it on the floor in such a way that I was lying above Even. According to Johansen, one night while we were sleeping I spoke to Even and he answered. We carried on for a while until I concluded the discussion with these words: "That's telling them, Eivin!" which became a stock phrase with us for a long time. This whole conversation amused Johansen greatly, and the others thought it strange that we could carry on a discussion in our sleep.

Early in December I began rooming with an American because I wished to attend a school in that neighborhood which was to last until the end of February. I wanted to learn English so as to associate with the people here; and, of course, it is the official language of the country.

*1841:* After leaving school in February, I stayed at home and helped with such improvements as are necessary to put new land under cultivation. Nothing remarkable or worthy of recording happened during this long period; our existence could be compared with that of hermits since there were hardly any people here with whom we could associate except the filthy Norwegian mountaineers who, in certain respects, were exactly like Indians.

In the autumn when the Norwegians arrived, there was almost a month when I could do nothing but run around in the woods hunting up the markers for the land they wished to buy. In this way I became well acquainted with the neighborhood for approximately six miles in every direction from our house, and no land was bought by the Norwegians without my knowledge.

Toward the end of November I went to Milwaukee to attend school in the hope of learning the English language better. I remained there that whole winter and until the end of April the following spring. The city is located in a marshy area near the outlet of the Milwaukee River, while the Menominee River flows through the middle of the city, which is thus divided by these rivers into three sections. The city is located ninety miles north of Chicago, a hundred and fourteen miles south of Green Bay, and about eighty miles east of Madison, the capital of Wisconsin. It was laid out in 1835 when the first settlement was made.

# 3. The Long Trip Home

*May 18, 1842.* WISHING ONCE MORE to see my old homeland and to visit my family and friends there, I left my home in Racine County today, accompanied by my man. This afternoon I reached Milwaukee where I have to wait a couple of days for a steamer.

*May 20.* The boat I was to take finally arrived from Chicago about eight o'clock in the evening. It anchored in Milwaukee Bay since the mouth of the river was too shallow for big vessels. Consequently those of us who wished to go on board had to be taken out in a little skiff belonging to someone here.

*May 21.* This morning I went on deck to have a look at the weather and to see what speed we were making. To my great surprise the boat was still lying in the same place as last night, but about eight o'clock, while we were eating breakfast, it finally weighed anchor and got under way. The weather continued misty and raw all day. We touched at several places during this voyage of nine hundred and fifty miles and arrived at Buffalo in very beautiful weather.

*May 25.* By six o'clock this morning we were in Buffalo, where I remained only three hours, taking the nine o'clock train to Niagara Falls, only twenty-two miles away. I therefore had too little time to see much of the city, but I made as good use of it as I could. Because of its location, Buffalo is one of the most flourishing commercial centers in western New York state. It is also the home port of most of the steamships which plow the waters of the Great Lakes.

As already mentioned, I left Buffalo about nine o'clock in the morning and arrived at Niagara Falls a couple of hours later. This marvelous and unparalleled work of nature is caused by a ridge of limestone which has been cut by the force of the water from the great lakes above. The ridge is one of a series of steps leading from Lake Ontario to Lake Erie. The difference in the elevation of the two lakes is said to be three hundred and thirty-four feet, the height of the great waterfall being one hundred and fifty-eight feet. The rush of the water begins near Burning Spring, about one mile above the cataract. The inclination of the river bed increases as it approaches the brink, thus accelerating the speed of the current and the contortions of the turbulent waters. No spectacle can be more awe-inspiring than a view of the immense falls and the rapid sweep of the waters above it.

In the center of the cataract is a little island which is connected with the mainland by a bridge. Several smaller islands are found both above and below the falls. They present a very beautiful sight covered as they are by a variety of deciduous trees, with an intermingling of cedars. In order to see the bottom of the cataract, it is necessary to go clear to the edge where the water breaks and rushes down. A very simple winding stairway has been placed close by, so that one can go down and get behind the falls. In the neighboring town, which is also called Niagara Falls, there are big comfortable hotels.

It is with a feeling of regret that I say farewell to you, mighty Niagara. Through ages of war and peace you have remained unchanged, and unforgettable will be my memory of you.

At four o'clock in the afternoon we continued our journey by rail to Lewiston, seven miles farther down the river, where I remained overnight. The town was beautiful but of no great importance, and everything was quiet there. Across the river on the Canadian side we could see a little town called Queenston. Although Lewiston is a small place, only a little village, in fact, it boasts two fair-sized churches. This would seem to be overly extravagant; surely one might have been enough. But that is how things are done here; the spirit of speculation is so vigorous that it brings forth great projects. Today's memorable experiences were made still more impressive by most beautiful May weather.

*May 26.* The steamer I was to take arrived in Lewiston this morning, and we left about noon, passing down the river between high banks until we reached the outlet into Lake Ontario. A town and a fort were located here. That was the last we saw of Canada because from now on we followed the American shore, being bound for Oswego. Late in the evening we stopped at Rochester a few minutes. I traveled as a deck passenger on this trip, and I got so cold during the night that I had to go into the boiler room to get warm. Fortunately I wore a good Kalmuck coat which kept out the chill quite well and prevented me from catching cold.

*May 27.* About five o'clock this morning I arrived at Oswego, approximately one hundred and twenty miles from Lewiston. I did not remain here more than two hours but seized the opportunity to catch a boat which was leaving at seven o'clock. I had breakfast at a place conducted by an Irishman and fell into conversation with his wife when he went out to see if he could drum up more trade. She asked if I was from Ireland, thinking I had the Irish brogue. I said no, but explained that I had come from Norway and that I was on my way back for a visit. Her highest wish, she said, was to return home again, and she added that Ireland was the most beautiful country in the world and other comments in that vein.

After breakfast I went down to the canal where a boat was ready to leave for Syracuse. There were no signs of any particular activity in Oswego; in fact, it was very quiet, even though this town is much larger than Lewiston. At the scheduled hour the boat left with quite a number of passengers on board. Along most of its course the canal follows a river and passes through some pretty little towns. Because I had stayed awake all last night, I was very sleepy. About three o'clock we arrived at Syracuse. The captain of our boat had a little box on his table, where he sat as if pondering great things. From time to time he stuck his nose in the air, gave a toss to his head, and looked about the cabin with an air of importance, evidently blind to the fact that he was nothing but a conceited fool. Many of the passengers bought their railroad tickets for the trip to Utica from him. The luggage was taken by horse and wagon to the station where it was loaded on a special car and then locked up.

This city is very beautiful and is important as a commercial center. A great deal of salt is made here every year and shipped inland, especially to points in the West. I was not here long since my train left about five o'clock.

Late in the evening, after having passed through beautiful country, we reached Utica where I wished to purchase a ticket for the remainder of the journey. I hoped I should be able to sleep on the train, but, as last night, I was unable to catch a wink even though we managed to keep the car tolerably warm. We passed through several places where coffee and pie were ready to be served to the passengers. This was most welcome for we had to sit up all night. But the eating had to be done in a hurry, only ten minutes being allowed at each stop, which proved to be quite enough for anyone quick in his movements. At Schenectady we stopped for some time before continuing our journey.

*May 28.* At Schenectady I hoped to catch a little sleep, but it proved to be impossible. At daybreak we continued our journey and arrived in Albany at six o'clock in the morning. The luggage belonging to the through passengers was taken aboard the steamer which lay at anchor close by. At seven o'clock we were off, and the boat began churning its way down the Hudson River. As I said on a previous occasion, the country along this river is very attractive, and on its banks are many fair-sized towns surrounded by green fields and woods. With the high hills in the background, they present a beautiful and romantic view. The governor has his residence in Albany, the capital of New York. This state is divided into fifty-six counties with a total area of forty-nine thousand square miles.

Usually two boats ply in each direction daily between Albany and New York, as there is much traffic between these cities. The weather was fine, and the warm sun made it difficult for me to keep my eyes open since I had not slept at all for two nights and three days — nor did I get to bed until late this evening either. By five o'clock in the afternoon I was in New York where there was a great competition among people offering lodgings, as is always the case in big cities here in America. Unacquainted with the city as I was, I of course had to take a chance on one of them, not knowing what my lodging would turn out to be. I accepted the offer of a negro who took me far into the city up Broadway, one of the greatest and most prominent streets in New York. There I took lodging with a widow. It was very expensive — a dollar and a half a day. Here I was, alone in a strange city, without any acquaintances, but it did not take me long to make new ones. I had the address of a Norwegian named Peder Säther, and today I managed to locate his office but did not find him there. By profession he is a money-changer.

*May 29.* Today being Sunday, I made no further effort to locate Säther. I thought it would be useless since I did not believe that he lived where he had his office. This conjecture proved to be true when I found him.

Going out to look around after breakfast, I started down toward the ships, but while I was walking along the church bells began ringing, and I decided to attend church. When the service was over I intended to return to my lodgings, but passed by the place three times without recognizing it. Then I went out to the Castle in order to get my bearings. There I found some Swedish ships and went on board. Leaving them, I finally made my way home, where dinner was being served. After dinner I went back to the Swedish ships and expressed my wish to travel with them to Europe, but nothing came of it because of their poor accommodations.

*May 30.* This morning I located Peder Säther, the money-changer I have already mentioned, at 96 Nassau Street. During my stay here I visited him every day and learned to know several other Norwegians who live in the city. He had his office boy take me around to help me with my few business affairs, which did not take long, all of it being finished in less than a day.

Among those whose acquaintance I made here was a Norwegian from Mandal by the name of Williams. He has been here since 1807 and is very well-to-do. I could probably have left New York for Europe almost any day, but I decided instead to spend some time seeing the city and the surrounding region. In this way I became much better acquainted with this country which every year receives so many immigrants from the old countries of Europe, the mother country of the Americans. Therefore, do not forget the mother who reared you and taught you the basic principles of manhood, thus laying the foundation for what you are and what you may become.

This city, the largest commercial center in America, covers the southern part of Manhattan Island. Among its public buildings are the City Hall in the park, the Stock Exchange in Wall Street, some baths and other structures, as well as three theaters. Directly across from the City Hall, facing three streets, is Astor House, the largest hotel, five stories high and built of cut stone.

The city administration is vested in a mayor, ten aldermen, ten associates, and a capable body of policemen. Almost every hour of the day steamers, packet boats, and mail cars arrive from and depart for every harbor in the United States.

Late this week I engaged passage on a Hamburg packet which is to leave in two or three weeks. The arrangements permit me to move aboard at once, which will be less expensive than staying in the city.

*June 6.* As this was Sunday, a Norwegian tanner named Hans Rees and I were invited to spend the day at Peder Säther's home in Brooklyn, which is located on the other side of Long Island Sound. Many of New York's most important businessmen live there with their families, away from the noise and turmoil of the big city. Brooklyn has quite a rural atmosphere, being beautifully located and very quiet. Here the weary businessmen can breathe a freer and more rustic air and spend their Sundays quietly in devout reflections. Even on Sundays, which are supposed to be quieter than other days, New York is so crowded that they cannot enjoy those reverent meditations which they desire, though the people here are not as religious as they are reputed to be in Boston or New England generally.

In the evening we returned home after enjoying the beauty of the day and the generous hospitality of this rustic place. Many of the houses in Brooklyn are surrounded by beautifully planted trees.

*June 9.* For several days I had been planning to take a little excursion during my stay here, but had not decided where to go. It was always my custom to wander around, and today as I returned from such a walk, I went to a steamer which lay quite close to my boat. I found that it was leaving this afternoon, so I went aboard and bought a ticket for Providence.

At five o'clock we started up Long Island Sound, which separates Long Island from the mainland and is about one hundred and two miles long from Red Hook to Montauk Point and from three to seventeen miles wide. Along its whole length there are lighthouses on either side to guide the sailor. When we had gone a few miles, another boat about the size of ours came along and passed us proudly. But before long it stopped and hoisted a flag. Our boat drew up alongside it, and to our surprise all its passengers came over to us. Something had gone wrong with the machinery, and the ship could not continue until repairs had been made. Our boat towed it to one side and then continued on its way. The passengers who had been transferred had to pay their entire fare again.

*June 10.* Last night a heavy fog appeared which lasted until nearly noon and forced the boat to proceed very slowly. In the morning the captain put out in a little boat to get his bearings. Finally, about eight o'clock we arrived at Stonington, but the captain did not venture to leave until the fog had lifted. Since we were still about forty miles from our destination, we were given free transportation there by railway, but those who had come from the other boat had to pay once more. Thus they had paid three fares during their journey from New York to Providence. After staying in Stonington an hour, we went on and arrived in Providence at noon. The country we passed through was unlovely, and the soil extremely rocky. The location of Providence is not beautiful either.

About two o'clock we continued our trip. We had with us a magnificent lion and three tigers — all full-grown — which were to be sold in Boston. On this part of the journey the railway ran through very fine country. The farms near the city were well kept, and around the beautifully located houses were gardens laid out in the European fashion. I arrived in Boston about four o'clock but did not look for lodgings until dark because I had no luggage with me. By railway we entered the western part of the city where a great public park or grove called the Common is located. It is very attractively laid out on a hillside with beautiful walks and lawns.

Boston is the principal city in the state of Massachusetts and the fourth largest in the United States. It is situated on a peninsula that runs northeasterly from the mainland with which it is connected by several bridges in addition to the so-called Neck. There are several thriving towns in the vicinity which must be regarded as a part of Boston, although they have separate municipal governments.

The most important of these neighboring towns are Charlestown, Lehemere Point, the Neck, and South Boston. As objects of interest in and about Boston must be mentioned Tremont House on Common Street, a great hotel with two hundred and two rooms, the State House just opposite the Common, a statue of Washington in the State House, and the Navy Yard. Breed's Hill is famous because of the battle fought there between the

British and the Americans on June 17, 1775, usually called the battle of Bunker Hill. There are a great many splendid private houses and churches as well as scientific and literary institutions in Boston which make it one of the most attractive places in the Union.

*June 11.* Although Boston has an extensive trade, it is not as important as New York, which is to America what London is to Europe. The central part of the city is located on highly elevated ground. The piers where the ships dock are very long and wide, because great warehouses owned by the merchants are built along most of them. The piers are well paved as are the streets, which, however, are narrow and very crooked since the situation of Boston does not allow well-laid-out blocks with straight, wide streets as in other cities less cramped for space. I left Boston about six o'clock in the afternoon and passed Providence, a city of considerable size, a couple of hours later.

*June 12.* Coming up on deck Sunday morning, we found the weather bright and sunny with a clear horizon. I arrived at New York about eight o'clock and then went to my old lodgings on the ship *Howard,* which was lying at the nearest pier.

I had breakfast on the boat and afterwards went up to see the tanner Hans Rees. Both he and Peder Säther were anxious to know where I had been. I told them I had visited Boston, as Rees had already surmised. I stayed with him until about noon, when I went back to the ship to eat. The mate told me that someone had been aboard looking for me. He gave me a slip of paper, and written there I found the name of Carl Corneliusen, whom I remembered having seen once in Christiansand. I kept asking myself what he might want but could find no answer to my questions. I was out a while and returned in time for coffee. Afterward the captain and I went up on deck, sat down on a bench close to the companionway, and chatted about things of no particular importance. While we were sitting there a tall, thin, dark-complexioned man came on board. He recognized me as soon as he saw me, but I did not know who he was and had to ask his name. He said he was Carl Corneliusen, which I ought to have known if I had only stopped to think.

He told us that he had come over last autumn and had been living in the city since then. "Are you a robber, a rascal, or what are you?" I was thinking to myself, suspecting that he had left his native town on account of some misdeed. I raised no questions, however, because I assumed that he would not tell the truth even if I did inquire. All three of us went down to the cabin, where the captain ordered coffee for him. Later I went with him to his lodgings. He told me that he had arrived last fall and had remained here since in order to earn some money. If he had only known where Johansen was, he declared, he would have looked him up sooner. As he now intended to go west to Wisconsin, I told him how to get there. His landlady, who was a Greek, praised his conduct highly, and as a result my early suspicions of him were replaced by full confidence. When the woman learned that I was acquainted with him, she invited me to stay for supper. I accepted the offer, and she took the same liking to me as to him and regarded me as a friend of the family. We agreed to meet after breakfast tomorrow and, having taken a short stroll together, went to our respective lodgings.

*June 13.* According to yesterday's agreement, Corneliusen came on board at half past nine, and I went with him and introduced him to the friends I had among our countrymen whom he did not know. Farther up in the city I also knew someone whom I wished him to meet, the aforementioned Williams. We visited him in the evening and thus spent the entire day as pleasantly as yesterday, when he had been happy to find me. I told him that if he had not found me yesterday he probably would have missed me since I had intended to go south this morning by train. We said good-by to each other in the evening, and he asked if I would take a letter to Norway, which I agreed to do. As I intended to start my journey south tomorrow morning and he would be gone before my return, I asked him to leave the letter with the captain.

*June 14.* The first thing I did this morning was to visit a well-known portrait painter, Mr. Theodore Lund from Denmark, who was married to a girl from Christiania. As I intended to catch the morning train my call was very brief, but even so I arrived a quarter of an hour late and had to wait for an afternoon train. After making certain of its time of departure, I called on Corneliusen, who had a good laugh at my unexpected appearance. I spent most of the time with him, and the landlady looked upon me as an old acquaintance. Whenever I came there at mealtime, she wanted me to eat with them.

By four o'clock in the afternoon I was down at the wharf and had bought my ticket; in half an hour the steam-driven ferry *Bergen* took me across the Hudson River to Jersey City where we boarded a train that brought us to Philadelphia about eleven o'clock in the evening.

The country was rather hilly until we passed New Brunswick on the Raritan, which we crossed by a bridge spanning the deep river valley. A three-story building with a high roof stood close by, but the gable was no higher than the bridge. We stopped a few minutes at New Brunswick for refreshments. This town is located about thirty-four miles from New York. Some twenty-six miles farther on we reached the Delaware River, which we followed. Night had already fallen, but the sky was clear, and we could see that the country on both sides of the river was low. When we reached a point opposite Philadelphia, we left the train and took a ferry across the river.

*June 15.* Since I had decided to visit Washington, about a hundred and fifty miles from Philadelphia, and wanted to be there before evening, I took a steamer that left at seven o'clock in the morning. We enjoyed fine weather as we sailed down the river to Wilmington in the northern part of Delaware. This state covers twenty-two hundred square miles, and its southern part is very flat. It is divided into three counties, with Dover the capital. By the constitution dating from 1792, the legislature is composed of a senate and a house of representatives, numbering twenty-one members, which assemble on the first Tuesday in January. The general election takes place on the first Tuesday in October.

We all disembarked at Wilmington after a short trip of thirty miles on the river. Then we took the train to the Susquehanna River, which we crossed on a ferry, the railroad cars being on the second deck and the passengers on the first. Here I had a breakfast of pudding, some oranges, and a good glass of cognac — my first meal after leaving New York. About two o'clock we arrived in Baltimore, where I had a dinner consisting of some cold leftovers.

Baltimore is the largest city in Maryland and is said to be the third largest in the United States. The most notable sights are the Washington Monument, one hundred and sixty-three feet high, at the crossing of Charles and Monument streets, and Battle Monument on Calvert Street. There are two theaters and a museum in the city.

About four o'clock I left Baltimore and reached Washington about half-past five after a trip of some fifty miles. I spent the rest of the day trying to see as much as possible. The Capitol, where Congress meets, is built on a high hill and can be seen for several miles before one arrives in the city. Washington is beautifully situated on the Potomac River, which separates the state of Maryland from the state of Virginia. Glancing toward the left after getting off the train, I saw a beautiful park in front of me; I walked through the open gate and up the gradual ascent to the Capitol where I stopped and gazed out over the handsome city.

*June 16.* After breakfast I made my first excursion of the day to the Capitol in order to see the magnificent interior of the building where the legislative bodies assemble. To reach the entrance I ascended a long flight of wide steps. On the platform outside stood many columns made of cut stone like that in the steps. Inside was a wide corridor leading to a very large room capped by a giant dome over the center of the building. According to the guide, the dome is one hundred and twenty-two feet high — a considerable height. To the left were two statues, and on the walls were pictures representing notable events in American history.

Since Congress does not assemble before ten o'clock I had a good opportunity to look around. The crescent-shaped assembly room of the House of Representatives in the southern end of the building is stately and spacious with a fine gallery for visitors. Close by, on the right, is the Post Office, and on the left, the Library. In a room between the Library and the corridor, good refreshments are sold.

To the right of the corridor, in the northern end of the building, is the Senate chamber, which is somewhat smaller than the corresponding room for the representatives. I had seen most of it before the senators assembled.

The guide took another person and me up to the dome, from where we could look out over the beautiful city and the surrounding country. When we looked down at the corridor through the windows, the people seemed very tiny. The building is three hundred and sixty-three feet long and has an open area of twenty-two and a half acres of land around it. From the dome we could see Alexandria, a town six or seven miles down the river, and Georgetown three miles to the west. It is estimated that the Capitol cost $2,596,500. It is built in the center of a park which gives it a splendid appearance. The cornerstone of the President's house, about a mile from the Capitol, was laid October 13, 1792. This structure is one hundred and seventy feet long and is built of white freestone. The Treasury, a very large building containing two hundred and fifty rooms, is situated near the President's house. The Post Office Building as well as the Navy Yard are magnificent. Besides the public buildings there are a theater, several banks, and a number of churches. Washington is planned on a grand scale. The streets radiate from a center and are from one hundred and thirty to one hundred and sixty feet wide. The greater part of the area within the city limits, however, is still undeveloped.

When the representatives had assembled, I went up to the gallery to hear the debates.[1] At present the number of representatives is said to be considerably over two hundred. Small boys were going from one person to another with papers. A chairman, or the "Speaker" as he is called here, had his place on an elevated platform. Occasionally, when the representatives became too noisy and the one who had the floor could not be heard, the Speaker rapped on the table with the gavel, which he kept at his side, and bade them be quiet. But he had to remind them frequently — just like a schoolmaster disciplining his pupils. Each territory also has a delegate in the House, elected by the people for a period of two years. Afterward I went to the Senate, which is composed of fifty-two members, two from each state, elected for a period of six years by the respective legislatures. One third are elected every two years. The Vice-president of the United States is the president of the Senate. In his absence the senators elect a president *pro tem*.

Thus I saw everything possible in the short time at my disposal. I was to leave at five o'clock by the same train on which I had arrived, and at six o'clock I was again in Baltimore, Maryland.

This state is divided into twenty-two counties covering an area of 1,150 square miles. General election takes place on the first Wednesday in October, and the legislature assembles on the

[1] Since Bache says nothing about the debates in either of the houses that day, the discussions evidently were of little significance. An examination of the *Congressional Globe* (27 Congress, 2 Session, 637–44) supports this conclusion. In the House, one man "spoke through the entire morning hour" on a resolution having to do with the expenditures made by the government in satisfaction of bounty land claims allowed by the state of Virginia, but, the *Globe* reported, he "was inaudible at the reporter's desk." In the Senate, a variety of subjects were under discussion from a pension for the widow of a Revolutionary soldier to a provisional tariff bill and a naval appropriation bill, but there were no debates of consequence.

first Monday in December. Under the constitution, drawn up in 1776 and revised in 1838, the General Assembly consists of a senate of twenty-one members and a chamber of deputies of seventy-nine members. It assembles on the last Monday in December in Annapolis. Each member receives four dollars a day. The state produces mainly tobacco, wheat, some cotton, hay, and hemp.

At seven o'clock I left Baltimore by steamer, going up Chesapeake Bay to Frenchtown, where I took the train to Newcastle, about sixteen miles up the Delaware River. We left the latter place by steamer and, as night had already fallen, I went to bed.

*June 17.* When we got out of bed and up on deck, we noticed that we were approaching Philadelphia. The banks of the river were low just as they are above the city. We arrived there at five o'clock, and, since we were not to leave until half past ten, I had breakfast and then wandered around seeing as much as the time would allow. The city has a fine location on a level stretch of land between the Delaware and Schuylkill rivers, about five miles above their junction. It is the largest city in Pennsylvania and, next to New York, the largest in the United States, having a population of approximately 220,000.

The state of Pennsylvania, with an area of 47,500 square miles, is divided into fifty-four counties. The general election takes place on the second Tuesday in October, and the legislative assembly meets on the first Tuesday in January at Harrisburg, the capital of the state. By the constitution, made in 1790 and revised in 1838, the members of the senate are elected for a term of three years, one third retiring and another third being elected annually.

At half past ten I crossed the river on a steam ferry that went through a little sound formed by two small islands in the middle of the stream. When we got to the other side, where we boarded the train, we were in the state of New Jersey. This state has an area of 7,500 square miles and is divided into seventeen counties.

The general election is held on the second Tuesday in October while the legislature, consisting of a legislative council of fourteen and a general assembly of fifty members, gathers in Trenton on the fourth Friday in October. The members of both houses are elected annually. The constitution dates from 1776.

After following the river for a while, the train switched to another track that cut across the state toward a place near Sandy Hook where we arrived about one o'clock. From here we traveled by steamer, enjoying fine, quiet weather. We passed Staten Island, the quarantine station for immigrants, and finally reached New York about four o'clock. The trips I wished to take hereabouts were now completed, and the voyage to Europe, on which I expected to start in a few days, lay ahead.

The state of New York covers an area of 49,000 square miles and is divided into fifty-six counties. Albany is the capital. By the constitution, adopted in 1821, the general election is held on any day in October or November chosen by the legislature. This body assembles on the first Tuesday in January. The senate, composed of thirty-two members, is elected for a period of four years, one fourth retiring annually. The house of representatives has one hundred and twenty-eight members, elected annually. They receive $3.00 a day; the president of the senate, $6.00 a day.

What little time I had left I spent visiting my acquaintances here. On returning from my last excursion, I asked the captain if he had received a letter from Corneliusen which I was to take to Norway, but he said there was none. I concluded, therefore, that he must still be here and decided immediately to go to his lodgings. When I opened the door his face broke into a smile, and I was very happy to see him also. I stayed with him until evening and received the letter unsealed together with a miniature portrait of him that was to be a present for his sister. In order to make our last days together more pleasant we visited some public places with which he was familiar. But I also took this occasion to see my other friends. Finally, on June 21, Cor-

61

neliusen and I said good-by to each other, for on the following day he was starting his journey to the interior of the country.

*June 22.* I went uptown today to say farewell to my friends, since the ship leaves tomorrow. When I came to Mr. Lund, he invited me to accompany him across the sound to Brooklyn in the afternoon to spend the evening with his pleasant family, con- sisting of the master of the house, his wife, and son. When I was ready to leave, about nine-thirty, he asked me to take a letter to Europe which he would bring tomorrow.

*June 23.* Lund brought the letter this morning, and I went with him to his studio where I stayed awhile and said good-by to him for the last time before going aboard the ship, which had already started to cast off from the pier. Besides a cargo of train oil, the ship carried six cabin passengers — two Americans, a per- son from Hamburg, two Jews, and me — and an equal number of steerage passengers. Just as we were ready to sail, our first mate left us to become captain on another boat. But finally at eleven o'clock we left New York aboard the *Howard.* The captain, P. N. Paulsen, comes from the island of Föhr. Since there was no wind today, we merely drifted with the ebbing tide and got no farther than Sandy Hook where, together with four or five other boats, we cast anchor and had to remain overnight waiting for a good wind.

*June 24.* Late in the forenoon, about ten or eleven o'clock, a mild breeze sprang up from the south, and all anchors were weighed. When we reached the open sea, we dropped our pilot. As the day advanced the wind increased, and before long we lost sight of land. Clear out to the horizon's rim there was nothing but sea and sky.

During the voyage nothing of moment occurred. We saw ships every day, and one morning about mid-ocean, we discov- ered a ship ahead of us which we passed shortly after noon. We finally came to a standstill, however, since there was no wind that day. The other ship had hoisted signals, but as we had nothing to signal with, we did not reply. After a while we saw them put out a boat that soon traversed the mile that separated us. They wished to buy bread and, having obtained this, took it back to their ship. Then they returned with the payment, consisting of sugar and some English newspapers. Among the sailors was a Norwegian whose home was somewhere west of Christiansand — I do not remember exactly where. The home port of the ship was a town on the eastern coast of Scotland, but it was now returning from Brazil with a cargo of sugar. We had rain only twice on this trip, and at no time did the waves flood the deck. One day the captain aroused a little excitement by harpooning a very large porpoise.

*July 30.* Sunday we saw the coast of the Isle of Wight rising steeply out of the water, the first European land sighted on the trip. Progress has been very slow lately since easterly winds have been blowing the last eight days or so. Because of the contrary winds, we had to set our course directly toward France.

*August 1.* Today we sighted the coast of France near Havre.

*August 4.* Today we passed Dover. The weather was fine and the water calm and clear as a mirror. For a long while we heard the boom of cannons from the English coast.

*August 8.* Late yesterday evening we saw the lighthouse on the island of Helgoland, and today — Monday morning — about seven o'clock we came to the lightship at the mouth of the Elbe River where we took on a pilot. He wore a pair of big baggy trousers and a blouse with a badge in front which undoubtedly was the sign of his guild. After we passed Dover and were out on the North Sea, we had beautiful weather with a gentle wind. The voyage was very pleasant; indeed it had been enjoyable all the way from New York, and this continued during our short trip up the Elbe. About two o'clock in the afternoon we cast anchor at a little town named Brunsbüttel. Having drunk our coffee, we followed the captain ashore in order to refresh ourselves with a bottle of wine and the feel of solid earth under our feet after more than five weeks at sea. Two of the cabin passengers transferred to another steamer which we had seen at the lightship. The first thing I inquired about after landing was how to make connections for Copenhagen. I learned that a steamboat for Hamburg was expected the next morning. After several hours ashore we went on board for our last night there.

*August 9.* When we got up this morning we noticed that the boat had been carried some distance by the current. About ten o'clock the expected steamer arrived and, after taking us aboard, continued on its course. Most of the passengers who had crossed the ocean with me transferred to this boat. When we came aboard we found a basket of fruit on the table from which we could help ourselves. The country above Brunsbüttel was low and flat, especially on the Holstein side of the river. We arrived at Hamburg about two o'clock, having enjoyed fine, warm weather all day.

One of my traveling companions and I had decided to stay together while in Hamburg, and as we came up from the pier we saw a carriage standing there. After asking the coachman about a good lodging place, we entered the carriage and were taken far into the city to a hotel near the theater and not far from the river Alster, which flows through Hamburg. After some refreshments, we went out to spend the rest of the day sight-seeing. Since I stayed here several days, I had a good opportunity to look about, but I soon tired of this because there were so many houses of ill-fame along some of the streets that I had to seek other sections of the city when I wished to be out.

Most of the houses in Hamburg were built in a very old-fashioned style of architecture. I also visited those parts of the town which had been ravaged by the fire [2] — a depressing sight.

[2] A fire in Hamburg, May 5–8, 1842, destroyed the greater part of the business quarter of the city.

A great number of those who had suffered losses had built houses beyond the city limits where there were also many beautiful country homes belonging to citizens of Hamburg.

*August 12.* As I was tired of wandering about here, I secured a passport from the Swedish-Norwegian consul, which I had failed to do in America, and about ten o'clock in the evening took the stagecoach across the Duchy of Holstein to Kiel, situated on a little arm of the Baltic. The distance was about twelve German miles. Since we covered the road by night, I had no chance to see the country through which we traveled, but I noticed that in several places the road was cut through hilly ground, making it fairly level.

*August 13.* About eight o'clock this morning we arrived in Kiel, and since the steamboat which I intended to take would not leave until afternoon, I made use of the interval as well as I could. The country around here is very hilly and rough.

In the afternoon another stagecoach arrived from Hamburg in which were two elderly Norwegian gentlemen, one of them accompanied by two beautiful daughters. I did not know what part of Norway they were from, but I took a seat in a corner near the door in order to listen to the conversation of the man and his daughters, which was amusing since they did not realize that I understood them. I was tempted to laugh but did not for fear of being noticed. Their conversation ran somewhat as follows:

"Father, let's have something to eat. We are awfully hungry."

"Oh, no," he replied. "What kind of talk is this? Let's wait until we get on the boat. Otherwise we will eat twice and that is not necessary."

"Oh, yes, Father, please let's have something to eat," exclaimed both girls at once. "We are starving."

The result was that he succumbed, and all three of them disappeared into the dining room. Then the other Norwegian gentleman came and sat down on the bench together with two Danes with whom he was talking. In order to learn the names and destination of these Norwegians I went to the vestibule and looked at their luggage. There I found the name of the man with the two daughters and noticed that they were bound for Arendal. But I went inside and asked the Norwegian sitting on the bench if he was Mr. So-and-so (I have forgotten the name) from Arendal. "No," said he, "I am Jacob Meyer from Christiania." This made me very happy, and I told him that I was the son of old Tollef Bache in Drammen. On learning that, he was as pleased as I, because he knew my father. He asked where I came from and where I was going, to which I replied that I had been in America and was now returning to Norway. After thus meeting and becoming acquainted with these people, I took a walk on a road along the coast where there were some beautiful country houses. About five o'clock I returned to the boat, anchors were weighed, and soon we were at sea again, enjoying the same fine weather as on previous days.

*August 14.* Sunday morning when I got up, the weather was still fine, and we were gliding easily over the surface of the water which was as bright as a mirror. All the elements were united, it seemed, to make this, my first trip on the Baltic Sea, a pleasant one. Eventually we sighted the white chalk cliffs of Moën, which we approached rapidly, speeded on by our one hundred and sixty horsepower steam engine. Later, in the distance, we could see the island of Zealand, forming the beautiful western coast of the sound we soon entered. At the northern end of Amager we turned toward the customhouse and dropped anchor in the roadstead, ending another lap of my journey. About two o'clock in the afternoon I came ashore and had my passport stamped and my luggage examined. The official asked if I had any dutiable goods, to which I replied that all I had was in my traveling bag. After these formalities I found lodgings not far away.

So I was in Copenhagen again, and soon I looked up a friend whom I visited every day during my stay here. One day I went to watch the civil guard training, but I was too late; it was their last day of drill, and I had to return without having my wishes satisfied.

*August 16.* This afternoon about four o'clock I left Copenhagen on the steamboat *Prince Carl.*[3] Again I happened upon the same people I had met in Kiel. We continued up the sound and passed Helsingør and Helsingborg late in the evening.

*August 17.* This morning at eight o'clock we arrived at Gothenburg and anchored at a place called Klippan until afternoon. Meyer and I rented a boat and went to the city, where we parted. I visited the shoemaker with whom Johansen and I stayed the last time we were here and, after several hours ashore, returned to the ship. All the other passengers who intended to take this boat also came aboard, and we sailed for Norway.

As I came out of the salon just after dinner, I met a man who asked if my name was not Bache. When I answered in the affirmative he introduced himself as a Mr. Hesselberg and informed me that he was in Gothenburg with a boat to get a cargo of timber. He said he had been watching me with a feeling that I was someone from Drammen. He made sure of this by asking an officer on the ship, who also told him that I was a Norwegian-American named Bache. Thus we became acquainted.

After relating this little conversation, I may as well recount another one. Mr. Meyer said he thought it was peculiar that a person would go to America, to which I replied that it was stranger yet that he would allow his daughter to go abroad. (On an earlier occasion he had told me that his daughter was married

[3] The *Prince Carl* and *Constitutionen* were the two first Norwegian steamships. They were built for the government in 1825 at a total cost of about 100,000 specie dollars. The *Prince Carl* (80 horsepower) carried mail and passengers to Göteborg and Copenhagen, making one trip every week during the months when the Oslofjord was free of ice. *Constitutionen* plied between Oslo and Christiansand.

to a foreigner!) He maintained that it was one thing to go abroad yourself and quite another thing to marry into a strange land, while I contended that it amounted to one and the same thing. Later he remarked that he still had an unmarried daughter at home, and immediately I asked if she was intended for me. "Well," he said, "you can always try your luck and see how you make out," which I admit was a very diplomatic answer. It promised nothing and offended nobody. Chatting in this way, we spent a very pleasant day and then retired.

*August 18.* I awoke this morning with a great feeling of joy. I sat up in my bunk and looked around the cabin. The light was burning on the table, and everything was quiet as in a dark, empty place. I began to wonder what the reason might be for I could not hear or see anything except what was in the confines of this little room. I thought it would be best to get up, because if I should go to sleep again the other boat that I was supposed to take might leave me behind. I had an idea that we must have anchored since everything was so much more silent on board than usual. So I got up, put on my best suit, and went on deck where I found everybody ready to go aboard the other steamboat, which was smaller than the one we were on. I cast a glance ashore to see if I could recognize old Norway after three years' absence, and I found it looked very familiar. With the others, I transferred to the *Carl Johan* and said good-by to the *Prince Carl*, which, by a coincidence, had taken me away from Norway and had now brought me back again.

From Fredriksvärn, the first port of call in my old homeland, we followed the Norwegian coast up the Christianiafjord and docked at Holmestrand about twelve o'clock after having touched at several other places. Here I dined with Hesselberg and a Swede at an inn where each of us also hired a cariole and horse with which to proceed upcountry toward Drammen. We stopped for a rest at Weierud farm in Sande parish and then continued on our way. As we passed Eeg farm in Scouge parish and looked up the valley toward Drammen and Lier, the distance between the mountains seemed much smaller than formerly. I suppose this was due to the fact that I had become used to the great open spaces in America. I parted with Hesselberg in Strømsø while the Swede left me after we had crossed the Drammen bridge.

The tollman at the bridge was the first of my old friends to greet me. Then I went up to see my brother-in-law E. Olson, who had moved into a new house on Bragernes Storgade during my absence. As soon as I got through the gate I jumped out of the cariole and ran up the steps into the kitchen. In my hurry I rushed by my niece Marie, whom I took to be some neighbor's child, but she ran out and shouted, "Mother, Mother, Søren has come!" By this time I was in the parlor, because the door was standing open; and soon I heard excited people running into the kitchen like a flock of sheep, so I rushed out again, and there I met my dear sister. She threw her head back and laughed in her joy. Here I also met Anne Brynildsen and several other people. Then I sent messages to my father and brothers telling them of my arrival. Soon my brother Tollef and Captain Hans Melsom came in to greet me. Naturally we talked much about America, since they were all anxious to hear about that country, which has been so widely discussed of late.

The day had been very warm and the roads dusty, and I was greatly in need of a general cleaning up after my long ride. I felt very happy to be at the end of my summer's journey and to be reunited with my friends and relatives after so long an absence.

*August 19.* After breakfast today I went to visit my brother Tollef. Things had changed so greatly during my absence that when I reached the street where he lived I had to ask directions from a man I met there. The house was pointed out to me, and I went in and greeted my brother. After staying there a few minutes I went on, and in the door of a near-by store I saw a stranger who, after I had walked a little way up the street, came running after me and started talking about his brother in America. On inquiring, I learned that his name was Ole Øvern, while his brother's name was Helge. He followed me to the gate of my brother Niels's farm on Landfaldøren. I had to search through every room before I found anybody, but when I came to the corner room facing the garden and the street, I finally discovered Miss Sophie Christensen sitting by the garden window. I inquired about my brother, who shortly returned from his lumber yard. After I had stayed for dinner with him, he let me take a horse and cariole out to Walle, my father's farm. A boy went with me to bring the horse and the cariole back. When I arrived there about three or four o'clock in the afternoon, I was received with great affection, and we were extremely glad to be together again. Anyone can imagine how happy father and son would be to meet each other in good health after so long a separation. Strangely enough, we had parted on a Friday afternoon and were reunited on a Friday afternoon. Of course, I had to tell him about all the journeys I had made during my absence.

After I had been at home a few days I suggested to father that I should like to visit the Storthing now that I had been in America. He thought the idea was a good one, and a short while afterward my wish was fulfilled, as we shall see.

*August 21.* Today, Sunday, my brothers and sisters came out to Walle, and we were all together for the first time in several years. In the evening when they left I went with them to the city for a few days.

*September 9.* This afternoon my brother Tollef came out to Walle to go with me to Christiania as we had previously planned. We expected our older brother Niels to accompany us, but since he did not come on time we left without him. It soon began to rain, however, and while we were seeking shelter and refreshment at the Asker Inn, Niels arrived accompanied by a merchant named Kapjon. They had some port, secured fresh horses, and continued on their way, while we followed a few minutes later.

Before long we caught up with them, and all of us entered the city together. It was already late in the evening when we got to our lodgings.

*September 10.* After taking care of some business matters for my father, I went to the Storthing where I spent most of the day. In the evening we went to an amusement place and had dinner.

*September 11.* Sunday morning Mr. Grimdal, representative from the district of Trondhjem, paid us a short call. In the afternoon I went to the farm Bredtvedt to see some old acquaintances of mine.

*September 12.* This afternoon I returned to the city and paid another visit to the Storthing, the second assembly of this kind that I had visited in two countries in two different continents, all within the same year or, more exactly, within four months. Thus another little ambition of mine had been satisfied.

*September [13?]* I returned to Walle today. My brothers went home last Sunday when I went to Bredtvedt.

During the latter part of this month my brothers and I, with several others, went on a two-day hunting trip in the forest between Mjøndalen and the paper mill at Eger. The weather was fine and we enjoyed the trip very much.

*January 24, 1843.* I accompanied my cousin Ole Olsen Bjoner on a little trip. First we took care of some business at Klommesteen, a farm half a mile east of Drøbak, and then continued on toward my cousin's home where we arrived late in the evening. As we were not feeling well, we rested here for several days. I spent the time quietly, and nothing noteworthy happened; indeed, I was rather bored.

*January 28.* Feeling somewhat better, we went on to Moss, where Ole Bjoner left me. I continued on to Søren Roer's home and stayed over Sunday.

*January 30.* I returned to Moss this afternoon and visited Smaaland, the dyer, with whom I spent the night. I also called on Mr. Thoresen.

*January 31.* After dinner I left town and went back to Bjoner for the night. An old friend of the family was there also, and we had a very merry time.

*February 1.* I went to Harrangen where Bjøn Spiketraad lives. The hilly roads were hard and slippery and driving difficult. I stayed overnight here.

*February 2.* Today I visited my cousin Ole Larsen on his farm, Storerud, where one has a good view of the fjord; otherwise it is located in an out-of-the-way corner. After dinner and an evening with his sister, who lives very near the fjord, we returned to Harrangen for the night.

*February 3.* Leaving this place for Drøbak, I crossed the sound and arrived at Walle this afternoon about four o'clock. The roads were icy and slippery almost all the way. Outside Moss in Rygge parish there was no snow, however, except where the road ran through woods.

*February 5.* My brother Niels invited me to attend a large dinner party at the Stock Exchange to celebrate the twenty-fifth anniversary of the coronation of our old king.[4] About one hundred and seventy-four people attended the dinner. In the morning ceremonial services were held in the church, with Pastor Arup preaching the sermon.

*February 7.* With my brother-in-law E. Olsen, I went to Christiania where a fair was being held this week. In the evening we attended a play called "The Lord Watches Your Steps."

*February 8.* On C. Blom's recommendation, Olsen bought a piano for his girls. We also visited the marketplace for a few minutes; business seemed to be slow. We then called on an old

[4] On being chosen crown prince of Sweden, Jean Baptiste Bernadotte, one of Napoleon's famous marshals, adopted the name of Karl Johan. He became king of Norway-Sweden as Karl XIV Johan on January 5, 1818.

acquaintance. In the afternoon I went up to look at the Royal Palace, which is not yet completed.[5] At five o'clock we left the city and about eleven reached Drammen where they were expecting us. The next morning I went out to Walle.

*March 24.* Friday morning, accompanied by my brother Niels, I took another trip to the capital, arriving there just before noon. In the evening we went to the theater and heard a three-act opera, "Luduvic." The next day we took care of all our business affairs.

*March 26.* We left the capital Sunday morning about nine o'clock and came to Asker Inn around noon. There we fell in with some other people going our way. When we had rested awhile we continued our trip, going over Røyken to Tangen, from where we followed the southern shore of Dramsfjord until we crossed the bridge at Drammen. As we passed through the town, one after the other left us so that we were alone when we got home about two o'clock.

[5] The cornerstone of the royal Norwegian palace was laid in 1825, but construction came to a standstill in 1827 and was not resumed until 1834 when a more modest plan was adopted.

# 4. *Return to America*

AFTER SEVEN MONTHS with my relatives, the time drew near when I again would have to part with family, friends, and fatherland, not knowing whether it should ever be my fate to return.

*April 14* [*1843*]. Today, Good Friday, we all gathered at my brother Tollef's home and had a very pleasant time.

*April 16.* Easter Sunday we all had a most enjoyable day at my brother Niels's.

*May 20.* Saturday morning at nine o'clock I said farewell again to my dear father at Walle since I am departing a second time from my native land. I was taken to Drammen by Andreas Larsen, a young boy who is going along to America. He took the horse back to Walle and on his return brought a letter from my father. I went into the garden to read it. What the contents of the letter were and what impression it made upon me under these conditions can well be imagined. I thought no one would find me there, but after a while Niels and the overseer of the sawmill at Mjøndalen joined me.

*May 21.* Sunday morning I spent quietly at my brother Niels's home, and in the afternoon we went down to the ship I was going to take to America, the *Johanna* of Bremen, Captain Luider Mensing, also from Bremen. When we came down to the water, we found boat lying by boat so close that a person could step from one to the other all along the harbor clear up to the ship. Thus it was all day — a throng of boats and spectators. In the evening we returned home.

*May 22.* This afternoon I took leave of my brother Niels and his family and went down to spend a short time with my sister and my brother Tollef. About five or six o'clock my brother-in-law was to take me down to the ship in his boat. Just as I stepped into the boat I looked around and happened to notice someone in the upper floor of the storehouse. I realized that it was my sister, but when she saw me looking up she stepped farther back so as not to be seen. Because of my own sad thoughts I could well understand what feelings must have been in her heart. But still I had a faint hope that I should meet her and be with her once again. At length we came down to the ship where the other passengers and I remained while the friends and relatives who had come down to see us off returned home.

*May 23.* About four o'clock in the morning we weighed anchor and began our journey. Since there was no wind, we got no farther than Svelvigen by eight o'clock. There we cast anchor, being unable to make any headway up the channel. Because of our slow progress during this short trip, we spent most of the time on deck with telescopes trying to get a good view of the countryside and the mountains along the fjord. Although there was no wind, Krogh, the gunsmith, managed to lose his hat, the first casualty on this trip. When we had dropped anchor, I went ashore with the captain and his wife for my first visit to Svelvigen. We wandered about there two or three hours before we went aboard again and then to bed for the night.

*May 24.* About half past four we got under way, and when I came on deck we had already passed Strømmen. Toward noon we passed Rødtangen and continued down the Christianiafjord, making very slow progress, however, because of poor wind conditions. At Holmestrand we chanced to see the *Prince Carl* touching at the pier. The weather was fine and our speed so leisurely that we had ample opportunity to watch the scenery along the fjord through our telescopes. It was very beautiful seen thus from the ship.

*May 25.* Today, Ascension Day, between nine and ten o'clock, we finally reached Färder light, where we dropped the pilot. The sky was clear except for a few pale clouds on the southern horizon, but by late afternoon most of the sky was overcast.

*May 26.* Today we had a favorable wind, enabling us to pass Christiansand shortly after nine o'clock and Mandal some two hours later. Through our telescopes we had a good view of these places. About three o'clock we passed Lindesnes, the southernmost point of my dear fatherland, which we now bade farewell.

*May 28.* This has been a stormy Sunday with rain and hail. We started sailing in a northwesterly direction since the captain intended to go north of Scotland; but because of the heavy storm he changed course so as to pass through the Channel. In the afternoon the weather improved, and the wind was favorable for the new course we had taken.[1]

*June 1.* Late in the afternoon we sighted land at Yarmouth. Through our telescopes we noted several towers, one being particularly prominent because of its great height, but we could not make out just what it was. Soon a pilot from the town came aboard, and in reply to our questions he informed us that what we took to be a tower was Admiral Nelson's monument. It must be of considerable height to seem so impressive even at a distance of three nautical miles. Our captain gave him a brief note to be inserted in the local newspaper to let the people at home know how we were faring.

*June 4.* Today was Whitsunday, and we enjoyed the finest weather imaginable. But in spite of the fact that there was little wind and the ship glided smoothly across the surface of the water, there was some seasickness aboard, though not as much as is the case in rough weather. Steamboats were plowing their way toward the mainland, creating a lively scene. The sailors had put on neat clothes today, as for a party. Even though we were afloat on this holiday it was very pleasant, and here and there on the deck you could see individuals sitting with their books, absorbed in devotional reading.

*June 5.* Today the weather was less beautiful, and there were

[1] See Appendix for the passenger list which Bache includes here.

contrary winds. We saw the city of Deal, which seemed to be located on a plain with high hills in the background. Because of the head wind we had to change our course so as to pass through the Channel. Sailing in this direction awhile brought us in sight of Calais, which appeared to have a location similar to that of Deal. Again we changed our course and now drew close to Dover.

*June 6.* Last night and this forenoon we were forced back some distance by the head wind and the current. In the afternoon, however, the wind became more favorable so that we could finally enter the Channel, which we had been trying in vain to do for several days.

*June 7.* We had advanced considerably during the night, and in the afternoon we passed Beachy Head about sixteen and a half leagues beyond South Foreland, located at the entrance of the Channel. Beachy Head lies about 285 feet above the surface of the water. Later in the afternoon we passed the towns of Newhaven, Brighton, and New Shoreham, making good progress westward; and this continued through the night.

*June 10.* Ever since Thursday, June 8, we have been facing such a strong head wind and current that the captain this afternoon decided to put into port at Dungeness about twenty miles west of Dover. This town was situated on a low, level plain, and close by was a high, round lighthouse painted red in order to serve as a landmark during the daytime. Behind it was an edifice that appeared to be a fortress. There were a great number of ships in the harbor, and while we were there another emigrant ship also arrived, presumably on its way to America. After we had cast anchor the wind changed somewhat, and we lay quiet throughout the night.

*June 11.* Today, Sunday, we sailed at about ten o'clock because the wind was now from the north. A great many ships were setting off in the same direction, and it was thrilling to watch them racing with each other, using every bit of sail they had. We passed almost all of them, only a few being able to keep pace with us.

*June 12.* Monday morning we passed the high cliffs of the Isle of Wight and in the afternoon, Start Point, seven miles southwest of Dartmouth.

*June 13.* At half past three this morning we passed Lizard Head southwest of Falmouth, the last land we would see before reaching America. The wind has been very favorable the last few days. At noon our bearings were 49° 15′ N. by 6° 38′ W. of Greenwich.

*June 23.* On Midsummer Night Jens Strøm, Amund Aamodt, and several others had a little spree. Jens Strøm had to "feed the fish" a bit but insisted that this was due to sickness since he had never been affected this way before.

*June 29.* Thursday evening between nine and ten o'clock, after most of the steerage passengers had gone to bed, the captain and I were sitting at the table chatting while the other four cabin passengers were sitting quietly in the storeroom. Suddenly Christopher Jaksland's wife came running to the cabin steps yelling that the passengers' galley was on fire. It gave us a peculiar feeling to realize that we were at the mercy of two elements. The captain and I rushed to the door. Just then the woman came tumbling down the stairs still yelling. The captain did not understand her, but when I explained to him, he cleared the stairs in a few jumps. We followed him, and when I got on deck I thought that the fire was more serious than it turned out to be since I saw the glow of a lamp within. Really, the fire was so insignificant that I went down to keep the captain's wife company. She had been sick the past days but had got up because of the excitement. I managed to convince her that there was no danger, and she calmed down a bit. Shortly afterward the captain and the others returned. Naturally we talked a great deal about this incident. As I have already stated, the fire was not serious, but Mrs. Jaks-

land had bolted out of bed too excited to put any additional clothing on, while Ole Gomperud had jumped right out of bed and
made for the pump.

During the night the weather was rough.

*July 19.* Toward noon our pilot came rowing out in a little
boat. The weather was calm and clear.

For several days the captain had been confined to bed with
rheumatism, and it was a pleasure to see how tenderly his wife
nursed him even though she was not well herself and had accompanied him on this trip in order to regain her strength. Many a
night she sat by his bedside to care for him. Every Sunday morning she would come up with a quart of raisins or prunes which
she distributed among the children by scattering handful after
handful on the deck. It amused us greatly to see them scrambling
and scuffling about for the fruit like a flock of chickens after
grain.

*July 20.* At five o'clock this morning we caught our first
glimpse of America. The weather was fine and enjoyable with
just enough wind for fair sailing. Today the captain was finally
able to come on deck after having been confined to bed for two
weeks. About noon we passed Sandy Hook with its many lighthouses and soon reached the quarantine station at Staten Island,
but it was almost five o'clock before we cast anchor. A doctor
and two customs officials came aboard to examine the passengers
and inspect our cargo. Fortunately all of us were found to be in
good health.

From a fortress on Long Island cannons were being fired at a
target far out at sea.

*July 21.* Friday morning the physician again came on board
and brought the captain some medicine for his rheumatism. Meanwhile I had received a letter from a man from Risør asking me
to get in touch with the agent of a transportation company here
on Staten Island to secure tickets for those passengers who were
going west with me. The sailors rowed the cabin passengers

ashore so that we might refresh ourselves after our long voyage. As soon as I landed I met the man from Risør accompanied by Cleng Peerson,[2] about whom I had heard rather unfavorable rumors in Illinois. Both of them praised the company in question as the very best one, which might well be true, for I had no knowledge of such affairs.

As we were going along we met two other persons who seemed to represent another company, and they offered me fifty dollars if I would induce my traveling companions to purchase tickets from them. To make me more favorably disposed, they took me in somewhere and treated me to a glass of cognac, which did me much good, indeed, but I stuck to my determination not to do business with anyone for the time being. Meanwhile we learned that two schooners were lying by our ship ready to take the passengers and their luggage ashore, so we returned aboard immediately. When I had been there only a few minutes, a messenger arrived asking me to go with one of the schooners that was to touch at a dock some distance from shore. This I did after having said farewell to our friendly captain, his wife, and the crew. When I came to the dock, there were some more agents who were insistent that I close a contract with them, which I would not consider until I reached New York. A representative of the company, George W. Anderson, then followed Christopher Aamodt and me to the city, where I wished to consult with a Norwegian broker named Balken. In his office I also met two other men connected with the company. After discussing certain

[2] As mentioned in the Introduction, Cleng Peerson was the first prominent leader of Norwegian immigration to America. He is generally recognized as having founded the first Norwegian settlements in the states of New York, Illinois, Missouri, and Iowa. He also tried to interest Norwegians in the state of Texas where he spent the last years of his life. Accounts of Cleng Peerson's activities can be found in the standard works on Norwegian immigration. See also Theodore C. Blegen, "Cleng Peerson and Norwegian Immigration," *Mississippi Valley Historical Review,* 7:303–31 (March 1921) and R. B. Anderson, *Kleng Peerson og Sluppen Restaurationen* (Chicago, 1925).

matters here we took a stroll in the city and then went down to the dock to meet my traveling companions. There I also met Peder Christensen from Drammen, who took me to his home for supper and the night. Thus practically the whole day was spent with this tedious business.

*July 22.* Last night I went to bed about eleven o'clock but did not fall asleep until nearly one, and even before I got up this morning there were two or three of the so-called "runners" outside keeping an eye on me lest I escape. After breakfast Christensen and I went down to talk with my traveling companions, and the runners kept trailing at our heels all the time like a pack of bloodhounds.

Yesterday Christensen and Christian Wold had proposed to us and the company representatives that we should not buy tickets for the entire trip but make arrangements for each stage of the journey separately. When we mentioned this to the agents this morning, however, they pretended never to have heard of such a proposal.[3] But after a great deal of arguing and debating, one of the runners finally offered terms that I readily induced my companions to accept after a few of them had expressed their willingness. The above-mentioned George Anderson grew very indignant when he learned this and accused me of double-crossing my countrymen, in spite of the fact that I secured lower rates for them than he or any other agents had offered. According to the terms agreed upon, an adult ticket to Buffalo was to cost $1.75. A hundred pounds of luggage could be carried free up the Hudson but only fifty pounds on the canal. There would be an extra charge of sixty cents per hundred pounds overweight. Children under twelve years of age were to travel for half fare while those under three could travel free.

About four o'clock in the afternoon we were finally through with this business, so some of us spent the rest of the day very

[3] The original passage is not wholly clear, but this translation renders its essential meaning.

pleasantly at a museum. There we met the captain and his wife, who kept us company until ten o'clock when we went to our respective lodgings.

It is a hard life to work like this all day for no compensation and with only one meal. It can be done for a day or two, but beyond that it is too strenuous.

*July 23.* Since I had been fortunate enough to finish those troublesome business affairs yesterday, I could spend today, Sunday, as I pleased. After a good breakfast and a shave I went down to Gasmann's ship and then to a public park or grove called Castle Garden where again I chanced to meet the captain just as if we had made an appointment. In accordance with his desire I went with him to the ship, which was still lying where we had disembarked. It took us about half an hour by steamboat to get there. He treated me to a good glass of wine, and while I was there I experienced a peculiar internal sensation which I shall not try to explain because such an odd case is too elaborate to describe. Down by the pier we had to wait some time for a boat, and in the meanwhile we had a few heartening drinks to celebrate the fine, warm weather. Back in New York we took a cab up to his lodgings in the City Hall on Broadway where I met his wife and had a good dinner. Shortly after the meal I bade them farewell and went down to my countrymen with whom I remained overnight.

*July 24.* This morning I learned the whereabouts of my old friend Peder Säther and immediately went up to see him. He had moved his office since last year. I accepted his invitation to spend the next night at his home in Brooklyn, but first I had to deliver a message to a Norwegian lady here who a few weeks ago had married a Frenchman named Brevor, a dealer in French and English goods. They received and entertained me well. In the afternoon at five o'clock they took an excursion boat to Albany, while I returned to Peder Säther's office as we had agreed. Soon we crossed over to his home in Brooklyn. On the way he showed me the house where he had first worked as a servant. I spent a very enjoyable evening with this congenial group.

*July 25.* After breakfast I took leave of the family and went with my host to New York to spend the day with some of my other friends. In the afternoon while visiting Mr. Rees, the tanner, I met Captain Overvind. At half past six, along with a brother of Mr. Rees who also was going west, I went down to catch the steamer *Rochester*, which started up the Hudson half an hour later.

*July 26.* Since we went up the river at night we did not have much opportunity to see the country, but after all I have taken this trip twice. By half past four we docked at the pier in Albany, and I went to a near-by hotel where I learned the whereabouts of my countrymen. When I got there some of them were just getting up while others were still in bed. They were all glad to see me, especially since I had kept my word and literally caught them before they could dress. After our luggage was sent, there was a lot of commotion, and we did not leave until six in the evening. Nothing unusual happened along the whole canal; the weather was fine all the way.

*August 2.* C. L. Clausen,[4] John Helgesen, C. Krogh, and P. Aamodt had arrived in Buffalo about a day before us, because they had taken the train from Rochester in order to be here early and arrange for the cheapest passage possible across the lakes. We arrived about seven o'clock this morning and found Helgesen on

[4] Claus Lauritz Clausen was born on the island of Ärö, Denmark, in 1820. After being educated as a school teacher he went to Norway in 1841 and became an influential lay minister. He had hopes of becoming a missionary in South Africa, but Tollef Bache diverted his interests to the Norwegian settlement in Muskego, which had been asking for a teacher. Shortly after his arrival there, however, he was ordained as a minister and served the community for a couple of years. Later he accepted calls from other congregations in Wisconsin, Iowa, and Minnesota. Besides taking an active part in ecclesiastical life he was also a pioneer editor of Norwegian-American publications and was one of the main promoters of Norwegian settlements in northern Iowa and southern Minnesota. Accounts of his activities can be found in the standard works on Norwegian immigration.

the pier to meet us. In reply to my inquiry he informed me that the price per ticket to Milwaukee would be two dollars with luggage free, which surely was very cheap. But I realized at once what kind of transportation this would be. If they were extremely lucky they might make the trip in two weeks, but if it should be stormy — as it frequently is on the lakes — they would not get to Milwaukee in less than three or four weeks. I wanted none of that, so I thanked Helgesen for his trouble and arranged for passage with a steamboat which I knew would leave at eleven o'clock.

Then Clausen also changed his mind and decided to go with me on the steamboat. He asked if I resented his conduct, and I could not deny that it seemed to me he had tried to arouse suspicion among the passengers by talking to them about the travel arrangements, thus hindering Christensen and me in our intention to go ahead of the rest and make the best arrangements for them that we could. Nothing came of our plan, however. During the last days at sea, so I heard, the passengers themselves had asked Clausen to request me to assume responsibility for the trip inland. This I refused to do but promised to help them all I could without unduly burdening myself.

We left at the scheduled time, while those who were going with Helgesen remained behind. As the other boat, carrying the rest of the party, had not arrived at the time of our departure, they also would have to go with Helgesen. The price per ticket on the steamboat was $5.50 with luggage free, making the total cost from New York to Milwaukee merely $7.25, plus luggage, which is the lowest fare I ever heard of for this trip.

*August 3.* This forenoon we touched at Cleveland in the state of Ohio, which is divided into seventy-six counties and has an area of 39,750 square miles. Columbus is the seat both of the higher authorities and of the legislature. A general election is held on the second Tuesday in October, and the legislature meets on the first Monday of December. The constitution was adopted in

1802. The Senate consists of thirty-six members with two-year terms, and the House of Representatives has seventy-two members elected annually.

Toward noon we reached Detroit, Michigan — a state that has forty counties and an area of 59,700 square miles. Here the general election is held on the first Monday in October, and the legislature assembles on the first Monday of January. The constitution was formed on May 11, 1835. Legislative powers are vested in a senate and a house of representatives. The members of the former are elected for two years, half of them each year, and their number is approximately one third of that of the representatives, who are chosen annually and cannot be fewer than forty-eight or more than one hundred. Detroit is the seat of the legislature and government. Late in the evening we landed near the tip of Lake Huron and took on fuel.

*August 5.* Today we passed several islands near the northern end of Lake Michigan, one of which was called Manitou. Someone told me that it was named for the god Manitou, and that in former times when there were thousands of Indians in this region they used to come to this island to worship him, because they believed that his spirit dwelt there. We stopped at Manitou to take on fuel.

*August 6.* Sunday morning at five o'clock we arrived at Milwaukee after four days of the finest sailing imaginable on the Great Lakes. Now I felt that I had come home again to Wisconsin.

On the boat Clausen had met a merchant from Madison who talked of hiring him as a clerk and Mrs. Clausen as housekeeper, a proposal which interested them very much. Of course I had to act as interpreter. This morning Clausen and I went up to the merchant's lodgings, but evidently he tried to avoid us. We returned again in the afternoon to find him still absent. Clausen wanted me to go with him a third time, but when I refused he finally gave up. If this plan had materialized, Clausen would not have been true to his original agreement to become a school-teacher among the Norwegians in America.

In Milwaukee I happened to meet Gasmann and his family.[5] Furthermore I was fortunate enough to meet some people from Muskego who had come in wagons, and so I was able to send some of my luggage out with them. I also asked that more wagons be sent up tomorrow to fetch the rest of my things.

*August* 7. About noon someone brought me a horse, while Even's two sons and several others arrived later with wagons. We began loading my goods and by eight o'clock were ready to leave town. The weather continued beautiful.

*August 8.* At one o'clock last night, long after everyone had gone to sleep and all was quiet, I arrived here on horseback. The dogs alone noticed me and began barking, but when I spoke to them they recognized me immediately and both of them came running out and jumped about me in their joy. After unsaddling the horse and caring for him, I went into the house. Johansen and Even got up to welcome me home, and we talked for a couple of hours before we retired to snatch a little sleep. About ten o'clock this forenoon a group including Mr. Brynildsen and Mr. Clausen with their wives also arrived. Our barn was crowded full of people who had just come; others were sleeping outside; and still more were expected.

[5] Hans Gasmann is well known in Norwegian immigrant history. In the fall of 1842 he sold his farm and mill near Skien and the next spring took passage for America with his brother Johan Gasmann, the captain of the ship *Salvator*. He took out a claim to 160 acres of land near Pine Lake, Wisconsin, and bought an additional tract of 1000 acres. Undoubtedly he had the future of his thirteen children in mind when he acquired all this land. Gasmann was a highly respected man in his home district and had twice been elected to the Storthing. Several of his letters sent home from Wisconsin were published in Norwegian newspapers and did much to advertise America among his countrymen. See Blegen, *Norwegian Migration, 1825–1865*, 206–208. The poet Pavels Hielm wrote a poem to Hans Gasmann which is translated with an introduction by Theodore C. Blegen and Martin B. Ruud in *Norwegian Emigrant Songs and Ballads*, 52–63 (Minneapolis, 1936).

When I returned I was told that the body of Johnsen, the Danish carpenter previously mentioned, was found this summer deep in the sand at the mouth of the Milwaukee River. There was no flesh left on his skeleton, but he still had his clothes on, and in his pockets were his money and his watch still in perfect condition after lying there four years.

*August 19.* Those of my traveling companions who had taken the sailing vessel to Milwaukee finally got here today. Thus they were on the lake thirteen days longer than I and those who came with me.

*August 20.* Today, Sunday, some of them came out to the settlement, and I learned that most of the group had become very tired of the long voyage and wished that they had taken the steamer instead. This would have saved them a lot of time which they could have used to good purpose instead of lying there idling on the deck. But so it goes when people ignorant even of the language of a country are too opinionated to listen to advice.

# 5. Ordaining a Pioneer Minister

*September 3* [*1843*]. AFTER THE SERVICES today, which were held in our buildings as usual since they are the largest in the settlement, a petition was signed which reads as follows:

Dear Pastor Krause: [1]

We, the undersigned Norwegian Lutherans settled in various parts of Racine and Milwaukee counties, Wisconsin Territory, have hitherto had no ordained Lutheran minister to preach the gospel or administer the holy sacraments among us, and consequently we have not formed a Lutheran Christian congregation but have lived like sheep without a shepherd, we as well as our children being constantly exposed to the danger of either lapsing entirely into worldly mindedness and a feeling of material security or of being ensnared by the well-nigh countless heretical teachers everywhere crying their motley wares — all of which lure us away from that meekness which is in Christ and lead unto spiritual death. We have long been aware of this, and, instead of indulging in mere wishes, we have sent written appeals to our fatherland hoping to induce some ordained Lutheran Christian pastor to come over for the purpose of gathering the dispersed flock and nurturing it with the good things of God's house. Up to the present, however, these efforts have been in vain. As recent settlers with modest means, we have not been able to promise a

[1] Reverend Leberecht Frederich Ehregott Krause was a member of the "Old Lutheran" faction in Prussia, which refused to abide by the royal decree of 1817 ordering the union of the Lutheran and Reformed churches in that kingdom. In 1838 he came to America and sent back enthusiastic reports to his fellow believers. The next spring a delegation led by Captain (later Reverend) Heinrich Von Rohr also came to this country further to explore the advisability of bringing the persecuted "Old Lutherans" to America. As Von Rohr agreed with Krause, about a thousand immigrants led by Reverend J. A. A. Grabau arrived in New York in October 1839. Part of the group settled in and near Buffalo where Krause was then located. The rest moved on to Milwaukee under Captain Von Rohr's leadership. A few settled in Milwaukee, but most of them went on to Ozaukee County where they founded the settlement of Freystadt (Freistadt). Before

rich living, and so far no one has been willing to brave the hardships of such a call.

Meanwhile some Christian friends in Norway who were acquainted with our situation and sincerely desired to relieve our
want spared no pains, especially after we sent them a written
appeal requesting and encouraging them to search for a spiritu-
ally-minded man who, even if not yet ordained, might have the
necessary ability and learning to come over and bring order out
of the chaotic conditions reigning here. At least as a beginning he
might do something for our children by organizing schools and
teaching them the fundamental truths of the Evangelical Lutheran faith; later, if we did not succeed in obtaining an ordained
pastor, he might seek ordination so as to administer the sacred
rites among us.

The choice of our friends fell upon the well-known Danish
Evangelical Lutheran school teacher, Claus Lauritzen Clausen.
This year, after he had received their offer and in the name of
God determined to follow the call, they sent him over to us with
the most favorable recommendations and testimonials. In accordance with our original plan he wished to begin teaching the children; but since it is far more important for us to bring order into
our church affairs, which under the present bad conditions must
become more and more chaotic, and since we have no more hope
than formerly of obtaining an ordained minister from home, we

long Krause also came to Freystadt and served as pastor there until 1848,
when he accepted a call at Martinsville near Buffalo. In 1845 the "Old
Lutheran" pastors, Grabau, Krause, Kindermann, and Von Rohr, met with
some lay delegates at Milwaukee and organized "The Synod of the Lutheran Church Which Emigrated from Prussia," more commonly known
as the "Buffalo Synod." This synod took an extremely high churchly, au-
thoritarian attitude toward ecclesiastical affairs. The Reverend Mr. Grabau,
dominant figure in the early history of the organization, "maintained that a
minister not called in accordance with the ancient 'Kirchenordnungen' was
not properly called; that ordination by other clergymen was by divine
ordinance essential to the validity of the ministerial office; that God would
deal with us only through the ministerial office; . . . that through her
Symbols and Constitutions and Synods the church at large must decide
what is in accordance or at variance with the word of God; . . . that Chris-
tians are bound to obey their ministers in all things not contrary to the
word of God." Edmund J. Wolf, *The Lutherans in America*, 413–14 (New
York, 1890). A brief account of the "Old Lutheran" migration to America
is in Wilhelm Hense-Jensen, *Wisconsin's Deutsch-Amerikaner bis zum
Schluss des neunzehnten Jahrhunderts*, 1:37–40 (Milwaukee, 1900).

have requested Clausen to seek ordination at his earliest opportunity and as our pastor to gather the dispersed Norwegian Lutheran congregation, nurturing it with God's pure Word and the holy sacraments. He received this proposal favorably because he knew that there were German Lutheran ministers near by whose language he understood and from whom he hoped he could obtain ordination.

Now that he has met you, Dear Reverend Pastor, and has discussed the local situation with you, and especially since our hope has been confirmed that you, together with another Lutheran minister, are willing to consecrate and ordain him as our pastor, it is our urgent and unanimous request that you, in cooperation with a Lutheran colleague, do ordain and consecrate this our brother in Christ, Claus Lauritzen Clausen, as our pastor and spiritual guide in accordance with the ordination ceremonial of the Lutheran church, pledging him thereby to preach the word of God, administer the holy sacraments, and order other churchly functions in accordance solely with the Bible and the symbolical books of the Norwegian and Danish churches. Hereby we also declare that when he is ordained we will gladly accept him as our pastor and spiritual guide, so to continue as long as he lives and teaches in accordance with his ordination vows. We further pledge ourselves to assume the responsibility of providing him and his family with the means necessary for their temporal welfare.

Racine County, Wisconsin Territory, September 3, 1843

This petition was signed by about seventy members of our settlement, some of whom were heads of families while others were single. The petition was written by Clausen himself, and in this connection I wish to say a few words about him. Judging by the impressions I got of him during the trip from Norway, he seemed to be very apprehensive and pessimistic about his temporal welfare, as is also indicated by a letter he sent my father from Denmark. I do not recall his exact words, but they were addressed to me since he was determined at that time to come to America and get a start in life here as a schoolteacher. In this letter I could detect an undue fear of travel in a foreign land as

well as much uneasiness about his material well-being. I sent him
a letter in reply which reads as follows:

To Mr. C. L. Clausen, Langeland, Denmark.

I have read your letter of September 22, from which I gather
that you wish me to assure you of a position in America as well
as a safe income for the future.

In view of your credentials, received from my father, I have
absolute faith in you as a man of good character and upright behavior. But you are still a total stranger to me, and I do not feel
that I ought to undertake any such obligations. You must not
believe that I lack faith in my father's recommendation. A thorough analysis of all facts involved, however, convinces me that
your request cannot be granted, as I shall presently explain.

Before leaving America I was well aware of the fact that the
Norwegians in my neighborhood wished to get a minister. Both
last year and this year Johansen, Even Heg, and Johannes Kure
wrote my father requesting that a seminary student be sent over,
who, to start with, might serve as teacher for their children and
later become their minister. The problem of finding a suitable
man for this position has occupied my father very much, but he
has had to inform the people over there that so far he has not
succeeded. I know, however, that their desire still persists, and
even though I have no children I wish to shoulder my part of the
burden so as to assist my fellow immigrants and help build the
future of the settlement. But since I have no authority to enter
into any binding agreements on their behalf I do not see my way
clear to offer you the assurances desired.

In America things are done quite differently from here. Not
only judges but also sheriffs are elected by the people for terms
of four years. If they are found satisfactory they are reelected.
Ministers are also chosen by the congregations, and a minister
without a congregation can not conduct weddings.

As for the land, it is very good and rich and bears all sorts of
grains without being fertilized. There is still plenty of government land to be had at $1.25 per acre, an acre being about the
same as a Danish *tönde*. All the people from various parts of
Norway with whom I have talked over there are very well satisfied. I believe that anyone who is not too emotionally bound to
his native place will be happy in America. The financial burdens

are much smaller there than here since our heaviest taxes amount to merely one per cent plus two days of work per year on the highways for men under fifty. No poor people are ever seen there.

Friendly greetings from

S. B.

Walle via Drammen, October 6, 1842

That was my answer to his request. But now, instead of starting a school, he aspires to become pastor and spiritual guide for the settlement. A pastor may, of course, be a necessity, but Clausen could also have accomplished a great deal as teacher. Although his manners and appearance create a very favorable impression, it is to be feared that his inner qualities do not correspond to his fine exterior. There always have been and still are those who under the cloak of religion do many things which have bad results. I do not venture to say that Clausen is one of these, though I might have my suspicions.

*October 12.* Thursday morning Even Hansen Heg, A. Hansen (the gymnastic instructor),[2] and I took a trip up to the German settlement in Washington County about forty miles from here and eighteen miles northwest of Milwaukee in order to be witnesses at Clausen's examination. Naturally the German language was used since the examiner, Mr. Krause, understood neither English nor Norwegian. An American named Mr. Leonard Martin, a surveyor and a good friend of mine, took us up there. We arrived late in the evening, and the minister was very

[2] Hansen had been a gymnastic and dancing teacher in Norway. When Pastor Dietrichson (see Chapter 7, note 1) came to Muskego in 1844, his visit to Hansen's cottage occasioned the following reminiscence: "After collecting myself a bit I recognized in Mr. Hansen the dancing master of my childhood years, and through my mind passed reflections upon the strange ways of life. On the bed in the hut lay Hansen's old violin with its bow. How vividly I recollected the many well-deserved sharp raps . . . which my spindly legs, adorned with white socks and dancing shoes had received from that bow when I tried to learn waltz steps to the tune of that same violin at the dancing school in the city of Fredrikstad. . . ." *Reise blandt Emigranter*, 25. One of Hansen's daughters married J. D. Reymert (see Chapter 14, note 2).

92

glad to see us. When it was time for bed he brought forth his books for devotions.

They started by singing, which was done in this fashion: first he read a stanza, whereupon the whole family joined in and sang it. Then he read the second stanza, and the whole family sang it. Thus they continued until they were through with the whole hymn. Next he read a chapter from the Bible, after which all of them knelt by their chairs and said some prayers. This finished, they resumed their seats and went through another hymn in the same manner as before. Not until then was it permissible to go to bed.

*October 13.* This morning devotions were held in the same way as last evening. After breakfast Hansen and I went out for a walk. A little earlier Clausen had shown us their simple little church. On the door was posted a notice which, according to Clausen, stated that late one evening when Krause and his family were returning from a visit with one of the parishioners some people who evidently had a grudge against him started throwing stones at them. It is not known who did this, but it is easy to understand how well Pastor Krause gets along with the people in the community when they pelt him with rocks. On this walk Hansen and I allowed ourselves plenty of time and found when we returned that they had waited a long while for us. By that time Martin had also arrived. He had spent the night in a German inn close by where conditions were not very satisfactory.

Finally we went upstairs to hear the examination. There we sat as stiff as wooden images. We heard something going on, but what was it? I do not know because I did not understand the language. Furthermore I was so sleepy that I had a terrible time keeping my eyes open. Late in the afternoon the matter was finished so that we could escape from our prison. Later Clausen came down with a document relating to the proceedings of the day which was signed by all who were present at the examination. During the rest of the afternoon we were liberally treated to things to eat, and this day was brought to a close in the same manner as yesterday. Hansen and I determined that next morning we would leave this place, which already bored us.

*October 14.* About ten o'clock this forenoon, in accordance with our decision, Hansen and I left the others at Pastor Krause's and went to Milwaukee, where we arrived at five in the afternoon. Here I visited old friends of mine.

*October 16.* I spent yesterday, Sunday, quietly here in Milwaukee, and today at ten o'clock the rest of our party arrived accompanied by Pastor Krause, who was going with us to the Norwegian settlement. We left the city about two o'clock and got home very late in the evening to find that everyone had missed us very much.

From Milwaukee up to Pastor Krause's home the country is covered by dense beech forests with a sprinkling of other varieties of trees. The population consists almost exclusively of Germans, most of whom do not understand any English at all. During my brief stay among them I got the impression that they associate very intimately with each other. This struck me as being a type of hypocrisy, especially all the unseemly kissing among the menfolk both when they met and parted.

*October 18.* This forenoon many of the Norwegians in the settlement gathered in our home to attend the ordination rites.[3] The ceremony began, but what Pastor Krause said none of us understood. When it was finished he drew up credentials of ordination, which Clausen translated into Norwegian. They read as follows:

[3] Clausen is frequently referred to as the first Norwegian Lutheran minister ordained in America. This is not quite correct, however, because Elling Eielsen had been ordained by a German pastor fifteen days earlier. "The validity of the ordination was later challenged by hostile critics of Eielsen, especially from within the camp of the Norwegian Synod, but historical investigation has completely sustained it." Theodore C. Blegen, *Norwegian Migration to America: The American Transition,* 137 (Northfield, 1940).

In the name of the Triune God:

I, Leberecht Frederich Ehregott Krause, Evangelical Lutheran pastor of the Evangelical Lutheran church in township 9, Washington County, and in the city of Milwaukee, hereby certify publicly by virtue of my office that the Reverend Mr. Claus Lauritzen Clausen, called to the ministry by the Evangelical Lutheran congregation in Racine County and Milwaukee County (i.e. called to the Norwegian Lutheran congregation there), has on this, the 18th day of October, 1843 A.D., been ordained at the request of the said Norwegian Lutheran congregation in Racine and Milwaukee counties in accordance with the rites of the Evangelical Lutheran church and has sworn a sacred oath on the Bible and the symbolical books of the Lutheran Church of Norway and Denmark.

May the grace and blessing of the Triune God prosper and aid him in preaching the Word of God and in administering the holy sacraments as well as in performing all the other pastoral duties whereunto the Reverend Claus Lauritzen Clausen hereby is declared commissioned and authorized. In the name of the Apostolic Lutheran church, in the name of which and by the authority of which I, the above named Leberecht Frederich Ehregott Krause, have conducted this holy ordination.

In testimony of the truth hereof I have personally set my hand and seal to this certificate.

Done in Racine County on October 18, 1843 A.D.

> L. F. E. Krause, Evangelical Lutheran pastor of
> the Evangelical Lutheran church in township 9,
> Washington County and the city of Milwaukee.

In order to officiate at weddings Clausen had to file an English copy of the credentials with the clerk of court and received in return a document which reads as follows:

Territory of Wisconsin — Racine County. So I, Henry A. Coos, Clerk of the District Court in the County of Racine, do hereby certify that the Reverend Claus Lauritzen Clausen has this day filed a translated copy of his credentials of ordination, according to the requirement of the statute, in my office.

In testimony hereof I have hereunto set my hand and seal of one [*sic*] court at Racine this 31st day of October, 1843.

> Henry A. Coos

From the preceding documents it will be seen that Clausen has received full power to perform all pastoral duties among us as clergyman and spiritual guide. On the two Sundays since his ordination when he conducted services he also administered Holy Communion, and on those occasions I noticed that he did not follow exactly the forms we used at home. When promising absolution he asked the questions which the ministers in Norway put to the candidates for confirmation: "Dost thou renounce the devil, and all his nature, and all his works?" Instantly I thought, "Perhaps little by little you will introduce changes. If that is the case you will soon find out how long you will continue as pastor here."

*November 6.* Today Even's son Hans and I took a trip to Burlington to sell some berries. We did not return until late in the evening. The country between here and Rochester was very rough.

*December 4.* When I heard this morning that Editor Reiersen of Christiansand had come here, I looked him up and brought him home with me.[4] According to his account he came here rep-

[4] Johan Reinert Reiersen was a liberal journalist who played an important part in the history of early Norwegian emigration. In 1839 he founded *Christiansandsposten*, which strongly advocated emigration and was thus instrumental in making this one of the most hotly discussed questions in the Norwegian press for several years. His trip to America in 1843–44, partly financed by a group of interested persons, was undertaken for the specific purpose of discovering the most favorable location for prospective Norwegian immigrants. He landed in New Orleans and went up the Mississippi to St. Louis, after which he traveled extensively in Ohio, Illinois, Wisconsin, and Iowa. He thought of going to California but was induced to go to Texas instead. After his return to Norway he wrote a book entitled *Veiviser for norske Emigranter til De forenede nordamerikanske Stater og Texas* (Christiania, 1844). This "pathfinder" gave a comprehensive account of conditions and opportunities in America. In a chapter on Norwegian settlements he speaks very unfavorably of the Muskego district. An English translation of this chapter by Blegen is in *Norwegian-American Studies and Records*, 1:110–25 (1926). Texas impressed Reiersen favorably, and in 1845 he and a group of his countrymen settled at Brownsboro in the northeastern part of the republic. In 1848 he founded a new settlement at Prairieville, southwest of Dallas. Before leaving for America in 1845, Reiersen began publishing a monthly, *Norge og Amerika*, which during the next two years served him and his friends as an organ for disseminating their proemigration views. In spite of the eloquence of Reiersen and his friends, the

resenting a group of three or four hundred Norwegians — farmers and others — who wished to locate together and thus form a settlement somewhere in America. So far Wisconsin seemed most attractive to him, he claimed. He stayed here several days studying conditions, but I heard that he was not favorably impressed with this district. I suppose, however, that his knowledge of soils is rather limited.

*December 14.* This morning a large number of settlers gathered in our house to enroll as members of the Lutheran church. At the conclusion of the business it was found that sixty-one farmers from Racine County had joined, which would make about two hundred souls counting men, women, and children, while twenty-three farmers from Milwaukee County had joined, adding some seventy souls more counting men, women, and children. Thus the congregation as today organized had a total membership of about two hundred and seventy souls drawn from the two counties. I did not join because I wished to see what would develop out of the innovations Clausen had introduced in the service. Four deputies or trustees were chosen from each of the two counties: Johannes Johansen, Even Hansen Heg, Johannes Skofstad,[5] and Anders Kløve from Racine County; Amund Hansen, Reier Nubberud, Gitle Danielsen, and Torger Luraas from Milwaukee County, a total of eight trustees for the congregation.

*December 24.* Today, the fourth Sunday in Advent, Ingeborg Sørine Jensdatter was married to Christopher Olsen Aamodt at two o'clock in the afternoon. To celebrate the occasion I invited

Wärenskjolds, who joined him in Texas in 1847, that state never attracted a great number of Norwegians. Reiersen died in Prairieville in 1864. See Anderson, *Norwegian Immigration (1821–1840)*, 370–86; Blegen, *Norwegian Migration, 1825–1860, passim.* A series of letters written by Reiersen have been translated by C. O. Paulson and the Verdandi Study Club and edited by T. C. Blegen under the title "Behind the Scenes of Emigration: A Series of Letters from the 1840's," *Studies and Records*, 14:78–116.

[5] In the manuscript the name is spelled "Schovstad."

some of the old acquaintances. Among the guests was an unbidden German whom Clausen had invited. He stayed around here some days. There were twenty-two people present besides the considerable number who live in the house. The party broke up about nine or ten o'clock. As the guests had to leave in damp, foggy weather, it was not in that respect a desirable wedding day.

# 6. Sickness, Misery, and Frontier Travels

SINCE I returned from Norway, we have been harried by much sickness. No fewer than seventy people all told died during the fall, so that conditions have been just as bad as they were in Illinois in 1839. One reason for this may be that after the immigrants landed in Milwaukee they came out here, wagonload after wagonload, most of them too poverty-stricken to go farther. They had nothing to live on, and the older settlers had to take care of them, with the result that fifteen to twenty people were frequently crowded into a house. One after the other was taken ill. There were many contributing factors.[1] Wells were few, and there was nothing to drink in most of the houses but brown marsh water. The newcomers were also unaccustomed to our diet which consisted mostly of pork, beef, milk, cheese, and wheat bread, while back in Norway they had been used to nothing but coarse oat bread. Added to all these things were the hardships of the long journey, aggravated by the poor food which most emigrants brought along, and the weeks of idleness enforced upon people generally accustomed to hard work. Finally, the climate in the new land was different from that of Norway. The continual care for the sick, both night and day, finally told so heavily upon those who were well that they too succumbed. In many houses one after another sank down upon his bed until there was no one left to tend the sick. It is easily understood how unsanitary conditions became in times like these,

[1] The reader of the diary may be interested, after noting the attempts of Bache to explain the causes and conditions of disease that harried the settlement, to read two modern surveys of the inroads made by malaria, cholera, typhoid fever, and other diseases in the pioneer colonies. See Blegen, *Norwegian Migration to America: The American Transition*, 54–68 (Northfield, 1940), and Knut Gjerset and Ludvig Hektoen, "Health Conditions and the Practice of Medicine among the Early Norwegian Settlers, 1825–1865," *Studies and Records*, 1:1–59.

and it is no wonder that matters went as they did. I do not recall any other year since I have been here bringing as much poverty and misery as this one. As an example I can mention that a certain man started out from upper Telemark with six or seven hundred specie dollars. He went by way of Havre, and on the trip across he helped so many that when he arrived here he had only sixty or seventy specie dollars left. That is the way it was with many. They had some money when they left home, but on the way across they helped others until they finally got into the same predicament as those who had to borrow. Whom could they blame but themselves for getting into a fix like this?

Of course misfortunes occur any place, and out here it usually happens that noxious fumes escape from the soil the first years it is cultivated. This is to be expected, for the ground here has been untouched ever since the creation of the world and whatever has gone out of the earth has returned to it. Then when the plow is put into the soil, it is only natural that these accumulated fumes should escape, and possibly this was another reason for the outbreak of disease. When the soil has been cultivated some years, the district usually becomes very healthful. As a matter of fact our neighborhood experienced no sickness until the outbreak last fall. Many who were then stricken lost heart and cursed the day they left their native land. They reasoned that if they had remained at home they would have escaped the plight in which they now found themselves. This may all be true, but it is also possible that if they had remained in Norway something equally bad might have struck them. While they were in this miserable state, they wrote letters home which were as full of venom as their hearts were full of hatred for this place.

*December 28* [*1843*]. Ingeborg and her husband left us today. They are moving up to his land close to Rock River. Both of them were rather sad at the parting.

The eight deputies, or rather trustees, were gathered here today to discuss some congregational matters. The first point taken up was the question of the pastor's salary. It was agreed that a list should be sent around so that the parishioners could declare how much they would be able to pay the minister the first year. Those who might wish to pay in produce should come to terms with the minister as to when deliveries would be most needed, what a day's wage should be reckoned at, etc.

The second point discussed was whether the congregation should buy a forty-acre piece of land which already had been used as a burial ground, the proposal being that a church should also be built there while the remainder of the land could be left for the use of the minister. No agreement could be reached on these points because the representatives from Milwaukee County wanted the church and graveyard located farther north at the place selected (and at one time also accepted) by the settlers in this neighborhood. This place would have a very fine location since it lay on a high hill in the southeastern corner of section 17, township 4, range 20 from which there is a beautiful view toward the north, east, and south. Toward the west, however, the view would be cut off by rising ground. Furthermore the place would serve well as a graveyard because the soil for several feet down consists of coarse sand intermingled with small limestones. The trustees from Milwaukee County argued that it would be too far south for them to bring the corpses to the place proposed by the men of Racine, but the latter countered that their place ought to be accepted because it lay right in the heart of a ten-mile stretch of territory coinciding with the settlement. They pressed their point still farther and argued that in the summer the people on the prairies farther south would have to travel some ten or twelve miles to reach the place though in the winter they would have only half that distance since they could then cross the lakes and big marshes on the ice and snow. Thus the contentions of the Milwaukee deputies were shown to be groundless. But they could come to no agreement, and the matter was tabled for the time being.

*December 31.* This, the last day of the year, a Sunday, is very beautiful with clear skies, bright sunshine, mild easterly wind, and clear, bracing air. It is not cold; as a matter of fact the snow is thawing slightly and the roads are rather soft.

Mrs. Brynildsen has not been well lately and has had to stay in bed, but today she has been up part of the time. Mr. Brynildsen had induced Clausen to try to persuade me to go back to Norway with him, but they failed in this even though Brynildsen himself had been after me some time earlier.[2]

*January 10, 1844.* Toward noon the portrait painter Theodore Lund arrived, accompanied by an American from Racine. They told us that some food and clothing which had been collected to relieve the want among the Norwegians in the settlement could soon be expected. This material will come in handy because the people here have been unable to earn a living as a result of the sickness spoken of earlier. It is true that the misery and poverty is extreme, the greatest which ever struck any Scandinavian settlement in the heart of this continent. Some of the goods are expected this evening so that distribution can begin in a few days.

[2] At this point Bache introduces a passage of some thirty pages, which he describes as "Brief excerpts of what I found in a book" having to do with the "organization, territorial arrangements and government of the whole country" in addition to "some less important things particularly with reference to some of the states through which I have traveled — their area and division into counties, their legislatures, when they are elected and when and where they assemble. . . ." The strange assortment of detailed and statistical information that follows is evidently copied from one of the almanacs or handbooks of the time, and is omitted from the present translation. From "a New York paper . . . called *Weekly Express*" he copies two long tables showing (1) the total indebtedness of each state and territory and (2) the amount of money that could be raised in each state by the sale of land at $1.25 per acre. Following this he gives "excerpts from the almanac for the year 1844" showing the population by states and territories, the total number of individuals on United States warships on June 1, 1840 (as well as the name and number of cannon of each warship), the proportionate population increase by decades, and a breakdown of population for both whites and colored people by age groups, sex, and occupation. After some tables showing the number of deaf, mute, blind, insane, and feeble-minded in the country, he ends with a list of the chief officials of the United States from the time the government was founded to his own day.

Undoubtedly the Norwegian immigrants were partly responsible for this catastrophe, because most of those who came to Wisconsin last year flocked in here, as if there were no other place to go, and lay around in idleness instead of seeking employment somewhere else. Furthermore, they prevented the older settlers from getting their work done on time, and so everything seemed to slow down. Thus one thing and another brought on the misery. It must be said, however, that as most of them had neither money, food, nor clothing when they came here, they may be excused. But if we go back to the time before they left their homes, we will find much to criticize in their whole procedure. Apparently many of them set out for America with very little money, thinking that their troubles would be over as soon as they reached Havre or New York. But it turned out quite otherwise. Then their difficulty began in earnest, and those who still had some cash left when they reached the end of the journey had to support those poor creatures who were entirely penniless. Thus upon their arrival in America those who had some money were reduced to the same level as those who needed help. This practice, of course, was designed to spread the misery — and that is exactly what it did. One suspects that such people have conceived the most fantastic notions about America. We could very well apply to them the old Norwegian saying that they expected roast doves to fly right into their mouths. If a person wants to live he must earn his livelihood by labor, which in certain respects may be easier to do here than in Norway.

*January 12.* The weather was cloudy and foggy but quite mild today. C. L. Clausen and Theodore Lund visited the homes of the needy, which by now were quite numerous since even some of those who had land were said to be in desperate straits. The distribution of supplies got under way, and some of the finest clothes were sold to raise money with which to buy more necessary things such as beef and pork. These fine clothes were of no use to laboring people who need something stronger and more durable to wear.

*January 13.* Today Lund and the American left us. They had very fine weather for their homeward journey.

*January 17.* This forenoon Brynildsen and I started out on foot to visit the Norwegians who last fall had settled up north by Pine Lake and Rock River. After we had walked about five miles we came to the home of an old American friend of mine where we rested awhile and had dinner. After having eaten and inquired about the shortest way, we continued our trip and by evening reached the little town of Prairieville, which I had visited about two years before. The weather was fine and the roads in good condition so that walking was quite pleasant. We stayed in Prairieville overnight.

*January 18.* About eight o'clock this morning we set out again and were fortunate enough to have the same kind of weather as yesterday. When we left home our intention was to visit Rock River first, but when we got about seven miles beyond Prairieville we changed our mind and went to Pine Lake instead, which was only some five or six miles away. Thus we came to Hans Gasmann's place about three o'clock this afternoon.

He was not at home when we arrived since he and several of his neighbors were meeting with some Episcopalian ministers from this area in order to get Mr. Unonius, a Swede, installed as minister for the local Scandinavian settlement.[3] The understand-

[3] Gustaf Elias Unonius (1810–1902) was born of a well-to-do official family and was educated at Upsala University. In 1841, accompanied by his wife and a small group of "better folk," he emigrated to America and founded the settlement of New Upsala near Pine Lake. Attracted in part by the writings of Unonius, immigrants from all the Scandinavian countries settled in this vicinity. The first Norwegian settlers arrived there in 1843. Having received a call from the Scandinavian settlers, Unonius took up the study of theology at the Nashotah Episcopal Seminary and in 1845 was ordained an Episcopalian minister. After serving several frontier communities, he moved to Chicago in 1849. There a group of Norwegians and Swedes united under his leadership to organize the St. Ansgarius congre-

ing was that before his ordination Unonius should spend a year at the newly opened Episcopalian school or seminary preparing himself for his pastoral duties. His salary of $500 was to be paid by the Episcopalian church, thus giving the Scandinavian settlers a minister with no cost to themselves. When Gasmann came home accompanied by *Lensmand* Bellerud, we talked much about this matter but rather in a joking vein since Bellerud was quite a clown.[4] He stayed until late in the evening, and when he left he asked us to visit him tomorrow and spend the night there.

The last part of our trip up here had taken us through country that appeared to be dry, flat, and poorly wooded, but as we neared the northern end of the lake whose western shore we followed, the woods improved. To all appearances it would be difficult to obtain winter fodder for the cattle here because there is no place within a distance of three or four miles where it can be gathered.

*January 19.* North of the house and slightly to the right there was a long slope from the top of which we could look over the trees and get a good view of the landscape for several miles around. In the afternoon we went over to Bellerud's, about a

gation. Besides serving as Swedish consul and engaging in turbulent conflicts with Lutheran antagonists, Unonius became an ardent spokesman for the Republican party as soon as it was organized. In 1858 he returned to Sweden, hoping to enter the ministry there. But as his Episcopalian ordination was not accepted by the Lutheran state church, he became customs collector at Grisslehamn, a position he held until 1888. The recollections of Unonius, published in Upsala in two volumes in 1861 and 1862, are now being brought out in a complete English translation by the Swedish Pioneer Historical Society. See Jonas Oscar Backlund, translator, and Nils William Olsson, ed., *A Pioneer in Northwest America 1841–1858: The Memoirs of Gustaf Unonius*, vol. 1 (Minneapolis: University of Minnesota Press, 1950). See also Blegen, *Norwegian Migration, The American Transition, passim*; George M. Stephenson, *Religious Aspects of Swedish Immigration: A Study of Immigrant Churches, passim*, (Minneapolis, 1932); Nels M. Hokanson, *Swedish Immigrants in Lincoln's Time, passim*, (New York, 1942); George M. Stephenson, *Letters Relating to Gustaf Unonius* (Rock Island, 1937); Mabel V. Hansen, "The Swedish Settlements on Pine Lake," *Wisconsin Magazine of History*, 8:38–51 (1924).

[4] A *lensmand* was constable of a parish in Norway.

mile farther north by a beautiful little lake called North Lake or Shunakee, which is one and a quarter miles long and three quarters of a mile wide. Pine Lake is two and a quarter miles long and three quarters of a mile wide. The Indian name of this lake is Chenaqua, which means "pine" in their language. It is supposed to have got its name from some pine trees that are said to have grown on a tongue of land jutting out into the water. We stayed at Bellerud's overnight while Gasmann and two or three of his sons, who had come along, returned home late in the evening.

*January 20.* This morning, Saturday, we left Bellerud's and set out for Rock River. On our way past Gasmann's place, we went in and got directions. Toward noon we reached a little town called Oconomowoc on the eastern shore of La Belle Lac or "The Beautiful Lake," which is both the lowest and the largest of the Oconomowoc group of lakes, being two and a half miles long by one and a quarter miles wide. A dam is built over the creek at Oconomowoc.

We had brought along a bottle of corn whisky and some sandwiches, and so we went into a mill to eat. After we had inquired about directions from the miller, he told us that Hans Ulen and Johannes Lie had bought twelve barrels of fine wheat flour, which he thought was peculiar. After our refreshments we continued on our way as directed and about three o'clock arrived at the place where Christopher Aamodt was living, about a mile from the junction of the Ashippun and Rock rivers.[5] The former river flows through the northern part of his land. He was now living with his brother Amund, who had put up a little sod

[5] Bache here spells the name of this river "Esborn" although he uses the various spellings "Aspborn" and "Asborn" elsewhere. Since he says the stream was near Christopher Aamodt's home and joined the Rock River, it is obviously the Ashippun River. This is the spelling used throughout in the translation. In Bache's day, the spelling of place names had not been standardized, and the contemporary maps of the territory show the river (or creek) variously as Ashipunn, Ashburn, and Ashippun. It is shown as flowing into Rock River or into East Branch, which joined West Branch (or Crawfish River) to form Rock River.

house on a piece of land he had claimed. The house was about the same size as the first one Johansen and I had built. Both Christopher and his wife Ingeborg were very glad to see us.

*January 21.* This afternoon we went over to Johannes Lie's and spent the rest of the day and the night. He had bought a considerable amount of land, about 320 acres, which struck me as being so low, marshy, and flat that there was little or no drainage. Consequently it will take a long time for this land to become dry and workable after the heavy rains which frequently fall during spring and autumn. But the people here were tolerably well satisfied both with their choice of land and with life generally in the New World. This neighborhood escaped the epidemic that struck so many other districts last fall. Even Pine Lake did not escape entirely, though the number of deaths there were few, according to my impression.

*January 22.* Today, Monday, we crossed Rock River and went over to Hans Ulen's for most of the afternoon. That part of his farm which we crossed was very fine, being high and well-drained, but the land south of his "smoke house," if I may call it that, was low and consisted chiefly of worthless marshes.

Late in the afternoon we left Ulen's and went back to Christopher Aamodt's where we stayed overnight. Several of the people who followed me to America last year settled here, and I have been told that some of them bought very marshy land. There was, for instance, Hellik Olsen, a mason, who is said to have bought a piece of land north of Johannes Lie's without even having seen it. According to reports it consisted mostly of swamps and marshes full of water as is usually the case with such land. Later he went over to take a look at his property, and as he caught sight of it he said: "Well, I see that I have got excellent wheat land." [6] Though he was not satisfied with it, he had to keep it as it was.

[6] A pun in Norwegian probably was intended here since *hvete* (wheat) and *väte* (wet, moisture) are pronounced alike.

Aamodt's house, as previously mentioned, is very small and its accommodations naturally limited. Three of us slept in the bed; the other three had to prepare themselves some kind of sleeping quarters on the floor. When this had been done there was no room left in the house. During the night there was a thunderstorm followed by heavy showers. Though the house was of simple construction, it was sufficiently well built to keep out the rain.

*January 23.* About eight o'clock this morning we said farewell to these people and started our return trip home. Peder Aamodt, Christopher's brother, went with us to Oconomowoc. Since we did not want to return by the same road as we had come, we took one to the right, and after going about three miles came to a little town called Summit where there was nothing but a grocery store and an inn. The surrounding country was monotonous. Within a distance of three miles or more there was nothing to be seen but this little dry stretch of prairie except for a grove of small burr oaks. The land was extremely flat with apparently no fall whatever, and the soil seemed to be of a dry, sandy texture. Presumably deep wells would have to be dug here because I believe it would be difficult to strike water in this vicinity.

From Summit we took off to the left. In a sense we had a pleasant trip for the roads were dry, but they were so icy that we found walking quite strenuous at times. About three o'clock in the afternoon we came to an inn where we had some refreshments. The long walk had already made Brynildsen tired, and he wished to stay here overnight. I was tired also but preferred to continue so as to have a shorter trip tomorrow. However, I had to give in, seeing that he was unable to go any farther today.

*January 24.* After breakfast we said good-by to these people and continued on our way. We soon covered the four miles to Prairieville. This town had not made as much progress during the two years since I had been here as many other small towns even though it is beautifully located near a fine waterfall which furnishes power for a big mill. Without any noteworthy happening, we finally reached home about four o'clock in the afternoon, tired from our long march and happy to be back again after an absence of eight days.

*February 10.* Anne Brynildsen has been kept in bed the last few days by an old stomach ailment.

Someone out on the prairie sent Clausen a puppy only two months old. When we went to bed it was put out in the kitchen, but before long it struck up such a concert of howls and yelps that Mrs. Clausen had to take it to bed with her. After that all was quiet. The puppy slept in her bed every night until Clausen returned from a three weeks' trip with Even Heg. From then on it had to sleep on the floor upon a pillow which Mrs. Clausen had made for this purpose. It took quite a while, however, before the puppy became reconciled to this treatment. The lady coddled the pup as if it were her own flesh and blood. And a nice child it was, indeed, because it never became house-broken. Magrethe Helgesen served as nurse for the "child" and had to dance to Mrs. Clausen's tune. Whenever the lady blew her trumpet Magrethe had to step briskly. I have a feeling that this "son" of theirs will become obstreperous as it grows up and when they move away from here. If this should happen it would cause Lady Clausen a grievous heartache which would be hard for the fond "mother" to survive. Various names were proposed for the "child," but when Clausen returned he called it Dan — and Dan it is.

*April 16.* Today Clausen moved over to Johannes Skofstad with all his belongings. From now on our household will be smaller. In time there may be no outsiders left here, which would probably be just as well.

*May 4.* Today Brynildsen and his wife left for Milwaukee on their way back to Norway. Since it was impossible for them to feel at home here, it was undoubtedly best that they returned to the old country. I went to Milwaukee a couple of days before they did so as not to be at home when they left. They arrived in the city late this afternoon, and I went to see them at their lodgings.

*May 5.* I spent most of the day as best I could with them in their lodgings though it pained me that she was going to leave me. I always entertained the hope that both of them would settle down to the steady tasks of life here in the far West as soon as it could take on that familiar routine which we were used to at home. In her I believed I had found a true friend who could give much good advice in feminine affairs. Naturally I wished that they would remain here a while longer. But now I had to change my plans and take new measures for the future. Perhaps this separation also will turn out for the best. Time alone will tell for no one knows what life will bring to him.

*May 6.* This evening they brought all their luggage aboard the boat, as it happened, the same one on which they arrived last year. Since I had decided to accompany them part way, I went aboard with them. At nine o'clock we left Milwaukee and took a northerly course.

*May 8.* Yesterday, which was very cold, was uneventful. This morning when I came on deck we were already approaching Mackinac, so I went back to the cabin where I found most of the people in bed.[7] My farewells said, I hurried ashore, and the boat continued on its way leaving me alone here.

I strolled around this strange place awhile looking it over and searching for a decent place to stay. The town was very small so that it did not take long to get acquainted with the people, mostly Frenchmen and a few Americans. As I had not eaten yet I went into a huckster's shop where I had breakfast and also obtained lodgings for my stay here. After breakfast I set off to explore the island. The road took me up a steep hill on the top of which was a fort. From there I had a fine view over Lakes Huron and Michi-

[7] The spelling in the original is "Mackina."

gan as well as the interior of the island, which appeared to be quite level except for an impressive looking elevation or hill a short distance away. I took a road to the right that ran along the side of the hill. When I had gone several hundred steps I caught sight of something through the sparse woods and turned aside to look at a natural phenomenon that seemed to be quite unusual. I stopped to get a hasty view of it from a distance and then went on to examine it more closely. There I stood gazing like a miser gloating over his gold while I mused about the wonders of nature, because what I saw was not made by man but by a higher omnipotent being. I pondered over this odd formation some time without finding an explanation. Even though I maneuvered around it like an enemy besieging a city, I had to rest satisfied with merely observing its outward appearance.

To come to the point, this impregnable thing which I had been trying to storm was a rock about ninety or a hundred feet in circumference shaped like an egg or a round haystack. It stood on an elevation surrounded by small cedar and beech trees. On one side of this elevation was a place where five or six persons could stand. On the western side was a similar place, possibly a little bigger. The elevation here was not as great, and there was a ladder with four or five rungs, up which I climbed. The rock resembled a bald pate with little bushes growing out of it here and there like hairs. Besides, it was gray in color with large white spots on it like the skin of an old man. I tried to climb the rock but had to give up since I could find no foothold. Many former visitors had carved their initials both on the rock and in the bark of the trees.

After examining this rock — called Sugar Loaf Rock by the inhabitants — I climbed the hill already referred to, which I found to be very long as well as quite high and wide. This height merged into a plain at the end of which were found remains of fortifications used during the war.[8] From here I had the most

[8] This probably refers to the War of 1812. In July 1812, a British force surprised and overcame the American garrison, which had not yet learned

beautiful view imaginable over the island and the surrounding water. Far to the east — about thirty miles, so I was told — could be seen islands belonging to Canada, and beyond these again was the Canadian mainland. After several hours of sightseeing I went back to town for dinner. Although the day was cold, as the previous days had been, and everything looked barren and wintry, the trees had begun to bud.

After dinner I went up to the fort, which was located close to the brink of a cliff. It consisted of a strong rampart built in the form of a square with barracks all along the inside walls. In the center was a big open space evidently used as a parade ground since it was always kept clear. I learned that the garrison consisted of one hundred recruits. The houses downtown were of the poorest sort, cheap frame houses with nothing but sawed-off lengths of trees between the girders. The roofs as well as the walls were generally thatched with moss-grown bark of elms or linden trees. I inspected a newly erected frame. It was so poorly constructed that by taking hold of a corner joist I could shake the whole affair.

*May 9.* I was told that a boat from the East was expected today which I could take back to Milwaukee. In order to pass the time I took another little excursion to a different part of the island so as to become better acquainted with it. I went up the same hill as yesterday, but instead of going to the right I took a road leading to the left. After walking about a mile I came to a fence which I decided to follow, figuring that it might take me to a house or something else worth seeing. Finally I came to a farmhouse where the whole family was out planting potatoes. I chatted with them, and the farmer told me that the island was about three miles long and three miles wide, which I judge to be nearly right. He also told me that there was a certain disease

that war had been declared. In August 1814, an American force under Colonel George Croghan attempted to recapture the island but was repulsed with considerable loss. By the Treaty of Ghent (July 1815) the island was restored to the United States.

on this island which killed its victims off very rapidly, and that as no cure had been found for it, anyone attacked was absolutely doomed.

When they were called in for dinner I went back to town and had my meal. Shortly after noon a boat arrived from Chicago, but none appeared from the East. To keep the time from seeming too long, I took another little trip this afternoon. Since I wanted to keep a lookout for my boat, I followed the shore to the eastern part of the island, strolling along in my loneliness, casting my eyes hither and yon so as not to miss anything. After a little walk I sat down by a gently flowing spring whose clear water soon mingled with that of the great lake a short distance below. Here I sat like a lonely bird bereft of all companions. I felt like a lone castaway from a ship engulfed by the roaring waves as he sits gazing out over the smooth, glassy sea during the calm after the storm.

I got up after a while and strolled along until I came to a place where the trees had been cut down. Here I stopped to look around, and discovered an opening shaped like a low, wide arch high up on the cliff. The path leading up there was very steep and had been eroded by the rains. I clambered up to inspect this formation which struck me as being very peculiar, and when I got there I discovered another one still higher up that stood at right angles to the first one. Curiosity forced me on. To the right of the path between these two natural gateways the cliffs were almost perpendicular straight down to the surface of the lake. When I had passed through the second arch, I found that it was no thicker than an ordinary brick wall. The top resembled an artificial mound with a hole in the center which could not be seen from the land side until you got right up to it. I was told that this formation is called Arch Rock. Here also former visitors had carved their initials into the bark of trees round about.

After having studied this odd formation awhile I started walking toward the fort, but when I had come about half way I went out to the brink where I had a view both over the town and the lake. Here green grass had already begun to sprout, so I lay down to take a rest but was careful to choose a spot from where I could see any approaching steamboat. By now I was anxious to get away from this tiresome place where everything seemed to be dull and dead. The weather, unusually cold for this time of year, was more like fall than spring. There was not the slightest breeze, and the water stretched like a mirror as far as the eye could reach. Here I lay out in the open, feeling like a prisoner because there was no sign of the boat I so longed for. There was nothing I could do but remain patiently in this free prison until the time of deliverance should come. Eventually I fell into a short, refreshing sleep using the earth as a feather bed and the sky as a blanket. Round about me was nothing but childlike innocence void of all cunning and deceit. Oh, unspoiled nature, how gentle and beautiful you are to behold!

When I got up from my sleep I looked about to see if there might be anything else of interest to explore but noticed nothing, and since night was coming on I went back toward town. I saw very few birds or other creatures on the island at this season, and I was told that nothing could be raised here except oats and potatoes. But the potatoes were the best I have ever eaten in America at this time of year. The soil on the island is sandy and very well suited to potato growing.

*May 10.* The weather has been cold ever since I set out on this trip, but today it is colder than ever. This makes it all the more boring for I must stay in by the fire to keep from freezing. I looked for a boat the entire day, but as none came I sauntered in here and there to pass the time away. It is a small place with a population of about 1400, not counting the garrison at the fort. The people make their living principally by fishing and trading with the Indians who come here every year in August and September to receive payments from a resident agent. I understand that they will receive payments from the American government for some twenty years more. Presumably this is for lands which they have sold or for other reasons that I am not acquainted with.

*May 11*. A boat that I could take finally arrived this morning between four and five o'clock. After several minutes it continued on its way but soon ran into a heavy fog which lasted into the afternoon. Toward noon we were to touch at Manitou Island to take on wood. The fog was so dense that we could not see anything beyond the ship. The passengers were taking life easy, aware of no danger, when a couple of jolts suddenly shook the boat — and there she sat as firmly fixed as if she were rooted to the place. What was now to be done? This was not getting us anywhere. Some believed that we had been grounded on a rock, and many of us went out on deck to see how things were. We could hear people on land talking since we were only about two rods away from shore and only four rods from the lighthouse. The Americans are dare-devils when it comes to handling a steamboat. They do not seem to care what happens just so they can make speed. There might be some excuse in this case as the fog was extremely heavy, but of course it was careless not to slow down as we approached land. I can also relate that while I was on Mackinac Island a steamer came into port full speed and did not stop until it rammed right into the shore so firmly that it took a long time both with engine and windlass to get the boat loose again. This particular case of playing with power was quite inexcusable for it occurred on a very bright day. But to resume our story: When the engine had been thrown into reverse to back the boat into open water, one of the passengers proposed that a number of us should run back and forth on the front part of the deck. The suggestion was acted upon at once, but after I had made two or three runs I decided to visit the bar. As I rushed toward the door a woman came out, and in the collision I flung my arms around her just as I shouted, "That's the way to do it!" in reply to a certain question from a fellow passenger. I do not know how the lady took it because I did not see her any more after I had given her a helping hand and then hurried in to the bar.

After two hours of work, the boat finally was freed. Soon the weather cleared, and we discovered that we were a mile or so south of the place where we intended to land. If we had gone two or three hundred yards farther south, we would have missed the island entirely. But now that we were afloat again we laid to at the pier, and the passengers went ashore to look about. While we were there another boat also came to take on wood. We stayed here quite a long time while they loaded on a lot of wood and the passengers amused themselves as best they could. A number of Indians were there also with their birch-bark canoes, which were surprisingly large and comfortable and at the same time very light in structure. They were equipped with sails to take advantage of the wind when opportunity offered. The wood aboard, we continued our voyage, and in the afternoon the sky cleared entirely so that the rest of the day was very beautiful. There were so many passengers that the floor of the salon, which covered the entire length and breadth of the ship, was filled with folding cots for those who did not have berths. The floor of the barroom was also covered with pallets, for our boat was well loaded with goods and a great number of passengers. All of us went to bed, the great crowd of people became quiet, and I fell into a deep sleep, which was most refreshing to my weary body.

*May 12.* The morning came clear and beautiful with brilliant sunshine, and everything promised a pleasant day. Most of us stayed on deck to enjoy the beauty of the water about us and the shores of Wisconsin off to our right. When the passengers were counted, I learned that there were seven hundred people on board, the greatest number I had ever traveled with on any steamboat. About ten o'clock we reached Milwaukee, and I immediately went to my lodgings. Four hundred passengers landed here intending to proceed inland. Since this was Sunday, I had determined to spend the day in town and visit some of my old friends. In the evening another steamer docked bringing about one hundred additional passengers for Milwaukee, so we see that quite a number of settlers from the East and from Old Europe arrived during the day. Wisconsin, like Illinois, is now a center of attraction for immigrants, and the population increases by leaps and bounds. As an example I can mention that in May 1842, when I left for Norway, Milwaukee was said to have about 3000 inhabitants while by September 1843, the number had increased to more than 6000. It would seem almost unbelievable that the population of the city could more than double in little over a year, but this is merely typical of the growth of the Territory as a whole, which increased in population from 3,245 to 46,678 between 1830 and 1842. In view of its rapid growth, Milwaukee will become a great city and play the same role in Wisconsin as Chicago does in Illinois. These two cities will compete with each other for the honor of being the greatest commercial center of the West. To be sure, Chicago is at present twice as large as Milwaukee, but she is not growing as rapidly as her rival.

*May 13.* I intended to leave for home today, but as it rained continuously I postponed my departure, hoping for better weather tomorrow.

*May 14.* Since it was a beautiful morning, I said good-by to my friends and set off for home where I arrived early in the afternoon in spite of the slushy roads following yesterday's rain. During the past year I had become accustomed to having many people in the house, and it seemed very lonesome when I came back. But after a while I suppose I will become used to this quiet life which now seems so cheerless.

Thus far I have written only about the traveling I have done since I left my dear father on June 28, 1839 — almost five years ago. Until then I had always been with him, never having left my native land. Indeed, I had scarcely been beyond the bounds of the district where I was born. But now I wish to write about

Wisconsin, even though I have already told something about it as well as about the United States as a whole. I took my material from American books dealing with these things which will also be largely true in this case. I believe, however, that the information is correct and will be useful to have at hand. To be sure, such great changes take place that after a decade or a century much of what we say now may have lost its validity. But still something of value will remain because even though the man-made institutions of a country undergo great changes, the land itself does not change. It endures from generation to generation, only slightly altered by the ingenuity of man. These alterations are inconsequential, indeed, when compared with the totality of nature.

To my mind there is no other country in the Western Hemisphere where greater changes are taking place than in the United States, which is to America what England is to Europe and the rest of the world. These two countries cover the whole globe with their trade, and they are leaders in the invention of useful industries and devices of a solid and genuine sort. I suppose the Americans must give England honor for what they now are able to accomplish, since they came here from the mother land as colonists, bringing the arts with them. They settled here under many great difficulties as they had to fight the natives of the land, who hated them fiercely. They also encountered hunger and disease which swept away great numbers of the settlers. Indeed, at that time they had much to struggle with. But now, after winning their independence in the Revolutionary War, they have progressed so that in many respects they are on a par with the mother country. It is good to see the child making rapid progress and occupying itself with noble deeds after leaving its mother.

The liberty and equality which reign here contribute not a little to the rapid increase in population that presumably is a blessing for the land. Liberty is a good thing when it is not misused, but since this has frequently been done, it may also, sooner or later, be done by the Americans. In former times the Israelites tired of being ruled by judges and chose kings to rule over them in order to be like the heathens. At the time when the Romans reached the zenith of their power as the mightiest nation in the world, they were ruled by consuls, but they, too, grew weary of this and chose emperors instead, whereupon they lost their glory. It is possible that in time the United States will also follow this course.

I will now turn to Wisconsin, which at present is the refuge for my countrymen here in the West, and write down the most necessary and interesting information. I have lived in this Territory most of the time since I crossed the Atlantic and should, therefore, be well acquainted with it. You usually find, however, that the reports are very biased and either praise or disparage the region altogether too much. The best policy is to follow the middle way and thereby approach accuracy as closely as possible. This is the surest course for a lover of truth to pursue.[9]

[9] There follows a lengthy account, covering some thirty pages, describing the Wisconsin Territory which he admittedly took from "American books" — evidently almanacs and statistical handbooks. The information is of a factual nature and deals with such matters as the boundaries, topography, geography, climate, history, form of government, division into counties, and resources. Of some interest to prospective emigrants was his listing of the three land title offices in the Territory and the first sale of land in each district. He included a table of land sales in Wisconsin, by acres and monetary amounts, from 1835 through 1841 which he took from the Reports of the Commissioner of General Land Titles Office in Washington. With the aid of a diagram, he explained the usual method of division of land in the West into sections and townships. Among odd and unrelated bits of information he includes: (1) Population figures of the various counties for the years 1830, 1836, 1838, 1840, 1842; (2) A table showing the number of men, women, colored persons, slaves, deaf and dumb, imbeciles, illiterates, etc., in 1840; (3) A long list of the "most useful or interesting plants in Wisconsin" with their scientific names and the names of those who named them; (4) A table showing the dates from 1836 through 1844 when the Milwaukee River was frozen over in the fall and when it was opened in the spring.

# 7. Summer and Autumn Rambles

*August 7 [1844].* THE LAST MONTHS I have spent quietly at home, living almost like a hermit, with Johansen as my only companion. Every day we have been busily at work, each on his own farm, and time has passed so quickly that we hardly know what became of it. In the beginning this mode of existence struck me as dull and monotonous, but after a while I found it to be very pleasant, which shows that a human being can adapt himself to strange circumstances and form new habits of life.

We expected this day to pass as quietly as the others, but as I was going to work this morning I met a strapping young man down by the road. His tall, powerful build and rosy cheeks reminded me of some young giant from the Norwegian mountains. We shook hands and introduced ourselves, and I then learned that he was J. W. C. Dietrichson,[1] a theological student, who was

[1] Johannes Wilhelm Christian Dietrichson was "an aristocratic, imperious, high-church divine, of a military family" who, arriving in America at the age of twenty-nine, quickly became a storm center in immigrant church life. "He was the first Norwegian Lutheran minister in this country who had been regularly educated at the University of Norway and regularly ordained by a Norwegian bishop." Dietrichson was inspired by missionary zeal, and shortly after his ordination he left for America (May 1844) on a subsidy granted by P. Sørensen, a dyer in Oslo. After working among his countrymen in America, he returned to Norway in the summer of 1845. While at home he published his *Reise blandt de norske Emigranter i De forenede nordamerikanske Fristater*. Both in speech and in writing he opposed emigration vigorously. Probably because of this he was given a grant of two hundred dollars by the Norwegian government to resume his missionary efforts among the immigrants on condition that he would also send back reports setting forth life in the American West "in the right light." He sailed for America in July 1846 and continued a stormy career there until 1850 when he returned to Norway. Shortly afterward he published another book entitled *Nogle ord fra Prädikestolen i Amerika og Norge* (Stavanger, 1851). He died in Copenhagen, Denmark, in 1883. Blegen, *Norwegian Migration, 1825–1860*, 250–55; Anderson, *Norwegian Immigration (1821–1840)*, 423–29; Einar Haugen, "Pastor Dietrichson of Old Koshkonong," *Wisconsin Magazine of History*, 30:301–18 (March 1946).

born in the town of Fredrikstad. In accordance with his desire, I took him up to the house and introduced him to Johansen and Even Heg. After about an hour, I took him over to Pastor Clausen, whom he was very anxious to meet and talk with. We stayed there until afternoon. He gave as his reason for coming to America that the Word, the Holy Biblical Word, spurred him on to visit his countrymen in the far West in order to maintain among them the Lutheran faith which they had taken with them from their homes. To support this undertaking, he said, he had received enough money from one of his best friends in Christiania to defray his traveling expenses for a whole year to be spent in America.

It would be well if he could accomplish something in this respect. Time will tell how successful he will be. It seems that he is not particularly satisfied with his trip so far, and apparently he is not well suited to life here since he strikes one as being too pampered to endure any hardships whatever. Furthermore, he has a sweetheart back home who tugs at his heartstrings.

*August 11.* On the tenth Sunday after Trinity, Dietrichson delivered his first sermon among us and prayed for the King of Norway and Sweden. Clausen read his *vita* and letter of ordination to the whole gathering. A large number of people had assembled to hear the new preacher.

*August 12.* This forenoon I set out on foot toward Racine to visit some friends whom I had learned to know during my stay in New York while en route to Norway in 1842. When I reached Mons Knudsen Aadland's [2] house out on the prairie, he asked me to stay overnight, which I decided to do even though it was only

[2] Mons Knudsen Aadland (Adland) came over from Norway in 1837 in the company of Ole Rynning and with him located at Fox River. Aadland was the last man to leave the ill-fated settlement. In 1840 he traded his farm for a small herd of cattle. With these and three dollars in cash he moved to Wisconsin and settled at Muskego. Eighteen years later he "was worth forty thousand dollars . . . and had eight hundred acres of land and much valuable farm equipment." Blegen, *Norwegian Migration, 1825–1860,* 129.

half past one o'clock when I got there. He was very busy — right in the midst of wheat harvesting.

Often today I feared that I would have to turn back because the latter part of my trip led across large marshes that were especially wet now as a result of the recent rains.

*August 13.* Somewhat late this forenoon I parted from these people and continued on my way. Before long I was very wet from wading marshes that were soggy with last night's rain. After a while I passed through a beautiful little grove, and beyond it the road crossed a fine, dry stretch of prairie only about a mile and a half wide. Toward noon I reached the home of Mr. Lund, the painter of miniatures. It lay close to a brook whose banks were low and marshy. Mr. Lund was not at home, but a Dane named Morier, who is reputed to be of noble blood, was staying there.

After a while Mrs. Lund appeared. She was born in Norway, but I had not seen her since I met her in New York in 1842. On my arrival here my feet were so wet that I had to borrow a pair of stockings from my cousin Berthe, who was working for the Lunds. When I left home I did not actually intend to go all the way to Racine, but as I had not been there for two years and Mr. Lund was not expected back from there until Friday, I decided to go down and see him tomorrow. I brought along and read to Berthe some letters I had received from Norway after she left us.

When bedtime came, a pallet was spread for me on the upstairs floor. After I had retired, the nobleman's hound came and wanted to be my bedfellow. As I would not agree to this, he evened the score by doing unmentionable things in a corner.

*August 14.* Late in the forenoon I said good-by to Mrs. Lund and, in accordance with my resolution of yesterday, set off for Racine, accompanied by a man named Bang, who was staying at Lund's. After walking a couple of miles we came to the home of a Dane named Lütchen, who had been back to the old country and found himself a wife. I had talked with him briefly in New York when he came over the first time. We visited here awhile and had lunch, after which we continued on our way, reaching town in the early afternoon. There I secured lodging at the place where Lund was staying. Racine had increased in size noticeably since I was here last, and several churches were being built. The town is beautifully located on Lake Michigan about twenty-five miles south of Milwaukee and ten miles north of Southport, which latter place has always outdistanced Racine somewhat in size.

*August 15.* Having spent the forenoon in town and eaten my dinner, I took leave of Lund and set off, intending to cover as much as possible of the twenty-five mile trip to my home. For several miles across the prairie the road was very fine since it was so constructed that it drained from the center to ditches along the sides. On my way I passed two peculiar houses whose walls were made of a mixture of clay and straw. The walls were extremely thick, and if they are durable they ought to make warm houses, which would be a blessing on these open prairies with their cold, piercing winds. By evening, twenty miles from Racine, I reached the outskirts of the Norwegian settlement. Very tired after my day's walk, I spent the night there with a Norwegian family.

*August 16.* I got home in the early forenoon. During my absence two brothers, Peder and Johannes Jacobsen, with their families had come to take up their lodging with us for some time. Peder Jacobsen was a master wheelwright at Laurvig for several years after serving his apprenticeship in Drammen.

*September 14.* At noon today Christian Wold arrived to have a look at the settlement. According to his account he had heard bad reports about Muskego when he was in Norway last spring. Many letters from here had been unfavorable, and in a letter from Cincinnati Editor Reiersen of Christiansand had advised people to avoid Muskego. But I believe time will show that this region is quite equal to, if not better than, the other places where Norwegians have settled. Here we have woods and good well water almost everywhere, and our meadows yield an abundance of hay — advantages which are usually lacking in the other regions. Wold wished to stay at our place over Sunday, which pleased us greatly since we expected to hear much about our homes and relatives from him. I learned among other things that my brother Niels had become head of the civic guard in Drammen and that my brother-in-law E. Olsen had gone to Paris to consult physicians about the serious illness that has plagued him for several years.

*September 20.* Friday morning Wold and I started off on a trip toward the north because he was anxious to see the land around Pine Lake which he had heard praised in terms so extravagant that they did violence to the truth. The weather was fine as we left home, but when we had gone some eight or nine miles threatening clouds rolled in from the west. There was a house a short way from the road where we decided to seek shelter and rest for a while. When we got there we found it empty and without either doors, windows, floor, or loft. Since we would not be able to reach the next house before the rain, we took some boards that were lying along one of the walls and spread them over the joists to make ourselves a place to rest. We took our shoes off to ease our feet, and Wold, who did not feel well that day, soon fell asleep. After a short, heavy shower the rain ceased for a few minutes, and we got ready to continue our trip; but it started to rain again, keeping us there awhile longer. Finally it stopped, however, and we resumed our walk, but we soon got soaked as the "road" we followed was merely a narrow path that squeezed its way through the dense growth of scrub oaks and underbrush. After having been driven to seek shelter in two other houses because of rain, we finally reached the little town of Prairieville about eight o'clock in the evening and found a small hotel. Wet as we were, we sat down by the stove to dry our clothes on our bodies — a slow process. After a while we went to the dining room to eat supper. At the table we continued to talk Norwegian. I noticed that a waitress who came to serve us tea stopped behind Wold's chair for a while as if listening to our conversation, but I had no idea that she could understand us because I did not expect to find any Norwegian girl here. Shortly after she had returned to the kitchen, a man came to our table. He said he understood that we were Norwegians and then informed us that he had two Norwegian girls working for him. We expressed a desire to meet them, and he obliged us by bringing them out immediately. They seemed very glad to see us since they rarely had an opportunity to meet fellow countrymen. We talked together for more than an hour, after which Wold and I retired, glad to shed our wet clothes and get a good night's rest after our long march.

*September 21.* After breakfast we continued our trip, the weather being fine. Having walked about four miles we stopped at an inn [three lines in manuscript illegible] . . . considerably, and in particular about the Norwegian immigrants who had passed here. Their clothes struck her as peculiar, especially because the skirts reached only to their knees. This had seemed odd to me also when I saw them for the first time last fall. In some respects she compared them with the Indians, who are very filthy, as the mountaineers usually are also. I could offer no excuse for them and had to agree that she was right.

After a short stay at the inn we continued on our way and around four o'clock in the afternoon came to the home of a Swede, Mr. Unonius. Earlier we had visited one of his neighbors — also a Swede — who had been much plagued with illness since coming to America. His ailment was not, however, the common ague but some form of bone infection. He told us that he intended to sell his farm and move to town.

For about a year Unonius has been preparing for the ministry at an Episcopalian mission school near by as he has received a call from the Scandinavian settlement in this region. From his account it would appear that the teachers have accomplished much around here during the summer and that many new members have joined the congregation. Dietrichson visited this settlement some days ago, and I judge was not well received. Indeed, it seems that he was even denied a house to preach in. I was told that before Dietrichson and his companion left Milwaukee for the Norwegian settlement at Muskego they stopped at an inn to get something to eat. When they sat down at the table with a number of other people, Dietrichson ordered a cup of water into which he dipped his spoon and then wiped it off with his handkerchief, which probably was not itself clean. The people of the house felt insulted at this, which is not surprising since Americans are generally clean even when they belong to the poorer classes. As already mentioned, this is usually not the case with the Norwegians in America, although there are some honorable exceptions.

We were fortunate enough to have pleasant, clear weather all day. The country hereabouts is hilly and more densely wooded than the region west of Pine Lake. The earliest settlers on this side of the lake were Swedes, and most of the people now living here are of that nationality. They do not adapt themselves readily to pioneer farming since most of them were city people in the old country and had spent most of their time with studies and similar pursuits. We stayed here until the next day, which was a Sunday.

*September 22.* After breakfast we set off with Unonius and his family, intending to visit Sheriff Bellerud, who lives on this side of the lake. It was a beautiful day, and the trip along the lake shore was very pleasant even though the country was rough. Here we had an opportunity to enjoy nature in her primitive beauty. A mild southerly breeze rustled the leaves of the trees, which had already begun to fade as if wishing to warn us that the sterner seasons of fall and winter were not far away. Having crossed many little hills and valleys, we arrived at Bellerud's shortly before noon. After eating our dinner there we went over to visit Gasmann about a mile farther south. We found Mr. and Mrs. Gasmann sitting in the doorway while the children were running about wildly, pelting each other with cucumbers, of which there seemed to be an ample supply. After an exchange of greetings, we entered the house but the children continued their wild chase with the result that cucumber after cucumber came flying through the door, some of them narrowly missing the windows. A Dane by the name of Fribert,[3] who lived close by, also dropped in and was greeted with shouts of joy by the children. In the old country he was editor of the paper *Dagen*, and it is said that he arrived in this country with a considerable amount of money reportedly filched from a safe entrusted to his care. As an old friend of the family he immediately started some tomfoolery which continued until he left in the evening. In the midst of all this hubbub they tried in vain to induce me to put on a mock wedding with one of the girls in the house. — Well, all this turmoil came to an end finally and we were able to go to bed.

On the day following, Gasmann was going to send several loads of goods up to a new house they had built some miles north of here. Wold and I decided to go along to take a look at their future home and the land out there, which is said to be so very fine.

*September 23.* When we got up this morning the wagons were already loaded, and everything was ready for our departure im-

[3] Laurits J. Fribert was a well-educated man of means. His published book entitled *Haandbog for Emigranter til Amerikas Vest, med Anvisning for Overreisen samt Beskrivelse af Livet og Agerdyrkningsmaaden, närmest i Viskonsin* (Christiania, 1847) strongly advised settlers to go to Wisconsin rather than to Illinois, Iowa, or Texas. The author "touched on nearly every side of the emigrant's problem, giving special attention to agricultural methods in the West." Blegen, *Norwegian Migration, 1825–1860*, 256.

mediately after breakfast. But no sooner had we come down to the living room than it started to rain; so the moving had to be postponed and the goods taken off the wagons. Wold and I therefore changed our plans. He decided to go directly to Milwaukee from where he would continue on to New York, while I decided to pay Christopher and Ingeborg Aamodt a visit.

After breakfast the above-mentioned Dane, Fribert, returned for another visit in the company of a certain Dr. Theodor Schytte.[4] Having paid his respects to the ladies, Fribert said, "You must excuse the Doctor's lack of manners" — a remark which did not escape the latter.

About ten o'clock in the forenoon we left the Gasmanns who again were busily loading the wagons, as the weather was clearing up. Wold accompanied me to the nearest farmhouse, and we parted with mutual good wishes for happy journeys. Quite a number of new houses had been erected since I was here last winter. They were occupied by Norwegians who had arrived during the present year.

Continuing on my way alone, I arrived at Aamodt's place about three o'clock in the afternoon, where they appeared glad to see me. Both of them were in fairly good health, and they were expecting a "blessed event."

*September 24.* This was a quiet, restful day. In the afternoon I sauntered about looking at the land, which seemed to be tolerably good and well wooded.

*September 25.* At their invitation I decided to spend several

[4] Theodor Alexander Schytte was born in Fredrikshald, Norway, in 1812. After attending local schools he enrolled as a medical student at the national university, graduating in 1840. In 1843 he went to America as physician on an immigrant ship. His practice among the Norwegians in Wisconsin did not prove lucrative, and he returned to his native land. In 1848 he was appointed district physician in Finmark, where he died the following year. After his return, Schytte wrote an emigrant guide called *Vägledning for Emigranter* (Stockholm, 1849). See Gjerset and Hektoen, "Health Conditions and the Practice of Medicine among the Early Norwegian Settlers, 1825–1865," *Studies and Records,* 1:42.

days with the Aamodts. I therefore planned to do something useful while staying here, such as banking dirt up against the walls of the house to make it warmer.

*September 26.* Today Aamodt and I put up a thin board partition in the house so that one part can be used as kitchen and the other as bedroom. We also changed the ceiling a bit, put the cookstove back in place, and made everything cozy and shipshape in the little cabin before evening came.

Later on a *"telebonde"* came in and asked for directions to the Ashippun River.[5] After we had answered this and many other questions, he suddenly inquired if we also were Norwegians, a fact which he should have been able to deduce from our long conversation with him in his own tongue. But it seems to be a habit of this class of people to ask inane questions.

*September 28.* This morning Aamodt and I took a trip beyond Rock River to visit Hans Ulen in his black little smokehouse. I call it a "smokehouse" because it looked exactly like the constructions used for this purpose in Norway. The roof and the loft seemed to be made of bark for the poles out of which they were constructed had not been trimmed, and so much smoke leaked through the huge chimney, which filled one fourth of the house, that everything looked black and dreary. Ulen had been expecting me the last couple of days, because he had heard from his brother-in-law Jens Hellum that I was visiting in the neighborhood. After a brief chat the three of us decided to go up the river for a duck hunt, since it was still early in the forenoon and we had brought our guns with us, hoping to run across some game. We had a very comfortable canoe with four seats in it, one in each end and two near the center. (Aamodt and I had crossed the river in a canoe which we found by the shore. We returned it to the place where we found it so that the owner would not miss it.) We hunted along this crooked river about

---

[5] A *telebonde* was a farmer or peasant from the district of Telemark in Norway.

four hours and shot quite a number of ducks. There is a lot of game in this western country such as ducks, deer, and rabbits, but the wild animals become scarce as the population increases. On returning to the house we put on dry socks and then ate the dinner which had long been waiting for us.

Among Hans Ulen's curiosities was a chicken that had fallen into a dish full of dough, after which the mother hen would not recognize it as her own offspring. Consequently, the people of the house had to wash it and nurse it as if it were a baby. It now strutted around the house at will, hopped up on chairs and table, and even felt free to use us human beings as roosts. If there was food on the table, it was not at all backward about helping itself to it.

Aamodt and I went out on the river again after dinner to shoot ducks, but luck had forsaken us. As we came down to Jens Hellum's place we decided to go up and have a look at his magnificent estate. The door was closed, but we saw him at work out in the field and went over to him. He accompanied us back, but no sooner had we entered the house than he picked up something and disappeared again. We sat down on a bench because he had no chairs. Everything was lying about helter-skelter in this little doghouse of a place. When it appeared that he would not be back for a long time, we went down to the river to start our return trip. As far as we could see in both directions, the land along the river was low and marshy with the exception of an occasional ridge that ran down to the stream from the higher lands in the distance. Some time ago the river had risen a few feet and flooded the marshy ground. Consequently, Jens Hellum had to use a canoe when visiting Hans Ulen as there is a particularly low stretch between their lands.

We arrived at Ulen's in good time for supper, and quite late in the evening Aamodt and I set out for his home. Through the beautiful moonlit night, our walk was very pleasant. When we arrived we found everything cleaned and tidied up like a doll's house even though Mrs. Aamodt was not feeling well these days. Thus the day came to an end, and we were glad to get to bed.

*September 29.* Today the weather was much milder than it has been for some time. Hans Ulen's wife came and stayed well into the afternoon. Because of her indisposition, Ingeborg had to remain in bed and the day passed very quietly.

*October 1.* This first day of October was mild and beautiful as a summer's day. Aamodt and I took a trip up north to see the land where a number of Norwegians had settled during the summer. We passed through some beautiful rolling areas that were not too densely wooded and seemed quite free of underbrush. This took us into Dodge County where the land was quite high until we reached the marshlands of the river valley. Our main purpose was to visit Ole Gomperud, and when we had met him and taken a trip up the river, we started for home, arriving in good time.

*October 2.* Today I finally left my friends and started homeward. Aamodt accompanied me about four miles along the way before we separated. From Summit I took a different road from the one I had traveled on my last visit. About seven miles on this side of Summit I went into a house to get a drink, and there I met Ole Gomperud's daughter, Sørine. She seemed to enjoy my company, and so I stayed several hours. As the people of the house were absent, I had a very good time. I finally said good-by to her and continued my trip. On my way I passed a beautiful little lake with steep banks; in the middle was an island all covered with trees.

About six o'clock I came to Elling Helgesen's house and entered since I intended to stay with him. Some fifteen minutes later he returned from work. There was no woman in the house, and we had to be our own cooks.

*October 4.* Yesterday was passed quietly here at Elling Helgesen's. About seven o'clock this morning I started off for home, hoping to cover the remaining twenty miles before too late in the day. A few miles farther on I came to a dry, beautiful plain called Eagle Prairie, which is about two miles wide and four miles long. East of it, where the road cuts in through the woods, lives a man who is said to own 750 sheep. I saw them grazing and judge that the estimate is about right. This is the largest herd of sheep I have ever seen owned by a farmer, although I am told that in the eastern states there are many farmers who own herds numbering several thousand. A couple of boys were herding the sheep.

About noon I passed the village of Mukwonago, situated on a little river of the same name.[6] At three o'clock this afternoon I finally got home to my good friends, who were anxiously awaiting me since they had not expected me to stay away so long.

[6] In the diary Bache spells this "Mequanigo." On the maps of the Territory in this period, it is variously spelled Mequnnigo, Mequanigo, Mequonigo, Mequanego, and Mukwonago.

# 8. *Speaking of Religion: Lutherans and Mormons*

FOR ABOUT A YEAR now a pastor has administered the affairs of this frontier parish with the aim of keeping the people united as far as the outward forms of the church are concerned. But in this country, where the law grants a man the liberty to worship his God in accordance with his own conscience, the conviction is firmly rooted that a faith which smacks of compulsion is no faith at all. Under these circumstances a person's fundamental principles can also be revealed for what they are. It seems to me that the basic ideas of Pastor Clausen as expressed in the following document, written to the church board, expose him as being quite pontifical:

To the Honorable Church Board of the Norwegian Lutheran Congregation of Racine and Milwaukee counties:

A year has now passed since I was duly ordained in accordance with the regulations of the Lutheran church and assumed my duties as your pastor in reply to a call from this parish. It was deemed urgent at the time to organize the congregation in conformity with the regulations of the Lutheran church. A beginning was also made in this direction, but our progress was soon hampered by the many difficulties which presented themselves at that time. Subsequently I was so busy traveling about in the other Norwegian settlements, ministering to their spiritual wants, that my time and energy were largely consumed in that manner. Knowing that there were no other duly ordained Lutheran ministers, I felt compelled to continue my itineraries without being able to settle permanently in any one parish. Therefore I decided to let the provisional arrangement I had made with this congregation remain in force until I could become better established as a missionary with this settlement as my main mission post. As you are well aware, this has been the situation up to the present. Of late, however, my relations with the other Norwegian settlements have undergone a great change because the Lord has sent unto us the amiable, capable, and zealous laborer in His vineyard, the very Reverend Pastor Dietrichson. This has relieved me of many of my former duties so that henceforth I will be able to devote myself more wholeheartedly to the service of one congregation. I will presumably have a few annex congregations to serve in the future also. This will not take so much time, however, as to prevent me from spending at least two thirds of the year in the main parish. To the latter, therefore, I will have to direct most of my attention, endeavoring especially to get it so organized that it at least can be classified as a well-ordered Evangelical Lutheran congregation from which, as my center of operations, I will be able to exert greater influence upon the annexes and attempt to elevate them gradually to the same high level. If, as I have reason to believe, the majority of the people of this settlement still desire to constitute that main parish in and for which I should especially labor as pastor and shepherd of souls, then I must honestly confess that this, for many reasons, coincides with my earnest desires. I must add, however, that this mutual desire can only be fulfilled on the conditions which I have indicated above, and which I will now proceed to elaborate more fully and clearly.

The Dano-Norwegian church ritual of 1685, with later amendments and ordinances now in force in Norway, must be the absolute norm of constitution both for pastor and parish. The entire ecclesiastical organization of the congregation must rest thereupon and be in concordance therewith; moreover, all divine service, public or private, including the administration of the sacraments and other pastoral offices, must be executed punctiliously in accordance with the precepts of the ritual, unless specific reasons necessitate omitting or changing certain nonessential matters.[1]

I wish especially to emphasize that the regulation concerning confession and absolution found in chapter four of the ritual must be adhered to strictly. A modification will, however, be

[1] *Note by Pastor Clausen:* For instance the ringing of church bells (see the Ritual, ch. 1, 2nd Article) must be omitted for the time being since we have no bell. Likewise the intercessory prayer for the Norwegian Royal House will here be changed to an intercessory prayer for the American government, etc.

necessary as far as the first article is concerned since we have no confessional in our church. Therefore it will be required of everyone who desires to partake of the Lord's Supper to present himself to me in my own house the day before the administration of the sacrament, or at some other convenient time if good and sufficient reasons make this arrangement impossible. In private conference with them about the most important concerns of their souls, I will thus be able to obtain from each one individually a spontaneous and freely given confession of the sins that oppress him. This is the real essence of confession and creates the condition under which absolution can be granted. Thereupon their names will be entered in a register kept for that purpose. On the day following – or on the day fixed for the ceremony – I will in accordance with Norwegian practice, first deliver a communion sermon for those who have been admitted to partake of the Eucharist, after which, in accordance with their confession and general deportment, I will grant them absolution as penitent sinners. To people who lead manifestly godless, profligate lives and are the slaves of sin – among whom I include not only murderers, thieves, adulterers, drunkards, etc., but anyone who is plainly guilty of fraud, falsehood, contentiousness, envy, cursing, swearing, loose and blasphemous language, in short, any person in whose life according to the Apostle Paul (Galatians 5:19) the works of the flesh have become *manifestly dominant* and who, according to the judgment of the same apostle *shall not inherit the Kingdom of God* – to such people I declare that I can neither grant absolution, administer the Eucharist, nor permit them to act as godfather at christenings as long as their life and behavior do not show that they have forsaken sin and are attempting, by the grace of God, to do His will. If it should come to pass that a sinner, because of his obduracy in wickedness, should have to be excommunicated (i.e., expelled from the congregation) but should later be converted and desire to be reinstated, then we would have to proceed in accordance with the second article of the fourth chapter of the ritual.

In accordance with my oath of office and my conviction founded upon the Word of God I cannot yield one jot or tittle as regards these points, wherefore, I have at this time, fully and explicitly, presented my views to the board and the whole congregation for their serious and conscientious consideration. Those who are not able to join me on these conditions had better look about for another pastor, whereas those — be they many or few — who are willing to join me on the conditions announced, can be enrolled on a certain specified day or else at any convenient time in my home. The latter will then constitute the local congregation to which I shall, for the time being, devote all my efforts, and whose further relations with me our dear Lord will, by His grace, so order that it shall redound to the glory of His name and our common good.

When the board conjointly has read and considered the foregoing document, I respectfully request that it be returned to me, accompanied by their written opinions of same.

Town of Rochester, Racine County, October 16, 1844.

C. L. Clausen<br>Evangelical Lutheran Pastor

These were his words, copied directly from the document which he sent to the board of the local Lutheran congregation. Several days later the members of the board (Johannes Johansen, Even Hansen Heg, Johannes Skofstad, and Anders Kløve) notified him in person that their convictions permitted them to remain members of the congregation. Clausen thereupon demanded the return of his document. This was refused, however, since the board members wished to retain it and thereby be able to show cause for their action. To discover whether the rest of the members would remain loyal, Clausen called a meeting at his house on October 30 and read another statement which was much milder than the former one. As a result all the members, with but a few exceptions, enrolled again in the congregation. Furthermore, many who previously had remained aloof, gradually joined the church, thus making the membership somewhat larger than it used to be.

One Saturday when I went to settle a certain matter with Clausen, he tried to persuade me to join him and become a member of his congregation. He maintained that my father would not have acted as Johansen and the others did even though they were not in exact agreement concerning the sacraments, which my father also had mentioned. When he proceeded further to accuse Johansen of laboring under certain delusions, such a fit of anger seized me that I almost cursed him to his face. I managed to control myself, however, and merely stated that the document he had drawn up was so popish in tone that I could not subscribe to it. The main reason for my refusal to join his congregation stemmed from the fact that my family had given a certain sum for the construction of a church here and now Clausen wanted one third of the amount to pay part of his debt to me. I do not know exactly what his intentions were, but the suspicion struck me that he was not entirely upright in character. On this occasion he also read to me the altered statement that had induced many people to join his congregation, but in spite of the fact that it seemed couched in much milder terms than the original one, I told him that I would remain firm in my determination.

I have already told about his installation as minister, a position which he seemed to covet unduly, and which has revealed his unstable character. At first when he absolved the communicants from their sins, he would begin by asking them if they renounced the devil and all his works and all his ways, a question properly asked at the time of baptism and confirmation. Furthermore, he would ask them if they believed that the absolution which he, through his holy office, was authorized to grant them was identical with the absolution that God, through His Holy Word, bestowed upon them. This question had to be answered in the affirmative. Later on in the summer he altered his procedure. One Sunday, after the sermon, he announced that henceforth all those who wished to partake of Holy Communion should come to him the day previously and confess their sins. After the communion service he would then announce that since they had made their confession he would grant them absolution. And now, after having issued his revised statement and enrolled the congregation anew, it is reported that he has dropped both the above described methods and adopted still a third procedure. It seems to me that this is a peculiar and rather disrespectful way of dealing with the great gifts of God. He has given me several reasons to suspect that he is not the most reliable of men. Among other things, I can mention that he is very free with his promises but very lax when it comes to fulfilling them.

I also have reason to believe that he leans toward Catholicism. As evidence of this I can cite an incident that just occurs to me. Last winter he and Johansen were discussing religious sects. In the course of the conversation Johansen said he felt that the Greeks had the truest Christian form of worship as far as outward forms were concerned. To this Clausen replied that if he should change faith he would join the Roman Catholic church, which had retained the Word in its purity from the very beginning. Of late he is reported to be more vacillating than ever, an indication that his behavior has not been as noble and consistent as it should have been but has swung from one extreme to another. He has a very pleasing appearance and can be quite ingratiating with his gentle manners, which would be well enough if these externals reflected those inner qualities that all true pastors of souls ought to possess.

Speaking of religion, so many sects spring up in this free country that they seem to be an expression of business enterprise rather than of a sincere religious spirit. No sooner is a faith transplanted to these shores than it immediately degenerates into a dozen or more varieties. But in all this welter of sects, none can be more miserable, degenerate, and blasphemous against the Holy Trinity or more despicable in the sight of man than Mormonism, which now has its main station at Nauvoo, Illinois, on the east bank of the Mississippi. There the Mormons have built a temple with a baptismal font which is said to rest on the backs of twelve wooden oxen, so arranged that they face outward. The main Mormon settlement was formerly located in Missouri, but they were driven out of that state. This summer their prophet, Joseph Smith, was shot by the Americans. They are reported to be a very thievish lot. This sect grew out of an historical romance, whose author had no idea that it would give rise to anything like this.[2]

At the head of the Mormon sect is a prophet, and next to him in rank are twelve elders, followed by many bishops, deans, and ministers who travel about to spread the faith. A fair number of Norwegians in the Fox River settlement as well as in Muskego have joined them. All their members come from the least enlightened classes, and they are accepted without any previous conversion or any improvement in their way of life whatever. Indeed, even the most hardened criminals are gladly accepted. They also claim that they can heal a patient by the laying on of hands if his faith is sufficiently strong; otherwise no cures are promised.

It frequently happens that a Mormon may be baptized more than once. If, for instance, he fears that either his father, mother, sister, or brother has died in a state of sin, he will let himself be baptized once for each one of them in order to save their

[2] Bache has inserted here the now well-known Spaulding-Rigdon theory of the origin of the *Book of Mormon*, using a statement said to have been signed by Spaulding's widow which was published by a preacher named D. R. Austin in the *Boston Recorder* in April 1839. This theory, which Bache seems to have accepted without question, is briefly as follows. While living in Ohio in about 1812, a retired Congregational minister, Solomon Spaulding, wrote a romance of prehistoric America purporting to show that the original inhabitants of the country had come from the Old World in the pre-Christian era. In the New World the tribes had divided and engaged in savage wars, burying their dead in the great mounds which had long aroused the curiosity of the settlers in western New York and Ohio. Spaulding's novel, called "Manuscript Found," included the fiction that the document had been found buried in the earth or in a cave. The manuscript was never published, but some four years after the *Book of Mormon* was completed, the Spaulding theory was advanced to prove that the Mormons' Golden Bible was a plagiarism of the "Manuscript Found." The supposed instrument of the unauthorized borrowing was Sidney Rigdon, an associate of Joseph Smith who had become a Mormon in 1830. The theory is full of inconsistencies, gaps, and obvious errors, and the best and latest authorities have dismissed it as entirely groundless. See Fawn M. Brodie, *No Man Knows My History, the Life of Joseph Smith, the Mormon Prophet*, Appendix B "The Spaulding-Rigdon Theory" (New York, 1945).

souls from eternal damnation. Thus they carry on, and by so doing they believe they can rescue many an expired sinner from the grip of Satan and bring him to God. When they preach they usually choose a text from the Book of Revelation and expound upon it. A Norwegian from Illinois, Gudmund Haugaas, who is one of the twelve elders, came up here to preach, accompanied by another Norwegian, a priest.[3] As a result three members of our settlement joined the sect and were baptized. This took place on December 13 in a little river which at that time was frozen over. It is said that one of the converts, Gitle Danielsen, has been very cruel to his wife since then and that he curses her for not having joined the new faith also.

[3] Gudmund Danielsen Haugaas (spelled "Houkaas" in the manuscript) was an immigrant on the sloop *Restauration* in 1825 and settled in Kendall County, New York, but in 1834 he removed to the Fox River settlement in Illinois. He is said to have been well educated and was one of the earliest lay ministers and doctors among the Norwegians in America. In the Fox River settlement, Haugaas, like many others, joined the Mormon church. According to Dietrichson he became "high priest after the order of Melchizedek" and "counsel of the highest Mormon bishop" (quoted by Anderson, *Norwegian Immigration (1821–1840)*, 428). Besides serving a church in his home community he also tried to spread the gospel of the Latter Day Saints in other Norwegian settlements. He died of cholera in July 1849.

# 9. A Manifesto, a Church Dedication, and a Critical Observer

*1845.* LAST YEAR, especially during the winter months, a very severe epidemic raged in our midst, carrying about seventy or eighty men, women, and children to their graves. As a consequence several ill-considered letters were sent home which brought discredit upon the settlement. To counteract this a manifesto was written by Johansen and signed by a number of the settlers. The manifesto, with affixed signatures, reads as follows: [1]

Something like a year has now gone by since the hearts of nearly all among us were filled with foreboding and discouragement, brought about by illness of various kinds and in part by want of the very necessities of life; a condition which at that time prevailed among us because of the crowding into our midst of large numbers of our poor immigrant countrymen who, lacking funds to continue their journey, found themselves compelled for a while to sojourn here. It was a season of sorrow, such as to try the patience of several of us to the utmost. A certain few, overwrought in mind, even spread the most thoughtless rumors, accompanied in some cases by curses and expressions of contempt for America, as much as to say that God had no part in creating this land, a land so highly endowed by nature that even its uncultivated condition must be regarded as in effect half cultivated when compared with the native state of the soil in Norway and many other European countries; a land which for centuries has been a safe refuge for exiles from nearly every state in Europe, exiles who have, almost without exception, found here a carefree livelihood after conquering the first difficulties that beset every pioneer community, provided only that they bent

[1] The manifesto appeared in the Oslo *Morgenbladet* under date of April 1, 1845. With the permission of the American-Scandinavian Foundation we present here the translation of S. B. Hustvedt, which appeared under the title "An American Manifesto by Norwegian Immigrants," *The American-Scandinavian Review*, 13:620–22 (October 1925).

their minds on gaining through industry and thrift the necessary means of subsistence. There are some who complain of the trials that immigrants at first must meet; but all such persons should feel a sense of shame when they recall what history has to tell of the sufferings of those earliest immigrants who opened the way for coming generations by founding the first colony in the United States, the Virginia colony. Not only were they visited by contagious diseases and by famine; they had also to fight against wild beasts and Indians. Through such misfortunes the colony was on several occasions nearly exterminated and had to be reenforced. At length, of some six hundred colonists about sixty were left; these survivors, facing certain death from famine, found themselves compelled to leave the shores of the country in boats which they had built in the hope of reaching the banks of Newfoundland and of meeting there with fishing vessels on which they might return to England. But, as it appeared, such was not the will of God. Just as they had embarked they came, at the mouth of the Potomac River, the gateway to the colony, across some ships that had been sent out from England for their relief. Thus encouraged they returned to continue the work of settlement that they had begun. So they fought and won their victory; and so they became the immediate occasion whereby it has been made possible for twenty millions of people to find abundant resources in the United States, a number which is supposed to be capable of being doubled more than once before the opportunities here shall have been exhausted. Should not we likewise, with brighter prospects than theirs, entertain the hope of winning by perseverance victories like theirs and of gaining what we need to sustain life! Or should God, who in his word has laid upon us the precept, "Be fruitful, and multiply, and replenish the earth," not crown such an undertaking with success, inasmuch as He has so richly endowed this land and made it more fitted to produce all manner of food for mankind than perhaps any other country in the whole world; more especially under the present conditions, when overpopulation in Europe, greater than at almost any earlier time, has made emigration a necessity.

The dissatisfaction that showed itself at the beginning among many of the immigrants at this place had its origin for the most part in an unseasonable homesickness more to be looked for in children than in grown people; it arose from such circumstances, for instance, as that they had to get along without certain kinds of food to which they had been accustomed, that this or that article in their diet did not have the same flavor as it had in the old home, that they suffered from the lack of some convenience or other, or that they missed certain of their friends with whom they had before had pleasant association. By taking such things to heart they permit their minds to be filled with unquiet longings that must remain fruitless. Meanwhile they lose sight of all those former difficulties, of the whole gloomy prospect of material success under which they labored heavily in the land of their birth; and so they now imagine the place where they were born to be that land of Canaan which at one time they supposed to lie in America. One who tries to forget bygone things and to look forward instead, and who pursues his lawful labors in patience and in the fear of God, will surely not find his hopes disappointed if he will only aim, so far as his material needs are concerned, to be content with his daily bread. We have no expectation of gaining riches; but we live under a liberal government in a fruitful land, where freedom and equality are the rule in religious as in civil matters, and where each one of us is at liberty to earn his living practically as he chooses. Such opportunities are more to be desired than riches; through these opportunities we have a prospect of preparing for ourselves, by diligence and industry, a carefree old age. We have therefore no reason to regret the decision that brought us to this country.

An attempt has been made to prevent people from coming to this country by representing America as a suitable refuge for released convicts or such men as seek to escape the wrath of the law. It is true that many persons of this type have come hither and that here as elsewhere there are altogether too many wicked men. Yet this state of affairs is unavoidable, inasmuch as good men and evil are permitted to come in, the one with the other; nevertheless, assault, robbery, and theft are much less common here than in the lands from which such men may have come. At all events, misdeeds of this kind are unheard of among us, and so no one need shrink back from America on this account. Attempts have also been made to frighten people away from this settlement because of the presence of illness among us last year; yet although the summer just past was unusually wet and cold for this latitude, we have not suffered from any epidemic, in spite of certain fears during the spring; and we have reason to hope that we shall continue to be spared.

Only a few words more. By reason of the circumstances just mentioned, namely the privations and the sickness that visited our colony and robbed most of us of the gains of our labor, some among us found it expedient to turn to our friends in Norway with a request for assistance in building the church of which we stood in such great need. The response to our request has been so unexpectedly generous that we have been enabled to complete after a fashion the church building that for some time has been under construction in this settlement. Wherefore we take occasion to express here our thanks to the honored donors, the following named men:

| | | |
|---|---|---|
| Hr. Proprietaer T. O. Bache, Walle pr...Drammen | 200 Daler |
| Hr. Stadshauptmand N. Bache .........Drammen | 100 Daler |
| Hr. Kjöbmand T. Bache ..............Drammen | 50 Daler |
| Hr. Kjöbmand E. Olsen ..............Drammen | 50 Daler |
| Hr. Kjöbmand J. K. Lykke ............Throndhjem | 10 Daler |
| Hr. Simen Svendsen ..................Lier | 15 Daler |
| Hr. Tollef Mörch .................... | 5 Daler |
| | 430 Daler |

The newspaper editors of Norway are hereby respectfully requested by the undersigned, their countrymen, to publish this account in its entirety and without change in their daily press, and to append our several names.

The settlement of Muskego, in Racine and Milwaukee
Counties, Wisconsin Territory in the United States,
Jan. 6, 1845.

About eighty signed the letter, and it was sent with the first mail on Wednesday. All were ready and apparently pleased to affix their signatures because the contents agreed so well with the truth. After the letter was mailed, several who were absent when it was drawn up have wished to add their names; hence there is no reason to doubt that the manifesto expressed the unanimous opinion of the people.

*January 21.* Johansen and I had frequently talked of driving up north this winter to the Norwegian settlements that he had never visited before. We therefore set out this morning at eight-thirty and, enjoying fine weather, arrived at Christopher Aamodt's about ten in the evening. They greeted us cordially. We covered some thirty-seven to forty miles during the day.

*January 22.* Today we went over to see Hans Ulen and remained there until nearly evening. Nothing special happened. Returning to Aamodt's, we spent the next night there too, because we intended the following day to visit Gasmann, who now lives only some four miles from here up the Ashippun River. This river is said to have derived its name from the great number of aspen trees which line its banks.

*January 23.* The day was so wet that nothing came of our plan for a trip to Gasmann's. Instead we walked over to visit Ole Øvern and his brother Colbjørn, a mile north of here. We stayed with them until after dinner and then returned.

*January 24.* On leaving we took our way through woods that in places were so dense that we had to clear away small trees blocking our passage. A little after noon we reached Gasmann's new place and stayed several hours. Mr. Gasmann was not at home but returned as we were hitching the horse to the sleigh. They wanted us to stay overnight, but we could not accept this invitation since we planned to get home next day, visiting several people along the way. We went down to Bellerud's, who now lives in Gasmann's former home at Pine Lake, and spent the night there.

*January 25.* We left Bellerud's at nine o'clock and, a mile farther on, came to the home of L. J. Fribert, the Dane. After an hour with him we continued our journey, reaching our home at Wind Lake just as the sun was rising. Thus ended our first trip of the year 1845.

At Rock River we were told that a man from Sätersdalen had discovered an easy way of killing deer. The tracks they left revealed that at night deer used to come to the fires where branches and other rubbish had been burned during the day. One evening this individual, who had never done any hunting before, built a fire in a somewhat secluded place and hid close by. Sure enough, along came a deer; he took aim, fired, and hit it a little below the spine, knocking it over. Then he made a rush, threw himself upon the animal, and plunged his knife into its throat, causing it to bleed profusely. But still the deer got up and ran a short distance with the man upon its back before it finally collapsed. The *Sätersdøl* lost his knife in the excitement but was well pleased with the exchange, for this was the first killing he had ever made. Since then he has caught several deer by the same method.

*February 3.* Last week was the coldest one we have had so far this winter, which otherwise has been very mild. About ten o'clock one evening during this cold week, a girl named Martine left Milwaukee and followed the shores of Lake Michigan. The next day she was found dead with her skirts pulled over her head. She was the granddaughter of old Anders Knive of Skouge parish. This girl arrived here last summer in a deranged condition and was thus a burden both to herself and others. She was buried last Thursday or Friday.

*March 1.* The first days of last month and the last days of January were the coldest ones we have had this winter. Generally speaking it has been mild, and the first day of this month brings clear, pleasant weather promising a fine and early spring, although we may still have some cold spells before summer comes. This seems like a solemn day. The sun rose about half past six this morning, sending its silvery rays over the land as if to reveal nature in all her beauty. How pleasant the warmth of spring is after the cold of winter! Everything seems to have regained its liberty. The birds twitter in the trees, the hens cackle, and the deer leap and gallop over fields and plains as if to give expression to that liberty and equality which reign in the land of freedom. Where are they to be found in Europe? Many who boast of liberty and equality nevertheless try to force their way to the pinnacle of glory from whence they can lord it over their fellow men. Though freedom is supposed to be limited by law, it is often misused in the land of liberty.

*March 5 and 6.* The beautiful spring weather has continued several days.

On March 4 the new President of the United States was inaugurated. He is the second president to hold office since I came to this country.

That day I went to see one of the vestrymen in the local Norwegian Lutheran church and delivered Johansen's statement of the money that my family in Norway, through me, had given for the building of a Lutheran church in the settlement. We expect it to be finished in a few days, and presumably it will be dedicated almost at once, because it is reported that Pastor Clausen is already making his arrangements.

*March 10.* About a year ago Even Hansen Heg promised the congregation that he would sell them, at cost, that part of his land on which the church is located. In this connection the church board sent him a letter last December. On January 8 he replied that if they could provide the required sum within two months of that date he would stand by his promise. The time expired last Saturday, and the board met to discuss the matter but came to no definite conclusion. Two members of the board, Syvert Ingebretsen and Peder Jacobsen, argued so strongly in favor of the purchase that they finally won the other members over. But the most difficult question still remained. Where should the money come from? The required sum of about seventy dollars seemed beyond their reach in spite of all their efforts. Another board member, Jørgen Larsen, told someone that they had tried in vain to obtain a loan of fifty dollars from me. This, however, is an untruth since no one spoke to me about this matter. The first-mentioned gentleman runs the whole board, holding the double position of chairman and secretary.

There is something peculiar and suspicious about this whole affair. As far as I know, it is not customary in this country for the congregation to buy land for the minister, the only exception, to my knowledge, being the German Lutherans north of Milwaukee. Now when the money given from Norway for the construction of a church is nearly depleted, the board sends out one list or order after another commanding the members of the congregation in a highhanded way to do all sorts of jobs. Sooner or later when the yoke becomes too oppressive at least some of the people will call a halt to this system. I recall hearing Pastor Clausen once state that his congregation should include the true Lutherans. As the people seem to believe this, it must follow that they regard the nonmembers as recreants. Of course there may be somewhat differing opinions among them, but generally speaking they are a very hypocritical flock who have an absolutely blind faith in their pastor and do not dare tell him the truth.

*March 12.* This forenoon Johansen, Even Heg, and I inspected the church, which is now almost completed. The interior is attractive, and the church is beautifully located on a high hill in the heart of the Norwegian settlement.[2] From there you have an excellent view in every direction for a distance of six to ten

[2] The Muskego church was the first Norwegian Lutheran church built in America, but the two churches in the Koshkonong settlement were dedicated earlier (see Chapter 13, note 3). The Muskego church "was built of oak logs hewed on both sides, six inches thick, and matched after the Norwegian fashion of building houses. On the inside the logs were dressed perfectly smooth and then fitted so close together that no mortar was used between them. Double doors in the front were made of black walnut. The pulpit was also made of walnut and was about seven feet from the floor. Galleries were built across the front and along both sides to about the middle of the church. These galleries were supported by six heavy columns turned out of solid walnut. In fact the church was pretty well furnished inside." Anderson, *Norwegian Immigration (1821–1840)*, 419–20. This building served the community until 1869 when a new church was erected. The old one was then sold to a near-by farmer. It was removed to the campus of Luther Theological Seminary in St. Anthony Park, St. Paul, where it stands as a shrine in tribute to the memory of its builders. A. O. Barton, "Muskego, the Most Historic Norwegian Colony," *Scandinavia*, 1:22–29 (Grand Forks, 1924); Hjalmar Rued Holand, "Muskego," *Symra*, 3:187–96 (Decorah, 1907).

miles. Toward the east the eye sweeps across what appears to be a vast green plain. Actually, however, it consists primarily of unproductive marshes dotted with tree-covered patches of dry land. Through this lowland winds a little stream that flows out of Wind Lake, farther to the north. Beyond the moors the land rises gently with occasional farmhouses along the hillsides. Indeed the scenery is very beautiful and will be still more so in the full bloom of summer.

*March 13.* Last evening Mr. Unonius and the Reverend Mr. James Levi Breck of the Episcopalian church came to our house to be present at the dedication of the church, which is to take place about ten o'clock this morning.[3] With them came another American, Mr. Abel Sanford, with whom I struck up a friendship last winter. About half an hour later Mr. Fribert and a young Swede named Petersen also arrived.

This forenoon at the proper time, I went up to the church, where I found that quite a group had congregated. Many had already taken their seats, but then the pedantic chairman, Peder Jacobsen, appeared with orders from Pastor Dietrichson that, until further notice, all of them should vacate the place.[4] This order was immediately obeyed. Most of these people came around to

[3] James Lloyd Breck (mistakenly referred to by Bache as James Levi Breck), prominent Episcopalian leader in the Middle West, was born near Philadelphia and studied in various eastern schools. In 1841, full of missionary zeal, he set out for Wisconsin where, the next year, he helped found the Nashotah Seminary near Pine Lake. In this district he came in touch with the Scandinavian settlers, and it was largely through his influence that Unonius joined the Episcopal church. Breck evidently hoped to find ready converts among the immigrants. "The Scandinavians, he believed, 'were themselves fully as ready to enter our door, opening into the American church, as we were to enter theirs, opening into their hearts.'" Like many of his other dreams, this hope also failed of realization. Some years later Breck became a bishop in Minnesota. In 1867 he went to California, where he died in 1876. Blegen, *Norwegian Migration, The American Transition*, 123, 125, 126, 128; Charles Breck, *Life of the Reverend James Lloyd Breck* (New York, 1883).

[4] Here Peder Jacobsen is referred to as chairman (*formand*), presumably of the church board. From the entry for March 10, however, it would appear that Syvert Ingebretsen was both chairman and secretary of the board.

the east end of the church and joined several of us who were sitting on the steps. When there was some expression of dissatisfaction at being put out in this fashion, I replied that clodhoppers had better be humble under the nose of a prince, which Nils Närum's wife thought was a pertinent remark. Soon another board member came and ordered the whole assemblage to go down the hill some distance, from which point they should follow the ministers back to the church. There Clausen appeared and said that the members of his congregation should proceed in pairs while the others could do as they pleased. Eventually all of them marched into the church in this way. The ceremonies were begun with an invocation and the singing of the hymn "In Jesus' name shall all our work be done." After this, several Bible passages were read and more hymns were sung. Then Pastor Dietrichson and Pastor Clausen delivered their sermons. The former spoke from the entry to the chancel; and a curious sermon it was indeed, apparently aimed at inspiring remorse or anguish in the hearts of the people for having left Norway, their dear native land. What shall we say of a clergyman who comes to the New World ostensibly to be a good influence among his countrymen and bring comfort to the brokenhearted, but instead does his utmost to dishearten them by tearing open the old wounds and arousing longings for their former home at a time when such longings cannot possibly be satisfied? I do not recall his exact words, but there he stood and with all the eloquence at his command tried to picture the idyllic life we had led among the mountains of Norway where only one religion dominated the whole land. All these blessings we had left only to find ourselves, after the hardships of an Atlantic voyage, in an American wilderness where many forsake the faith of their fathers and join erring sects. He asserted, however, that even if all but two or three should become apostate, the church which we dedicated today should belong to the chosen few. It must be said that the sermon as a whole was mixed with too much nonsense.

When Pastor Dietrichson was through, Pastor Clausen mounted the pulpit over the altar to deliver his opening sermon in the new church. As his first point he dwelt at length upon baptism as the door which gives admittance to the communion of saints; then he discussed the Lord's Supper and, finally, the importance of the ministerial calling, concluding by forbidding anyone but a Lutheran pastor to set foot in the place where he then stood — a dictum that may not be so easy to enforce.

In view of this sermon and what has previously been related, I believe that Pastor Clausen has reached the height of his grandeur. Or how did the great men of history fare? Were they not humbled when they reached the zenith of their glory? Clausen and Dietrichson are grasping for so much power that sooner or later they will lose it. Their sermons were largely a condemnation of those who had not joined their church and a cry of woe over those who had withdrawn from it. Once as we were parting Clausen told me that his congregation should be genuinely Lutheran, but according to my opinion it is becoming genuinely Roman since he is striving rather to be a dictator than a true minister of the Gospel.

During the ceremony Clausen officiated at the altar while the board members sat at one side of it and Dietrichson and Krause directly in front of it. After the service Mr. Unonius, Pastor Breck, and Fribert went home with Clausen and remained there until fairly late in the evening. After supper my friend Abel Sanford and I took a walk, hoping to meet our other guests whom we were anxiously awaiting in order to get an account of the religious discussions of the afternoon. According to their account they were given permission to hold services in the church, in direct contradiction of what had been stated in the dedication sermons. Thus they swing from one extreme to another, unable to arrive at a definite decision. As already related, Clausen altered his confessional procedure, another evidence that he has an unstable character.

We finally went to bed and had a good night's sleep. Thus ended the events of this day which will be long remembered because of Clausen's and Dietrichson's bravado and sorry behavior. If their thoughts and deeds are recorded in history they will be a poor example for the coming generation to follow.

*March 14.* This forenoon the Reverend Mr. James Levi Breck, Mr. Unonius, and Abel Sanford set out for home. They asked us to visit them, and we promised to do so. Mr. Fribert also said good-by and left for Milwaukee in the company of Pastor Krause, who had been staying with Clausen. They had fine weather with a clear sky and a cold west wind for their journey.

*March 21.* A bright day dawns to announce that it is time to get out of bed after a refreshing sleep. The earth seems to rejoice in the warmth of the sun this Good Friday morning while people wend their way to church to hear the Word of God. Everything seems peaceful as if nature herself wishes to praise the Creator for the passing of winter and the coming of summer with its verdure and renewed life. The birds are singing, on the other side of the lake the ducks are quacking to each other, while down by the shore some children are playing. In the distance smoke curls up from various places where last year's withered grass has been set on fire.

*March 26.* During the Easter holidays the weather was pleasant, as it has been through the whole month, although the last couple of days have been unusually mild. Christopher Aamodt came down last Saturday to pay us a visit. He went home today.

Yesterday afternoon Johansen received a letter from the local church board which reads as follows:

Town of Rochester
March 25, 1845

The board met today to examine the expenditures of the church and to determine whether the bills presented actually concerned the church and if they had been properly discharged by the person concerned. In Johansen's account is entered an item of

THE INTERIOR OF OLD MUSKEGO CHURCH

[From a photograph made in October, 1940, by Mr. Paul Hamilton, Minneapolis Institute of Arts. The building is preserved on the campus of the Luther Theological Seminary, St. Paul, Minnesota.]

expenditure amounting to $13 to cover Clausen's ordination. The board held that this sum did not concern the church and was confirmed in this opinion by a statement appended by Johansen:

"S. Bache reserved the right to hold the congregation responsible for the $13 mentioned above as having been spent in connection with Pastor Clausen's ordination."

To defray this claim is none of our concern. If the disbursement had been made for the church, the congregation would as a matter of course pay for it. We hold that it is wrong to withhold the funds of the church as in this case, because the minister and the church are two separate entities. We therefore demand the $13 outstanding, which the church needs immediately since there are many matters that should be attended to.

Peder Jacobsen, Syvert Ingebretsen, Jørgen Larsen,
Ole Aslesen

These were the words and such were the contents of the letter. Johansen replied today as follows:

In reply to the board's communication of yesterday I wish to state that I have verbally notified one of the members, Mr. P. Jacobsen, of the fact that Mr. Bache has withheld the $13 in question as payment for the sum expended by him in connection with Pastor Clausen's ordination. The same information was also conveyed in my written statement of the disbursement of the voluntary contributions made by the undersigned and others toward the construction of a church in our midst. The board, therefore, knows very well unto whom it must address itself if it feels justified in demanding said sum as being withheld on a mistaken premise. I must repeat that I am in possession of no document entitling me to extort said money from Mr. Bache. Furthermore, it seems to me that it reflects little honor upon the congregation in general and the board in particular to be so insistent in a matter that in no way concerns Mr. Bache, who has never been a member of Clausen's congregation and consequently is under no obligation to help defray its expenses. Least of all should he be held solely responsible for an account that otherwise would have to be met by the whole congregation. This is all the more true since it is practically to his family alone that the congregation can be grateful for the contributions that made the church possible. The board's pressing demand for the $13 has altogether too much in common with the methods of habitual beggars, who, the more they get, the more ungrateful they become in trying to wring gifts from people who owe them nothing.

Wind Lake, March 26, 1845
Johannes Johansen to
The Muskego Church Board

The thirteen dollars referred to was a sum that I had advanced as payment for our conveyance up to Pastor Krause's at the time when Clausen was ordained minister for the local congregation, as previously related. It was reasonable to expect that I would be reimbursed either by Clausen or by the congregation, but I had been given no security of any kind. Inasmuch as my family in Norway, through me, had advanced $430 for the construction of a church in this community, it was only natural that I should withhold a sufficient amount to reimburse me for the sum in question.

*March 28.* The last two days have brought the finest and warmest weather of the month, though it is not as warm today as yesterday.

The first wedding ceremony in the new church took place today when Thore T. Mørch married my cousin, Berthe Olsdatter (Bjoner). They passed here about one o'clock, and about a quarter to four they returned from the church, accompanied by Pastor and Mrs. Clausen and Johansen, who drove, and by Even Heg and Helgen, who were afoot. I was invited, too, but I did not feel like going because of an insult connected with the bride. People say that she was the one who was most eager to force the wedding through. In a few days she will start westward with her husband to a place called Rock Run in the state of Illinois, not far from the Wisconsin border. His land is located there, but, as far as we are able to gather, he does not own much of it. The money she brought to America was placed at his disposal last year, but nevertheless I have learned that he still has to pay for the land at the land office. This sum, we may guess, will not be so easy to raise just at present.

*March 30.* Last night we had a fine gentle rain. This is very good for the soil, which was getting dry. The wheat has now had enough moisture to turn it quite green, and the grass has already begun to sprout. Today the weather is very mild, and it looks as if we are going to have rain tonight also, probably by evening. If rain at night and mild weather during the day continue to alternate, there will soon be enough food for the cattle. Work in the fields was started last week, and some seeding has already been done, especially of spring wheat, which is usually the first crop sown.

Confirmation was held in the church today for the first time. It lasted until well into the afternoon. After services Pastor Clausen announced that no outsider should be allowed to preach in the church while he was away on a trip he had to make. Every Sunday during his absence a member of the board should conduct services by reading the text for the day from Luther's *Book of Homilies.* This should be preceded and followed by the singing of a hymn for general edification. Clausen and Dietrichson have rented a Methodist meetinghouse in Chicago. Still they maintain that they will not let anyone but a genuine Lutheran make use of the church here. How greedy they are for power! This can of course go on for a certain time, but it may not last very long.

*April 1.* The day is beautiful, but a rather cool west wind is blowing.

Last evening Berthe Bjoner came over to visit me as I had asked her to do. She spent the night here and left at seven o'clock this morning for her lodging, presumably to pack before setting off with her husband for their new home in Stevenson County, Illinois. About eleven-thirty, as Even Heg and I were walking down the road on our way home for dinner, they drove by with all their luggage. She did not seem at all displeased, but the husband looked somewhat dejected. They were going to spend the next night at the home of Syvert Ingebretsen Narverud's,[5] whose wife is a cousin of Thore Mørch. Thus we parted. The distance to their new home is about seventy miles.

The early spring flowers are already in bloom, a certain indication that summer will soon be here.

*April 8.* These last days we have had real winter weather with cold wind from the west and north. Yesterday at daybreak a little snow fell.

Last Sunday night a whole block in the heart of downtown Milwaukee, reported to be insured for $100,000, burned down. The fire is said to have started in a German warehouse.

At eleven-thirty this forenoon I set off on foot for Pine Lake to see some people reported to have arrived there who left Norway with Captain Gasmann shortly after Christmas.[6] About seven-thirty I reached Silver Lake where Helge H. Øvern and Elling Helgesen live. I had supper there and stayed overnight.

*April 9.* Last night about one o'clock, while we were sleeping soundly, someone knocked at the door. Our late visitors were none other than Ole Gomperud's wife and her oldest daughter, who was married a short while ago to a blacksmith named Knudsen. The reason for their coming was a love affair which Elling had with Mrs. Gomperud's daughter Sørine. This case was now settled.

[5] He has heretofore been referred to by Bache as Syvert Ingebretsen.

[6] Captain Johan Gasmann was the brother of Hans Gasmann (see Chapter 4, note 5), whom Bache visited at Pine Lake, Wisconsin, in the summer of 1844. The account he wrote of his trip has been translated by Carlton C. Qualey in *Studies and Records*, 5:30–49. It is said that Captain Gasmann had been rather skeptical about the wisdom of emigrating but that this trip changed him into a "booster." In a letter of December 18, 1843, to a royal commission, Captain Gasmann described conditions aboard his ship *Salvator* and offered practical, humane suggestions for the improvement of life on the emigrant vessels. It may be of interest to mention that J. Gasmann, a brother of the two Gasmanns already mentioned, served as a member of this commission. Blegen, *Norwegian Migration, 1825–1860*, 214–38.

I stayed here during the day and learned that there were no newcomers from Norway.

*April 10.* Today I continued my walk up toward the Ashippun River to visit Christopher Aamodt. I arrived there about three o'clock in the afternoon.

*April 12.* I left Aamodt's today and started for home. In the afternoon I came to Helge Øvern's again but found no one there. Since I had the whole house to myself I peeked into every nook and cranny and finally discovered a letter from a son of Hans Gasmann regarding Helge's courtship of his sister Julie. Through her brother the girl rejected the suit. Helge finally came home somewhat intoxicated and rolled into bed.

*April 14.* Today I continued on my way and reached home just as my friends were eating supper.

The food supplies among the Norwegians at Rock River and Ashippun River are low at present, and it seems as if our countrymen up there will have to continue tightening their belts because pork costs $18 and wheat flour $5 per barrel (*tønde*) at a time when they are practically stripped of these most essential staples. Lately I have been tortured by a terrible toothache which sends pains through a large part of my head.

Some people who came from a district in Illinois about a hundred miles south of here report that sickness is raging down there. One epidemic is even said to be so severe that a number of patients have died only eight hours after being attacked. It is to be feared, therefore, that this will be a bad summer; there has been little or no rain so far, and the water in the lakes is unusually low.

*April 29.* During the last few days it has rained considerably, causing the fields and meadows to turn quite green. The trees are also in full leaf, and everything proclaims that summer is at hand.

*May 2.* Nature rejoices because the cold, bleak winter is gone. She revels in her beauty and praises the Creator for having freed her from her prison. Animals are frisking about in the green pastures. The horses gather into groups and roam through the woods. Thus everything reminds one of freedom and equality. But I notice that the horses organize rival factions and will not admit any outsiders. Our little Indian mare is the leader and hates all those who do not belong to her group, even the minister's horse. Two colts, a two-year-old and a three-year-old, were castrated today. We turned them out into the fields with the others because the man who did the castrating said they would be killed if we left them in the barn. It did not take him very long to do this job — only about half an hour.

*May 4.* The day is fine, though somewhat cool. Johannes Skofstad was here this afternoon. He told us that Mons Knudsen Aadland's daughter, who married her uncle last fall, is reported to have died in childbirth. It seems that she was alone at the time of her death. Her husband was away, and they lived so far from other people that no one was at hand to care for her. Apparently the husband would not recognize the child as his own, claiming that it had arrived too early for him to be its father. It is a question how far his suspicions are justified, but it seems to be true that she died. The laws here forbid marriage within such close degrees of kinship, and the neighbors also thought it a scandal. This undoubtedly explains why they moved so far west into the Territory.

*May 9.* About one o'clock this afternoon while Johansen and I were sitting in the house, we suddenly heard a wagon approaching at great speed, but it seemed too close to be down on the road. I went to the door to learn who was out driving and what should I see but a runaway horse trailing a three-wheeled, empty wagon behind it. Just then the left hind wheel smashed into a stump, and about fifteen or twenty yards farther on the horse was stopped by a fence. By that time it was freed from the wreck as completely as if it had been unhitched. Soon a boy came running with tears in his eyes and asked me if I would help him catch the horse. This was quickly done. When we came to Even Heg's, he told me that the woman who was with the boy claimed that one of our horses had caused the accident. She said they were visiting at a house about a mile north of here and had tied their horse to a fence near by. Another horse had then come up, and, in the excitement, their horse broke loose and started the runaway, accompanied by the other one. Fortunately the horse which caused the commotion is not ours. It belongs to a man south of here, and we call it the "snorter" because it has the habit of snorting continuously. One of the wheels and the seat had fallen off on the way down, and one of the rear axles and part of the harness were broken. When all these things, which had been in pretty poor shape even before the runaway, were assembled, the boy had to patch them together again. This job was finished by about five o'clock so that they could return to their home, not very far from here. If one of our horses had caused the accident, the woman would undoubtedly have done everything in her power to make us pay for the repair of all these things, but since this was not the case she had to content herself as best she could.

*May 19.* A couple of days ago Pastor Dietrichson arrived here on his way to Norway. We, and several other people in the settlement, wished to send letters home by him, but he refused to take them unless they are unsealed. This being the case, most people are likely to send their letters through the regular channels and forego his services. A man from Numedal by the name of Gunnul Vindeg is taking him to Milwaukee.[7] According to Vindeg, his brother-in-law, Halvor Funkelien, had started a law suit

[7] Gunnul Olsen Vindeg is known in Norwegian immigrant history as a writer of boastful but influential America letters. He was born in Numedal in 1808 and emigrated to America in 1839. The next year he settled in what is now Christiana township, Dane County, Wisconsin, and thus became one of the founders of the Koshkonong settlement. See Anderson, *Norwegian Immigration (1821–1840),* 335–55, and "Koshkonong og Vindeg-slegten," *Numedalslagets Aarbog,* no. 2, 91–101 (1916).

against Dietrichson in order to delay his trip to Norway.[8] The circumstances connected with this incident were briefly as follows:

For some reason or other, Dietrichson put Funkelien under the ban of the church and tried to heap shame upon him by ordering him to sit on a bench back by the door during services. This went on for a while, and Funkelien reasoned that if he could merely drape the bench with velvet and silk there would soon be a great rush of people to join him. He does not seem to have experimented along these lines, but one Sunday he made bold to join his fellow worshippers in the front part of the church, whereupon he was immediately thrown out by the pastor's assistants. After this summary expulsion, Funkelien had the pastor hailed before a court and won judgment against him.

This affair reminds me of another story I heard a couple of months ago about two men who came to church drunk. After services they got into a fight, and Pastor Dietrichson went over to separate them. But when he got there, the fellow on top jumped up and started to chase Dietrichson, who ran yelling

[8] Halvor Christian Pedersen Funkelien came from the district of Kongsberg in Norway. Dietrichson describes him as a drinker, brawler, and scoffer who paid no attention to gentle means of persuasion. In accordance with the church ritual the minister and the congregation read Funkelien out of the church, allowing him to attend services only on condition that he occupy an assigned seat by the door. At this Funkelien threatened to burn the church and kill the pastor and declared that he would take a bottle of whisky to service and sit next to the altar. He also began to associate closely with John G. Smith, a Swedish immigrant, who disliked Dietrichson heartily. (See Chapter 14, note 4.) On Whitsunday, when Dietrichson was to preach his farewell sermon, Funkelien made his first appearance in church after his excommunication. He marched to the front bench and seated himself as close to the altar as he could on the men's side of the church; and when the sexton, Ole K. Trovatten, asked him to take his assigned seat, Funkelien replied that he would sit wherever he pleased. Evidently to make his defiance more emphatic he shifted to the front bench on the womens' side just before the service began. Fearing trouble, many of the women left. Dietrichson then confronted him and directed him to take the prescribed seat, but Funkelien repeated that he would sit wherever he chose. Thereupon Dietrichson appealed to the congregation, and Funkelien, shouting threats and curses, was forcibly ejected by the sexton and two assistants. The next day, Funkelien,

that he should not beat his pastor. When the race was over, the man pulled a dollar from his pocket and said to Dietrichson, "This one I would have given you if you had been a nice boy, but now I will go and spend it for some good liquor." A few days later the minister sent a couple of his elders over to fetch the delinquent to him for reprimand. But when they got there, the transgressor treated them so liberally to the bottle that the elders were quite drunk before they left — and that was the end of the story.

These are examples of Dietrichson's behavior among the Norwegians in Wisconsin. Although he came here as a pastor of souls to lead people away from evil, the result has been quite otherwise. A minister of the Gospel should be an example to others of the harmony between life and doctrine. It is better to have no minister at all than to have one who prefers power and grandeur to humility and meekness. Even without a pastor a man can live according to the Word of God. He may not comprehend everything, but that part of the Bible which is essential unto salvation is clear enough. As for the rest, why should he brood over it

accompanied by two constables, served summonses on Dietrichson, the sexton, and the two assistants, ordering them to appear before the justice of the peace on a charge of assault and battery. A large crowd of Norwegians and Americans attended the trial. An American farmer named Brown, who had been read out of the Methodist church, acted as prosecutor, while another farmer by the name of Parmer [*sic*] asked to plead the case for the defense, probably because his father, a Presbyterian minister, had had a somewhat similar experience with one of his parishioners. The prosecution urged the jury as free-born Americans to resist with all their power the growing "papistry" in America. It asked them especially to declare Dietrichson guilty — "the pope," "the black coated gentleman" who had been the ringleader of the group which laid violent hands on his client. Mr. Parmer argued that under the American system of separation of church and state the secular authorities had no right to interfere with church regulations. Furthermore, he pointed out that Dietrichson could not be guilty of assault and battery since he had not even touched the person of the complainant. But the jury returned a verdict of guilty. The judge ruled that each of the four defendants should pay a fine of five dollars, plus costs — about twelve or thirteen dollars. The defendants appealed the case to the district court, but it was thrown out on a technicality. See Dietrichson, *Reise blandt de norske Emigranter*. 57–69, 122.

when God alone is the one who can give the true interpretation? Different men explain these matters according to their lights, but all may be equally far from the truth.

The behavior of Dietrichson and Clausen among the Norwegians here is rather aristocratic, or at least it leans in that direction. As an instance of this can be mentioned Clausen's manifesto to the church board of October 16 last year. To be sure, in a well-ordered congregation, there must be some kind of authority in accordance with the Word of God; but this authority must not smack of Romanism. Indeed there are but few sincere and true teachers who live in harmony with the Christian precepts which they profess. This they should do because they are regarded as examples by the common man. I believe there are more pastors who lead men toward perdition than there are pastors who lead men toward salvation. Those who have been teachers among the people will have much to answer for on the Day of Judgment, when they will have to render account of every word they have preached as well as of the life they have lived.

*May 20.* We rather expected that Dietrichson would call on us today and say farewell as he passed by on his way to Norway, but about eleven o'clock he drove by like an absolute stranger. In spite of the fact that he enjoyed much hospitality from Johansen and Heg in this house last fall, he would not show them the courtesy of parting with them in a friendly manner. I suspect from his strange behavior that he took offense at their withdrawal from Clausen's congregation. It is said that he visited none of his acquaintances in the settlement except Clausen; he came here as a friend and left as a fugitive. Possibly he suspected we had heard about his experience among the Norwegians farther west which I mentioned yesterday, and this also kept him from coming in. Thanks be to you, Dietrichson, for your brief sojourn among us, and may you have a safe trip back whence you came. He was not in the least fitted for his work in America because of his haughty and overbearing manners. Such airs do not befit a pastor who is supposed to lead people from the world to God. This can be done only through good examples, exhortations, and inducements, as when a person tries to persuade a child to do that which is right. Strictness and severity drive many a noble soul which might otherwise be saved to iniquity and damnation. According to reports, he made himself hated by many people and even received blows. Many who joined his church withdrew later. It is probably not wise to accept such rumors indiscriminately, but nevertheless there is always some foundation for them. Dietrichson had much the same opinion about America as Brynildsen. Such people had better return to the old country, and when they have nothing else to do they can sit and twiddle their fingers and take comfort in the fact that they have at least been across the Atlantic and seen the land of the immigrants.

The justice of the peace fined Dietrichson fifty dollars (which the congregation was supposed to pay) and advised him to get away from here lest the case become a serious matter for him. Such an affair does not reflect honor upon the clergy. It is best not to have anything to do with them when they are so anxious to dominate. Usually they are afflicted with this ambition, though there have been some gifted men among them who have done much to improve the lot of others.

*June 16.* Since Easter we had been waiting for letters from Norway. Frequently we sent someone down to the Rochester post office, but always in vain. We were unable to understand this long silence and feared that something might have happened at home. Probably father was sick and they would not write until they knew how he would fare. Today Even Heg sent his youngest boy down to Rochester to buy something. While he was there the mail arrived, bringing among other things, a letter to me. When he came home and told us that there was a letter from Norway we were extremely happy. It was dated May 9;

only thirty-eight days had elapsed between the time of writing and the time of delivery, which is very quick service.

*June 22.* In response to an invitation, Even Heg and his children, Johansen, and I attended the christening of Johannes Skofstad's little daughter. There we met several good friends who had also been invited. It should be noted that not all who gathered there were members of Clausen's congregation, the congregation which he says is genuinely Lutheran but which, according to the opinion of me and my friends, is genuinely Roman. I cannot imagine that Luther wanted a person to kneel down before a minister and confess his sins unless his spirit moved him to do so. But this is not the matter I wish to discuss. I was going to tell about the event of the day, the christening of Skofstad's little daughter. It may seem strange that she was baptized at home rather than in the church when there is such a building in the settlement. The explanation is that since Skofstad is not a member of Clausen's congregation the latter did not feel that the ceremony could take place in the church. He places much emphasis upon baptism and wants the ministerial profession to stress this sacrament strongly. I will let this pass for what it is worth, but if baptism is so important, then the ceremony should have been performed in the church so as to give the child power to withstand the forces of evil. According to Clausen's own explanation the child would now lack that power, and if we are to accept his teachings, the infant must, therefore, be doomed to eternal damnation. But God must be absolutely powerless if he is unable to save a child through such a baptism just as well as through a baptism performed in a church. The first part of the ceremony was impressive, and Clausen made appropriate opening remarks. But after performing the act of baptism, he said that this would have to suffice and that the ceremony had been conducted in accordance with apostolic usage. Then he added that the child would not be able to partake of the blessings of the church for the reasons given above; neither would the child have power to withstand the Devil or other temptations encountered and would, therefore, necessarily be damned.[9]

*July 9.* Yesterday the first immigrants of the year reached the settlement. They came from the Stavanger area. The trip across the ocean had taken nine weeks and three days. During the next two or three months we may hope for weekly contingents of immigrants from old Norway. As yet we have not heard anything about the arrival at Milwaukee of the long-awaited group led by Captain Gasmann. We are expecting them to bring us some copies of *Morgenbladet*, which we have been looking forward to eagerly.

The usual summer heat made itself felt a week or two ago, but as far as I know the health situation has been good. There may have been some cases of illness in the neighborhood, but if so they have been very few.

We have good prospects for a fine crop this year. The corn especially looks very promising.

*July 30.* Extremely warm and dry weather this month had caused the corn and potato vines to wilt. During the latter part of last week, however, we got some rain, and in the cool period which followed these crops have picked up considerably. We have already harvested the small grains such as wheat, barley, rye, and oats. The last loads were brought under roof today.

Recently I have read in the papers about an extraordinary case of fecundity. On June 22 the wife of Elyah Marshal of Silver Lake Township, Susquehanna County, Pennsylvania, gave birth to quadruplets. All four of them were girls and according to last reports they were doing well. Even though Mrs. Marshal is only twenty-six years old, she has given birth to eleven children. The *Montrose Democrat* states that such cases are few and far between.

The papers also say that it is practically certain that Texas

---

[9] The details in the original are not entirely clear, but we believe that the translation conveys the meaning of the passage.

will join the Union as a state. The Congress of Texas has already passed the necessary resolution, and it is expected that the President of the Republic will grant his sanction very soon. . . .[10]

*July 31.* I received a letter today from my brother Niels wherein he tells something about my father's illness. He still has to stay in bed. The letter was written on June 27, about five weeks ago.

*August 2.* Today another letter came dated May 15. It was brought by Niels Tollefson Rae, an emigrant from Gol parish in Hallingdal. He also brought copies of *Morgenbladet* and *Drammens Addresse* covering the period from January 15 to May 12. These papers will certainly provide us with interesting reading.

*August 20.* This afternoon I visited one of my oldest acquaintances in the northern part of the settlement. There I met an American justice of the peace. I was told that he had been in pursuit of an Irishman who all but raped a Norwegian widow down on the road some days ago. Presumably he will land in the penitentiary when he is caught.

*September 26.* This is the time of year when climatic diseases such as fever, ague, and biliousness are at their worst. Large sections of the population in Wisconsin and Illinois, but especially in the latter state, have suffered. Of Norwegian settlements, Muskego was most heavily stricken in 1842 and 1843, but this year it seems to have been the least afflicted. Even though there have been quite a few cases among us, we have escaped lightly compared with Pine Lake and the neighboring settlements along the Ashippun and Rock rivers. The settlers at Koshkonong have also been severely stricken, some of them fatally. There is much sickness among the Americans in this area. The doctors have also succumbed, and it is difficult to secure medical aid.

[10] The resolution was inserted here in the diary, but is omitted from the present translation.

# 10. A Debate with the Pastor

[*September 26, 1845*]. THE ENTIRE CONGREGATION assembled at the church this afternoon upon order of Pastor Clausen. He wanted to know whether they wished him to remain as their minister. Those who so desired would have to enroll anew and agree to the condition that this parish should become a sort of chapelry where he would hold meetings at irregular intervals as he found convenient. In return they could pay him whatever salary they were able to. These conditions were accepted.

It will be remembered that quite a number of people withdrew from Clausen's congregation last fall after having contributed substantially to the construction of the church. These also appeared at the meeting to present their case since the minister had declared their rights forfeit, maintaining, as is true, that the money was contributed for the building of a Lutheran church in the settlement. Even though he is aware that they gave materials for the building quite as freely as those who remained loyal to him, he argues that they want to have nothing to do with the congregation and consequently have no further claim to the church. This is a very perverse doctrine since property rights assuredly are sacred. Mr. Heg, who owns the ground on which the church is located, stepped forth and expressed his opinion, after which the rest of us who shared his views got up and, before the entire assembly, declared that although we could not accept Pastor Clausen as our minister we reserved our rights in the church and would feel as free to make use of it as those who had remained loyal to him. Clausen replied that as part owner of the church he was willing to let us borrow it from time to time, whereupon Even Heg wanted to know if we had to borrow what belonged to us. The answer was that we had seceded from the Lutheran congregation, to which I replied that the ritual

167

was not the words of Luther. Johansen declared that it would be disgraceful for Clausen to deny others the use of this church for divine services in view of the fact that he himself had to borrow an assembly place in Chicago.

Finally Clausen wanted to know if we had come there to disrupt his conference. We replied that we had come merely to proclaim, in the presence of the entire gathering, that we reserved our rights in the building, which was our property as much as anybody else's since we had contributed our proper share to its construction. A man from Sigdal then queried, sarcastically, which sect we were trying to reserve the church for, to which Johansen retorted that we wanted to reserve it for Christianity if we were allowed to. That silenced him, but outside the church after the meeting the man was still further taken to task, and it was found that he could not justify his question in the least. After all, the Norwegians around here have Johansen to thank for most of the contributions which have been made to the church. Without his aid the task would have been much more difficult. But that is the way of the world. Those who do well are rewarded with ingratitude. It seems as if they are trying to heap scorn upon the contributors. I feel convinced that if the contributors could have foreseen Clausen's popish ways they would have taken precautions to prevent things from going the way they have. All his dreams and ambitions apparently have as their object the attaining of papal authority over the members of his congregation. He is also trying to enrich himself. We hear of him both claiming and buying land and having people work it for him. Instead of fostering peace and unity among the people as a pastor ought to, he sows dissension and strife among them because the ritual seems to be his main article of faith. He maintains that at the time of his ordination he took an oath to observe its forms closely, which no one can contradict because none of the delegates who witnessed the ceremony understood a word of the language in which it was conducted.

John Helgesen was the first man to step forth and announce his willingness to sign again when Clausen, as already mentioned, had explained his new scheme that neither he nor the congregation should be bound to any definite terms. This is the third time that Clausen has made his congregation enroll since he became minister in the settlement.

The next day, a Saturday, Johansen went over to Clausen to collect some money which he had coming from him. A little later in the forenoon I went over to Johannes Skofstad's, and shortly after my arrival Anders Kløve also appeared with the news that they had arranged a meeting there for two o'clock that afternoon to thresh out matters with Clausen.

When the group which consisted of Clausen and seven others had assembled, Johansen opened the discussion somewhat as follows:

"As it does not seem at all possible for us to get along together, we had better express our opinions frankly and then part as friends. We should bear in mind, however, how quiet and friendly the first year was. But then you, Clausen, started with the ritual and since then there has been nothing but cliques, strife, and contention."

This brought forth the reply from Clausen that he had taken an oath to observe the forms of the ritual, to which Johansen retorted:

"Then you have already broken your oath and changed the form of the confession three times in addition. At first you asked: 'Do you forsake the Devil and all his works and all his ways?' Later you said: 'Whereas you have previously confessed, I promise you . . . etc.'; finally you adopted a third procedure and used neither of these forms."

Another member of the group, Østen Meland, claimed that he had heard the minister pray from the pulpit that those who had strayed from him might again be united with the fold. This made the preacher quite excited. "That's nothing but a lie," he exclaimed; "I have never prayed for anything like that." But Meland replied that he had heard it as well as many others who could testify to the fact, and several members of the group supported Meland. After a while Clausen asked why they analyzed his every word so closely, to which Johansen replied, "You who have assumed the responsibility of being a teacher to others must live accordingly; you are in a difficult position. People are usually guided fully as much by a minister's life and behavior as by his preaching. And as for your praying that we should return to your congregation, that's about as if someone raised a rumpus in a house and scared some people out, and then, after having bolted the door, asked the people outside if they please would not come back in again."

After they had been disputing this way a long time, Berthe Skofstad came in and sat down with her two- or three-month-old daughter on her lap. Then Johansen turned to Clausen and said: "Why would you not allow this child to be baptized in the church? Its parents lead just as decent a life as a great number of people in your congregation. And you would not have needed to worry about sponsors; you could have got enough of them. The first prayer you said at her baptism was very beautiful, but the last one was very bad and spoiled the whole ceremony. You said at the time that there was nothing essentially wrong with this baptism and that it was in accordance with the teachings of the Apostles. If that is the case, why can not this child be saved?" Berthe also pressed him for an answer to this. Clausen replied that undoubtedly the child could be saved by the grace of God, but it could not partake of the means of salvation which are the blessings of the church. "Why not?" they wished to know. "Because the child is not incorporated into the church," he replied. Thereupon Berthe became so insistent that Clausen had to explain himself more minutely, to the great amusement of the others. He did not do any too well, but somehow he seemed to believe that the child would lack the power to resist evil.

After this Johansen told him that it did not seem as if he came to America with the idea of being a teacher. "While crossing the Great Lakes," Johansen said, "you were dickering for a position with a merchant from Madison." Clausen asked immediately who had told him this; on being informed, he said that Bache was not to be depended upon because he gossiped about so many things. These may not have been his exact words, but there was no doubt about his meaning despite the fact that he tried to tangle everything up by putting different interpretations upon what he had said. Johansen followed up his attack by saying, "It seems as if you are more concerned about enriching yourself than about preaching the Word of God, because you are far busier buying and claiming land than caring for your congregation." Clausen replied that a person would not get rich from buying land on credit or by staking out claims for four shillings. Then this little exchange of words ensued:

Johansen: "You accept into your congregation without examination people who during the week fight and drink while you refuse to admit people like these parents when they wish to have their child baptized in the church."

Clausen: "I am not aware of having accepted any such people, and furthermore I have no time to do any more examining than I have been doing."

Johansen: "No, you want to gobble up everything! Why do you take on so many jobs? If you want decent people in your congregation you will have to do fewer things and do them well. But, of course, you want to get rich."

Clausen tried to maneuver Johansen into using expressions which might lay him open to libel, but without success. Frequently he became very excited and wanted to leave. He had not come here to be reviled, he said.[1]

[1] Considerable freedom has been used in wording and arranging various passages in this chapter which are confused in the manuscript. We believe, however, that we have rendered the exact meaning of the original.

## 11. From Neighbor to Neighbor

*October 27* [*1845*]. TODAY I decided to take a long walk. I left home about half past eight o'clock this morning and passed through the village of Mukwonago to the town of Ottawa where Helge and Elling Helgesen live. I wanted to see Helge's wife, a German woman whom he had married some six months ago. When I got there about seven o'clock in the evening, Helge was away from home, and both Elling and their hired man were sick with fever or ague. After about a quarter of an hour Helge returned.

It has been a very beautiful day.

*October 28.* I spent the day here with the Helgesens. They told me that there is much sickness in the localities I plan to visit. Indeed, there is much illness throughout the whole Territory.

That new wife of Helge's is only twenty-one years old and so full of spirit that she cuts all sorts of capers before her husband out of sheer deviltry and wantonness. Whenever she had an opportunity she would tease him and carry on in a way which was positively indecent. Elling said that she put on her worst demonstrations in the presence of strangers, who often blushed at her behavior.

*October 29.* After breakfast I said good-by to the Helgesens even though they wished me to stay several days. I was tired of seeing the woman carry on. About twelve o'clock I reached Summit where I met a Norwegian carpenter whom I knew slightly. He treated me to a glass of whisky and a cigar. After an hour I continued my walk, now in a steady rainfall, and came to Christopher Aamodt's on the Ashippun River about half past three o'clock. By that time the rain finally ceased, and the sky began to clear. On the way out here someone told me that Mrs. Aamodt was sick, but I found both her, the husband, and the child in fairly good health.

*October 30.* Today I went over to see Johannes Lie from Gausdal, who had returned home on September 20 from a trip to Norway last spring to bring his wife and little boy across. Both of them are very well pleased with their new home. He also is so satisfied after having brought his family that he never intends to take any more such trips nor does he want to move away from the farm where he now lives. He has a fine piece of land which slopes gently from the center. The woods on his farm consist mostly of Norway maple, from the sap of which sugar is made. Oak and other varieties of trees are scarce. He said he was exceedingly fond of sugar and had purposely picked this kind of land so that he could make it himself and not have to buy it. He had two hired men at work splitting fence rails and posts. One of these men, Lars Iversen Thorstad, was a very well-informed fellow whom it was interesting to talk with because he philosophized so wisely about things. He had a real passion for knowledge and was determined to master the English language. We spent a very enjoyable evening together chatting until all the others had fallen asleep. Finally we also had to go to bed.

*October 31.* This forenoon I bade these people farewell and started off homeward, but when I came to Christopher Aamodt's they wanted me to stay over Sunday and hear Pastor Unonius, who was going to conduct services among the Norwegians of the neighborhood. I accepted their invitation.

*November 1.* Aamodt had some matters to take care of down by Rock River, and I went with him. While he took care of his affairs I visited at J. Lie's. After dinner we returned home and spent the rest of the day quietly.

*November 2.* Around ten-thirty the minister arrived. After having some refreshments we went to Christopher O. Svendsrud's where the services were to be held as he had the largest house in the community. Some people were already there, and the services soon began. With no one to lead the singing they had to get along as best they could. This really turned out to be a comical affair because instead of decent church music they used popular tunes. Being an Episcopalian, the minister read Anglican prayers, of which he had made a poor translation. As text he took I Kings, 18:21: "And Elijah came unto all the people, and said, 'How long halt ye between two opinions? If the Lord be God, follow Him; but if Baal, then follow him.'" His interpretation of this passage was not very lengthy. He is a poor speaker, but he did his best. After the meeting I went with some acquaintances to their home about two miles farther north. I had dinner with them and after a while returned to Christopher Aamodt's. Soon afterward I saw the minister go by, and about half an hour later Christopher and his wife came home. We spent the rest of the day quietly.

*November 3.* About eight o'clock this morning I left my friends and set off for Pine Lake through some dense woods by a road which was new to me. I ate dinner at Niels Gasmann's. Only the wife and old Hans Gasmann, who was visiting there, were at home. After I had eaten and attended to some little matters, I continued my trip. By sundown I reached Prairieville and stayed overnight in a hotel. The day was very beautiful.

*November 4.* At eight o'clock this morning I took my cane and bag and set my course eastward toward home. The morning was radiant but not quite as cool as yesterday. Toward the south the horizon was covered with threatening rain clouds, but later on it cleared up. At eleven o'clock I came to the home of a friend of mine, an American named Martin. His wife asked me to stay for dinner, which I did, and then continued my trip, reaching home about two-thirty o'clock.

*November 22.* Summer with all its beauty is now gone, and today winter announces its arrival by spreading a sheet of snow over the earth. With the fall of the snow, a silence also seems to settle over everything. No more do we hear the song of the birds or the tinkling of cowbells. Nature has fallen asleep under her blanket of snow until spring again shall stir her from her slumbers.— Who knows what the winter will bring?

The evening was very stormy with a strong wind from the west accompanied by snow.

*November 23.* This is the last Sunday of the church year, a beautiful day with a clear sky but very cold as if winter had come to stay. Of course this is to be expected so late in the year. And now we shall see whether a dry summer will be followed by a dry winter. It is seldom that two years are alike.

*December 3.* Yesterday I asked the surveyor to subdivide my land on the other side of the brook. Today I rode out on the prairie to notify some Americans about this, since I had promised to sell them a forty-acre piece. But this deal failed to materialize. On my way back in the afternoon I met a *Vossing* and stopped to talk.[1] While we were chatting he suddenly exclaimed: "Well, look!" I did not know what was up, but merely stared at him. Abruptly I found myself standing on the ground with the horse between my legs, so quietly had he lain down. I freed myself from the saddle, got the horse up again, and rode home.

*December 9.* Today Johansen decided to go to Milwaukee to take an oath in connection with a deed of partition which he became partner to last summer when the estate of a dead Norwegian of this neighborhood was settled. Martin Knudsen and I went with him. We arrived there in the evening. I had not been in Milwaukee since May last year and found that great changes had taken place in the meantime. A fire had ravaged part of the city, and on the sites of the destroyed buildings new three-story brick structures had been erected. Indeed, brick buildings seemed to be springing up everywhere. We took lodgings with a Swede named Dreutzer and there met a man from Bamle parish who was very drunk. After making a lot of noise he fell asleep in a box where he remained for a while. The Swede smeared his face with oil and then painted him with soot, making him look like a "tough customer." Finally he was taken to bed, and we also retired.

[1] A person from the district of Voss in Norway.

*December 10.* Today I finished what little business I had to take care of and in the evening took lodgings with a Norwegian by the name of Nordbøe. Later my friend Martin Knudsen and I were treated to a glass of eggnog, which gave us indigestion. In spite of this we had a very pleasant time with our little group of friends.

*December 11.* About ten o'clock this forenoon I said good-by to my acquaintances and started for home. I visited several places along the road and got here in time to crawl into bed about half past ten o'clock. I found Johansen already sound asleep there.[2]

*December 21.* As this was Sunday and the air very heavy, we spent the day in quiet meditation on the Scriptures. Snow fell all forenoon and part of the afternoon but not enough to make good sleighing since the ground was already frozen and slippery. So far this month has been continuously cold.

*December 25.* During the last days we have had some snow and fair sleighing. It snowed again Christmas Eve and this forenoon, thus improving the sleighing. It is not as cold now as it was earlier in the month, which is fortunate. About twelve o'clock the weather cleared, and the rest of the day was fair. In the afternoon I visited Niels Närum.[3]

*[Undated.]* The last days of the year have been mild so that the good sleighing we have had for several days will disappear with the melting snow. The severe cold during the early part of

[2] In the original a copy of a land deed is here inserted which records the fact that Søren Bache had made full payment "for the West half and the South End quarter of Section twenty eight, in Township four North of Range twenty East, in the District of lands subject to sale at Milwaukee. . . ." The certificate, numbered 9,172, was signed by the recorder on December 10, 1844.

[3] After the entry for December 25, 1845, Bache inserts a Norwegian translation of a long account of the reform movement known as "German Catholicism." This passage is omitted from the present translation. The German movement that Bache reports seems to have been related to the liberal spirit sweeping Europe in the 1830s and 1840s. Bache's own interest in it probably arises from the fact that its leaders, Johannes Ronge and Johann Czerski, seemed to him to be fighting authoritarianism and "papistry" in the same way

the month has left the lakes covered with a thick sheet of ice. On the whole this has been a good year. The crops were fine, and the oak trees yielded an abundance of acorns on which the pigs could fatten. As a result the people in this settlement have brought a great amount of pork to town without further expense and have netted some twenty, thirty, or perhaps even forty dollars per trip. From all around, farmers have hauled so much pork and wheat to market that for a long while last fall as many as a hundred and fifty wagons per day rolled toward Milwaukee over a road some four or five miles north of here. People ought to make money now when they get a dollar per bushel for wheat and almost five dollars per hundred pounds of pork.

that he felt he was combating similar forces on the local front in Wisconsin. His final comment, however, is one of reserved judgment, for he says of the movement, "If it is of God, as I hope it is, it will remain, but if not it will collapse by itself." For an account of the German movement, see the *New Schaaf-Herzog Encyclopaedia of Religious Knowledge,* 4:466–68 (New York, 1909).

# 12. A Business Trip to Jefferson Prairie

*January 1, 1846.* THE NEW YEAR begins with thick foggy weather. In the whole vast expanse of the sky not a single bright spot can be seen. A drizzle falling from a heavy mantle of clouds is causing the snow to disappear rapidly. By noon today only a few patches of it remained. A great silence broods over everything as if the earth were a dark and deserted place incapable of sustaining any living thing. At this time of year nature seems barren and dead, but in a few months the hidden life will be freed from bondage and rejoice as it unfolds itself in new forms.

This afternoon it rained quite heavily, which was a blessing since we hear from many quarters that there is such a shortage of water that the cattle must go great distances for it.

*January 5.* With the exception of the first day the new year has been just like spring even though we are in the middle of the winter. The traffic on the road has been very light compared with what it was during the earlier winter months.

*January 31.* The last day of the first month in the year is clear though rather cold. As a whole, however, this month has been unusually mild, in fact the mildest January I can remember. Yesterday forenoon, for instance, was as balmy as a summer morning, but it cooled off in the afternoon when a chill wind sprang up. Earlier we had another day equally fair.

*February 10.* During the night of February 4 my friend Johannes Johansen was taken sick with a severe cold. Both his chest and liver were badly affected, and throughout his whole illness he suffered from a continuous cough. He was very short of breath and during the last days had a pain in his right side. The last two hours he lay in a coma and passed away about eight o'clock in the evening. Four hours before his death, he signed a statement in my presence which cost him great effort, especially the last three letters of the name "Johansen." Two hours later he uttered his last words.

*February 14.* Today, Saturday, all those who were invited came to pay their last respects to Johansen and to follow him to the grave. When the coffin was to be taken out of the house, hymn number 194 in Guldberg's hymnal was sung: "Come with me, Jesus, I am your companion," after which Clausen, who happened to be in the settlement, said a brief prayer.[1] At the grave we sang hymn number 328: "Who knows how near me is my death," and in the church the three first stanzas of hymn number 384, "When my time is at hand." Clausen then delivered a sermon, taking as his text Psalms 107:28, 29, 30: "Then they cry unto the Lord in their trouble . . . so He bringeth them unto their desired haven," which he expounded very effectively. After the sermon the fourteenth verse of the last-mentioned hymn was sung. Johansen's best friends, a group of more than twenty people, were invited to our home after the funeral. Before they left in the evening we sang hymn number 56: "How blessed is the man who is prepared for death," and Clausen closed with a brief prayer befitting the occasion. A few people remained until the next morning.

*February 16.* Since I had determined to seek the probate judge who has jurisdiction over the proof of wills, I set off on horseback for Racine this morning. The weather was bright though cool as I left, but when I was some twelve or fourteen miles from home, out on the open prairie, the clouds gathered and a violent snowstorm followed, through which I had to ride for quite a while without finding shelter either in a wood or a house. But after some two miles of this I came to an inn where I stayed awhile to get warm. Then I continued my trip and arrived in

[1] *Guldsbergs Salmebog* was published in 1778 by the Danish Minister of State Ove Högh Guldberg and Bishop L. Harboe. Since it reflected the rationalistic spirit of the time, it was never universally accepted either in Denmark or Norway. In the latter country it was superseded by *Landstads Salmebog*, published in 1869.

Racine shortly before sunset. I took lodgings in a hotel called Racine House and there inquired about the people I wished to see next day. After supper I asked the hotelkeeper if he had any Norwegians working for him. He said he had, and a few moments later he motioned for me to follow him upstairs. There he took a little bell from a window sill and rang it. Soon a girl came who was Norwegian. She told me where the Norwegians I was looking for lived and even took me over there, returning immediately to the hotel. My visit over, I too went back and enjoyed a good sleep even though the room was cold.

*February 17.* This morning the weather was cold but not as unpleasant as yesterday. I soon finished my affairs in Racine, and since I had to go to Southport to find the probate judge, I mounted my horse and started off again.[2] It was a ride of some ten miles, and I got there about twelve o'clock. After stabling my horse I went to look for the office of the judge. The door was locked, so I assumed that he had gone home for dinner. I therefore took a stroll through town to its southern end, which is about six miles from the Illinois boundary. The houses are scattered. The street I followed is called Main Street, and I should estimate that the entire length of the town from north to south is about one mile. It was founded in 1836 and has a population of about two thousand. The location is not particularly beautiful. Two small rivers or creeks run through the town. At their mouth a sandbank has been deposited by the water, and there the beginnings of a harbor have been made by the construction of a ramshackle pier. As a mass of stone was lying close by, it is possible that they are going to build a better one. South of this one there were two other piers which extended well into the water, but they were not in too good shape either.

Since the judge did not appear at the office, I went to his house, after a long wait, to present my business there. When I

[2] This is the present-day Kenosha. On the early maps of Wisconsin Territory it is shown as Southport, Pike, or Knosha.

finished my account, he wrote an announcement of Johansen's death for publication in the Racine paper. This matter taken care of, he flattered me by saying that Franklin, one of the great men of the American Revolution, had married a young lady named Bache. I finally left after it had been agreed that I should meet him in Racine on the first Monday in April. His name is Volney French, and both he and his wife seemed to be cultivated people.

Farther up the street I went into a little shop and had some refreshments — a glass of beer, cookies, and a cigar — before I went back to the hotel and got my horse. After a ride of about five miles I reached an inn where I decided to stay the night. The name of the proprietor was George Leet. He was very cranky when I arrived, but two other fellows and I had a merry laugh at him which seemed to improve his temper a bit.

*February 18.* The inn was located at the edge of a dense forest that hemmed it in toward the north and east, while the prairie extended off toward the south and west. At breakfast time this morning a threshing machine arrived to do some threshing there during the day.

After eating I mounted my horse and continued the trip. To return home by a different road, I took one going northwest which I also judged to be more direct than the other one. A mile or so from the inn, out on the prairie, I saw a windmill on a high hill. The eastern part of the sky was covered with dark clouds but along the horizon they were beautifully gilded by the rays of the rising sun. As I rode along I recognized a grove where Johansen and I had camped under the open sky in our wagon several years before. This brought back many memories of my former companion, which, combined with the beauty of the sunrise in the eastern sky, made me nearly oblivious to the silent, wintry landscape round about me. When I reached the main road from Racine, I met an Englishman with whom I struck up an acquaintance. We accompanied each other some ten miles, chatting about inconsequential matters. Around three o'clock I got back to my cozy home, happy at having completed a long ride which at this time of year was none too pleasant. The rest of the week I spent quietly, writing letters to Norway, one to Christiansand and one to my family in Drammen, to let them know what had happened.

*February 25*. The weather was bad during my trip and has continued cold and stormy ever since. Some snow has fallen, and sleighing is good, the best in three winters. This week, however, we have had clear days with crisp, clear air. Today the sun is shining but not warmly enough to cause a thaw, though there is no wind.

We have finally begun to examine Johansen's and my accounts in order to reach a settlement of our joint undertakings of many years. At last we shall learn how our affairs have prospered in this land which for decades has been a haven for Europeans seeking refuge from their harsh lot in the Old World. Many people miss Johansen for he was always ready to help others and had a way of maintaining a fair degree of harmony among the Norwegian mountaineers in this settlement. He was a sort of father whose advice they sought when they were in trouble. During our many years together I learned to know him as a man of noble and upright disposition who always tried to be just.

*February 28*. It is milder today than it has been for some time. Now that a change has set in perhaps spring will soon be here. But that cannot be counted on, because even though March is not severe, it is usually cold enough to keep vegetation from sprouting in all its beauty. Clausen and some other Norwegians stopped in a few moments this evening. They rode in a sleigh drawn by a team of two horses.

*March 8*. Yesterday Thore T. Mørk paid us a visit. Since his arrival in the settlement he had been staying with a certain Niels Katterud, a good friend of Mørk and his wife. But we asked him to fetch his horses and wagon, which he did without much delay. I had already received a hint as to the real reason for his visit and had learned something about the difficult position he was in. He stood in danger of losing his rights in one half of a claim of 320 acres and all the improvements he had made on the land. His friend, John Christensen, a smith's apprentice from Drammen (born in the parish of Eger), had paid for, or rather redeemed, this claim at the land office. Now able to do as he pleased, he had given Thore until May to meet payment on a sum of a hundred and fifty dollars which they had borrowed on a note in order to pay for a part of the land. The rest of the land the smith had paid for with his own money, and he also had enough money out at interest to redeem the above-mentioned note whenever he might wish. Knowing something about this, I asked Thore how things were going, and because he hoped that I would be willing to help him he told me frankly everything I needed to know about the matter in case I decided to act. I also learned that early last spring Clausen had promised to lend him some money the following May, but when the time came neither Clausen nor the money was in evidence. At the time he promised the loan, Clausen told Mørk that it was of no use to go begging Bache for any money. But now a year has already passed and he has not yet been able to get any money from Clausen. This is one of Clausen's sly little tricks. When Thore came to the settlement early last week, he met Clausen and reminded him of the loan, but the latter could make no promise until he returned to Rock Prairie. Thore said that on several occasions he had told Clausen that he must have a very definite promise or he would have to seek the money elsewhere. Finally he came to me, and I promised to accompany him home to see what could be done. If I were to solve his problem, I must get security either in his land here in America or in his wife's inheritance in Norway until the loan should be repaid a year hence.

Clausen furthermore has advised Thore to sign a release giving Pastor Dietrichson power to draw the money in Norway on his arrival there. Dietrichson should then either bring the money if he returned to America or forward it some other way. But the worst complication, it seems to me, was that Thore had signed a release for only half the sum while, as far as I can gather from my brother's letter about this case, the whole sum should have been released, which sounds reasonable. I have heard that Dietrichson is coming back next summer, but as matters now stand it is not at all certain that he will bring the money along. In any event it is a great loss for Thore, who has to wait so long before he can get a clear title to the land he has improved. And he would have lost it entirely if I had not helped him. He will come out of this scrape wiser but not wealthier, which is always the case with such affairs. Through Clausen's sage counsel he has lost much and gained nothing but the knowledge that he should depend upon people who are worthy of his trust.

*March 9.* This morning Thore left to visit a cousin of his who lives south of here. He is to stay there overnight, and tomorrow we will ride down to settle the matter of his land. While selecting clothes for the trip, I chose among other things a shirt that had been put into my chest when I left for America in 1839 and that I had not yet worn.

*March 10.* I left home Tuesday morning about five o'clock. A mile and a half or so out, I met Thore, whom I was to accompany westward. We stayed in Waterford about an hour and at nine o'clock continued on our way, going through Rochester from where we struck off in a southwesterly direction. As we proceeded I found the land to be hilly and sparsely wooded. Every now and then we passed fine farm houses, beautifully painted. About five o'clock in the afternoon, as we were passing through Walworth County, we came to a beautiful plain called Spring Prairie. There were fences along either side of the road. Trees had also been planted along some stretches of the highway, and, as earlier in the day, we noted many fine farmhouses. About halfway across the prairie we struck a crossroad where there was a two-story brick inn on one corner and a combination store and post office directly across from it. Near the western edge of the prairie we passed through a little grove consisting partly of young oak and ash trees. Immediately beyond, the land became low and marshy and appeared to be unclaimed. At least nc houses were to be seen for some four miles until we reached Elkhorn, the county seat. We got there about half past seven o'clock and decided to stay for the night. The town is located on a slightly sloping plain. There are not many buildings in the place — only two stores, two inns for travelers, a courthouse, and a few other houses.

With the exception of the low area referred to, the land we saw today was fine and rolling with many well-kept houses.

When we had cared for the horses and looked after some other matters, we were ready for bed because we were very tired.

*March 11.* Having fed the horses and eaten a tasteless and poorly prepared breakfast, we continued our trip across a prairie which, though high and well drained, was as sparsely populated as the four miles mentioned yesterday. After a ride of about six miles we came to a town called Delavan, which was also very small but still contained a few more buildings than Elkhorn. There is little to say about the place except that a river, or rather a creek, flows through it and furnishes power for a mill. Five or six miles beyond the town, at the eastern edge of Turtle Prairie, we came upon a large and attractive inn. We stopped there for about an hour to give our horses a rest and then continued on and eventually reached Jefferson Prairie where, in the fall of 1839, I had visited some Norwegians who lived in the settlement there. Actually, the road we were supposed to take ran two miles farther north, but we decided to make a detour so as to spend the night with one or another of these families. We finally stopped at the place of a man named Thosten Kjerkejorden, who had a good house and, besides, was building a new barn.

Yesterday the weather was quite pleasant, but this afternoon we had several heavy showers. The forenoon was not so bad though the air was heavy.

*March 12.* Immediately after breakfast, we set off toward Beloit, arriving about noon. We stayed there awhile to give our horses a rest and to buy some little things we wished to take along. I will admit that Beloit has grown somewhat since I was there a little over six years ago but not as much as the Norwegians around there always boast. I remember that the inn we stayed at now was under construction the last time I was in Beloit. A beautiful stone mill as well as a church and quite a number of other buildings have been erected. Furthermore, in recent years a bridge has been built across the river. The town lies partly in Wisconsin and partly in Illinois. The land around there is mostly rolling prairie, being highest to the west of the Rock River where there are rocky or sandy elevations.

Our purchases made, we continued toward the northwest and after a ride of about twelve miles came to the Norwegian settlement out on the prairie. The land between the river and the settlement is rolling, the hills are sandy and rocky, as already mentioned, and the soil seems to be very poor. What oak trees there are remind a person of some decrepit old fellow who has had just enough nourishment to hang on to life. They could hardly be used for anything but firewood for it would take about two of these trees to make an axe handle.

We went to the home of Peder Gaarder from Land parish, who had accompanied me on my second trip to America. His farm is located in S.36 T.2 R.10, seven miles from the Illinois boundary. At the home of one of the Norwegians here I met a certain Mr. Jørgensen, formerly a merchant in Skien, who last year conducted school for the children in the settlement.

The last part of the day was rainy, which made the trip all the more unpleasant, and we were happy to reach the house of a friend.

*March 13.* Not yet at the end of our journey, we had to leave after breakfast this morning also. The weather was fairly good as we set off. We followed a westerly course until we were two miles beyond Sugar River, after which we turned toward the south. Here we struck another dry rolling prairie, but the soil was of different texture from what we found yesterday. The woods also were better though there were a lot of poplars. On crossing Sugar River, we had covered only seven or eight miles, and as we still had to ride some ten or eleven miles toward the south, we did not complete our trip until sundown. Although the people here had believed that I would pay them a visit sometime, they had hardly expected me before fall or winter. They were therefore quite surprised to see me. My cousin Berthe seemed very pleased at my arrival, and I was very happy to see that she as well as the others around here were getting along well.

*March 14.* Today I was shown through the wood on Thore's land by his friend, John Christensen. It consisted mostly of oak trees, but there were also a great number of poplars as well as a lot of practically impenetrable underbrush. Since I soon tired of this, we returned to the house. After dinner Thore and I went over to see a Norwegian by the name of Andreas Erstad. He was not at home when we arrived as he had driven over to a near-by saw mill this morning to get some lumber. After sitting there awhile we decided to stroll over to a hill in the direction from which we expected him, and we had not gone very far before we heard the rumble of his wagon in the distance. We greeted him and accompanied him back to the house. After he had eaten I handed Erstad a hundred and fifty dollars and thus redeemed the papers which he had been given as security for the loan. When this business had been transacted we were ready to leave, but they persuaded us to stay overnight.

*March 15.* As soon as Thore got up this morning he started for home in order to straighten things up, because he had invited the Erstads to pay him a visit. When breakfast was finished and these people had put on their Sunday best, Andreas Erstad went out and hitched his two fine-looking horses to the wagon, and we set out. As the distance to Thore's place was only about three miles, we were soon there. The rest of us got out, but Andreas drove off to attend to some matter. He soon returned, and we spent the day here having a very fine time. John Christensen, in whose name it will be remembered this land was originally bought, had been over to the surveyor's yesterday and obtained his promise that he would be here next Wednesday or Thursday to divide it now that Thore's part had been redeemed.

About sundown the visitors left us, and thus the pleasant associations of the day came to an end.

*March 16.* I had planned to visit Clement Stabäk [3] today, one of the first Norwegians to settle in this community, but various circumstances prevented. Thore had certain matters to attend to before he could go along, and on the way he stopped to try to collect from a Norwegian who owed him some money. So as not to disturb them in their business, I sauntered out on the prairie a mile or so. There I rested for a while by a fence to get an impression of the land round about, and I must say that it looked pretty fair. Having surveyed things, I returned to the house and found them still engaged in their financial affairs. As a matter of fact it was late evening before they finally reached an agreement, hence my plans for the day came to naught.

*March 17.* The forenoon passed very quietly since the men of the house were away hauling material for a schoolhouse which is to be erected in the neighborhood. About three o'clock this afternoon Clement Stabäk came over and asked me to accompany him home. I had to decline this invitation, however, since we

---

[3] Clement Torstenson Stabäk (spelled "Clemmet Stabek" in the diary) is regarded as the real founder of the Rock Run settlement in Stephenson and Winnebago counties, Illinois, where he and three companions located in 1839 shortly after his arrival from Numedal, Norway. He is referred to as a man of considerable means. Anderson, *Norwegian Immigration (1821-1840),* 255, 259, 366.

were expecting the surveyor tomorrow or the next day. Clement soon left, and I saddled my horse and whiled away the rest of the afternoon by taking a little jaunt about the neighborhood.

*March 19.* We looked for the surveyor yesterday, but he did not come until this morning. As soon as he arrived I took him to the southeastern corner of the land where we placed the compass. After a while the others also came. One of them and I, who were to handle the chain, had to take an oath before we could start. We worked all day but still did not finish.

*March 20.* As already mentioned, we did not finish the surveying yesterday, and so we were at it again this morning. Since we had to work through the woods, we did not get done until after noon. When dinner had been eaten the question arose as to how the land was to be divided between them. It was finally agreed that Thore should take the southern part if by so doing he could obtain the southern half of the west forty. The title deed was then drawn up and signed, and thus this particular trouble was ironed out.[4]

The surveyor was John Hiran, who, according to his own statement, was born in the state of Maine. He was quite a well-read man and was particularly well versed in history. The people of the neighborhood respected him as an honest man who is absolutely dependable in all his business dealings. He was very anxious to talk about Europe and other matters of interest, and the conversation continued well into the evening. When many subjects had been discussed and all business affairs settled, he took a friendly leave of us.

*March 21.* Since I had been invited to Clement Stabäk's, I saddled my horse this morning and rode over, arriving there shortly before noon. He was out on the prairie after a couple of loads of stone at the time but was expected back soon. His wife asked me to sit down at the table and have dinner, which I did,

[4] The passage in the original is not clear.

and then I went out to look for him. He came shortly, but in the meanwhile an American and his son had also arrived to discuss some matters with Stabäk. The Yankee told something about a cow he had last fall and summer, but it all sounded like a tall tale to me so I shall not waste any ink on it. Since Stabäk wanted to get two more loads of stone in the afternoon, I went with him to get a look at the prairie even though he urged me to stay at home and take it easy. The quarry where he had been working was about a mile from the house. He had piled the rocks up in layers about four inches thick. When we had been there awhile, I went up on a near-by hill from where I hoped to have a fine view. His dog accompanied me but soon went back to his master. I looked about in all directions and saw the rolling prairies lying there still in their winter's sleep. Toward the north were plowed fields, some of which had been fenced in and seeded to winter wheat. I walked about a bit more and then returned to the quarry. When the wagons were full, we drove back to the house, unloaded the rocks, and stabled the horses for the night. After that we went out to burn the dead grass off the plains. This took us about a mile and a half from the house, and it was nine o'clock when we got back. Therefore, after eating supper, we went to bed and enjoyed a sound sleep.

*March 22.* I awoke with a feeling of contentment this morning. It is my birthday, the second one I have spent in the state of Illinois. The other time was six years ago, about a hundred miles from here. I am far from the place where I was born, but my father and my brothers and sisters are all alive back in my native land, unless some one of them has passed away since I heard from home last summer. I feel uneasy about my father who, I understand, has been sick in bed for quite a while.

After breakfast I inspected Stabäk's cellar, which was constructed of the same kind of stone as the rest of the building. The cellar was very deep as is usually the case in farm houses out West. A chimney stood near the outside entrance. Stabäk explained that he intended to build an addition on this side and use the present house as a brewing house or for some similar purpose. Near one corner of the building there is an excellent spring of clear water. Shortly after dinner we took a look at his woods — mostly oaks and poplars together with rather thick underbrush that made walking difficult. I also examined his fields, about seventy acres in all, of which fifty had been seeded to winter wheat and some rye. Although he had fenced in a considerable part of his land, much was still lying open.

Stabäk's main reason for asking me to visit him was to obtain a loan or to get me to take over a loan which in 1839 he had extended to a university graduate named Walour.[5]

When we got back to the house I decided to return to Thore's place. I therefore saddled my horse and said good-by to the folks. The road led up a hill covered with fine woods, and as I rode down the other side I could see through the trees a plain below me, beyond which rose another hillside sparsely covered with trees. It was a beautiful view, and this, together with the mild weather, put me into a very pleasant mood. Since the sun was still high in the heavens and I had only some three miles to go, I

[5] This is probably the "university graduate in theology, Peter Valeur," who in 1839 accompanied Ansten Nattestad's party aboard the *Emilia* from Drammen to Göteborg. As the ship passed out through Drammensfjord he delivered a touching farewell address. About a week earlier this emigrant group had petitioned the church department to ordain Valeur for service among them in America as a minister. "Valeur had declared his willingness to accept such a position and the majority desired him to be ordained first. . . . The church department was in a quandary, for this 'call' did not originate in an organized congregation and no departmental control could be exercised in America. Nevertheless, after getting opinions from the theological faculty of the university and from a bishop, it moved the authorization of the request, and on December 23 it was granted by royal resolution." On November 6, however, Nattestad had written Valeur that he feared the settlers would be too scattered to support a minister. "Thus ended what was probably the first move looking toward Lutheran church organization among the Norwegian immigrants in the West. Valeur, so far as is known, never came to America." Blegen, *Norwegian Migration, 1825–1860,* 120, 121, 122. See also Gunnar J. Malmin, "Litt norsk-amerikansk kirkehistorie fra de norske arkiver," *Lutheraneren,* January 16, 1924, p. 75.

rode along very leisurely. After a while I met Thore and Berthe, who had been out visiting one of their neighbors. We went home together, and when I had cared for my horse we took a trip out over his land.

*March 23.* My intention was to start for home today, but because of the cold, rainy weather and certain other circumstances I changed my plans. In the afternoon Thore had to see one of his Norwegian neighbors, and since he was driving over I decided to go with him to pass the time. Our visit turned out to be rather brief. We left as soon as we had done our errand and had been served some refreshments.

*March 24.* In spite of the cloudy weather and the sleet I set off today across very sparsely settled country. The woods through which I passed on my way to Beloit were rather poor, and some of the land here also failed to please me. Because of the cloudy weather I lost my way. I intended to cross the Rock River at Beloit but struck the stream four miles farther down at a little village called Pecatonica,[6] where there also was a mill. Consequently I had to follow the eastern shore of the river in order to reach Beloit. About half way I ran into a hail storm that kept on until I reached the town. After staying there an hour I continued on my way in the same unpleasant weather. Toward evening I came to an inn at the eastern edge of Jefferson Prairie where I stayed overnight. Here someone told me that a person had to pay $2.25 for one hundred fence posts. At this rate the cost of fencing forty acres would exceed the government price of the land.[7]

*March 25.* Although snow fell this morning as it did yesterday, I had to continue the trip since I was on my way.

Later in the day the weather cleared and I rode on without

---

[6] The spelling Bache uses is Pikkatanic. On the maps of the period various spellings are found, such as Pekatonica, Pickatonokee, Peekatonokee, and Pekatalikee.

[7] There is obviously something wrong with Bache's figures here.

any experience worth mentioning. I followed the same road and passed through the same towns as I had on my way out. When I came to Elkhorn a little past noon the innkeeper with whom I had stayed asked me to come up on the porch. I tried to excuse myself by saying that I was anxious to go as far as possible today. But he protested that I could certainly come up a little while and chat a bit. So I got off, and then he invited me to come in and have a drink. After this refresher I continued my trip. By eight o'clock in the evening I reached Rochester and passed the night there. The last three or four miles it was so dark I could hardly see the road. As I sat in the dining room eating supper, I became acquainted with a Norwegian girl of whom I had already heard some talk. I have no desire to say anything else about her except that there are relatives of hers in our settlement.

*March 26.* After breakfast and a trip to the post office I rode on and reached home by about half past nine o'clock. There everybody had been anxiously awaiting me and was happy to have me back again. This also turned out to be a cold, cloudy, rainy day. But in the evening I visited one of my friends and thus ended the day as well as the journey in good health and spirits.

# 13. To Madison for the Fourth of July

*April 5 [1846].* IN SPITE OF THE FACT that this was Sunday, I had to set out on another trip because of arrangements made more than a month ago. It was a very pleasant day, and I left home around noon, arriving at Racine about seven o'clock in the evening without having had any unusual experiences. After caring for my horse I decided to take a trip about town for it was a very beautiful evening and I had nothing particular to do until bedtime. While strolling down one of the streets I chanced to meet three girls whom I knew by their conversation to be Norwegian. I spoke to them, but they immediately set off on a run. I induced them to stop, however, and got into a conversation with them. As we walked along we were soon joined by three other girls, and in a short while by still three more, making nine in all. We then went to the home of a Norwegian family close by. They told me that no less than thirty Norwegian girls were employed in Racine. When we had been talking awhile, a fellow came over to me and asked to see me alone in another room. There I learned that he merely wanted to give me a glass of whisky. I accepted the offer and then returned to my lodgings.

*April 6.* The real occasion of my coming to Racine this time was in connection with the estate of my friend, Johannes Johansen. Toward noon I went to the courthouse where the probate judge has his office. He asked me to go to the printer to obtain, under oath, a certain affidavit. An Irishman who was administrator of another estate was to accompany me to secure a similar document. But when we got there we found that the printer had gone away to the country and that our trip was in vain. After a while I returned to the shop and managed to obtain the affidavit. I took it to the judge, who declared it to be correct.[1] The Irish-

[1] The affidavit, in English, is inserted at this point in the original diary.

man, however, was ordered to go to the printer's a second time for the same purpose but returned again with the same excuse. When he was to settle the estate he did not know how many days he had spent on the job. The judge made an estimate of eighteen days for him and allowed him a dollar per day for his work. After the Irishman had left, the judge complained that it was difficult to do business with people like that, who had had no experience.

Throughout the day the streets were full of people raising a great hubbub. From what I could gather, the majority of the citizens were Democrats while the Whigs constituted a minority. They were now busy electing town officials as the term of the present officeholders was coming to a close.

Having finished my business by about five o'clock in the afternoon, I saddled my horse and started for home. The weather was very muggy and rainy. By half past seven I reached an inn some thirteen miles from town where I decided to spend the night. As I was very wet, I dried my clothes before going to bed at nine o'clock. The name of the innkeeper was Mr. Parson.

*April 7.* About eight o'clock or a little earlier I left the inn and continued on my way. At Lodgin Inn I stopped awhile to warm up and get some refreshments, after which I rode on until I was about a mile from Muskego Creek. There my four-year-old mount threw me off. But I got back on again and continued my trip without further happenings until I reached home about ten-thirty. The day was cold and nippy, but it did not rain even though the sky was overcast.

Since I have been appointed administrator of Johansen's estate, I will have to take care of those matters from now on. I hope I can perform my duty to the satisfaction of all concerned.

*April 8.* Today I had some writing to do in connection with my duties as administrator, but as I may enter it into my diary later I will merely mention that I finished this particular work in the early afternoon.

This evening while I was with Even Hansen Heg, Dr. Theodor Alexander Schytte, and another person whose name I do not even care to mention, Hans Heg (one of Even's sons) brought a swan (*anas olor*) which he had shot. For several days it had been swimming around on Wind Lake close to the shore. The boys had shot at it several times both with shotgun and rifle without hitting it. The swan remained very calm and paid no attention to the shooting. But today Hans and another boy went down to the lake with loaded guns. Both of them fired at the swan at the same time and then sent their dog out to fetch it. But the dog did not dare tackle the swan, and so they had to row out and get it. The left wing was broken and quite useless. It was a large bird, weighing about twelve pounds even though it was not fat. From the beak to the tail it measured about five feet. They said this swan had been on the lake last year also. It was more timid then. It belongs to the duck family and the third class of aquatic birds (*anseres*). They plucked off its feathers, which were white and very soft. Swansdown is regarded as being of especially fine quality.

*April 17.* During the last days signs of spring have made their appearance. This gentle weather is no less pleasing to animals than it is to man. On the tenth (Good Friday), however, we had terrible weather with wind and rain all day from dawn to dusk. On the morning of the fourteenth what was probably the last snow of the season fell; the air now definitely seems to promise summer. From now on all living things can rejoice in their liberation from the harsh bondage of winter.

*May 8.* (Rogation Day). The weather is clear with only a few clouds in the sky. A pleasant cooling wind is blowing. Peder Helgesen and his wife are here today to say good-by, as he expects to leave in a couple of days for the Norwegian settlement some miles northwest of Beloit where he hopes to get better employment.

Just now while I am writing these lines, Martin Knudsen, who formerly was with Bang, the broker, in Drammen, is lying on the bed. His left hand is pressed against his side, his right hand rests upon his brow, his right leg is tucked under the feather bed, while the left knee is raised a bit. I have a notion to say some more about him, but I shall let it go with this.

*May 14.* All this week I have been busy appraising Johansen's estate. Since I finished part of the work this forenoon, I decided to go over to the land he owned in Milwaukee County and obtain an appraisal of it also. I left in the afternoon and by evening I arrived at an inn kept by an acquaintance of mine in that neighborhood. I spent the night there and also learned which officials I would have to deal with. After eating supper and chatting with some American friends, I went to bed and slept soundly.

*May 15.* Hoping to get my business affairs settled, I set off immediately after breakfast by a different road than the one I followed yesterday. After a walk of three or four miles I found the man I needed to see. He was too busy, however, to do anything about it today but promised to fix matters up next week without any further assistance from me. Accordingly I paid him the necessary fee, for which he gave me a receipt. This done, I continued my walk toward Milwaukee and spent the rest of the day among my old friends there. I also learned to know a man from Christiansand named Kildahl, of whom I had heard previously.

*May 16.* As I had decided to leave by steamboat I asked the innkeeper to call me if one should come before I awoke. At four o'clock this morning someone opened the door and shouted that a boat was coming. So I got up and prepared for the trip. After breakfast I went down to the pier and boarded the steamer, which had just laid to. About nine o'clock we left and reached Racine a couple of hours later. After a short stop there we continued on toward Southport, my destination, arriving at half past twelve o'clock. I went ashore and wandered about the town awhile before I went up to the probate judge to deliver my documents.

He was not at home, but I delivered them to his pleasant wife. She told me that he was expected back from Chicago with the first boat. Having given the necessary information, I went to a hotel and drank a good glass of beer. I had decided to go on foot to Racine, but as I was leaving town I heard the boat coming and turned back. Just as I set foot on the pier the boat docked. I boarded it and managed to exchange a few words with the judge before he went ashore. We headed north, and when we reached Racine I went up on second deck and took a seat. While sitting there I noticed three Norwegian girls who evidently had also noticed me. Farther off there were three others, one of whom joined the first group. I did not hear what they said, but by their expressions it was plain that I was the object of their conversation, especially since they smiled at me, a compliment which I repaid in kind. I left my place to escape their attention, and I also observed that they had withdrawn behind a pile of wood where they remained until the boat left. By seven o'clock we were at Milwaukee, having covered a distance of seventy miles. The afternoon was cold and stormy so that the boat trip was not particularly pleasant.

*May 17.* After eating dinner and making a few purchases I left the city. About sundown I reached home without any interesting experiences.

*May 23.* The newspapers these days are full of reports concerning the troubles between Mexico and the United States. Among other things there is a proclamation from the President in this connection. [*Here follows President Polk's proclamation of May 13, 1846.*]

It is further stated that the President has been empowered by the Senate to put in the field 50,000 volunteers and regular troops. Ten million dollars will be raised to meet the costs of the war. We are informed that Mexico and the United States have declared war, and General Z. Taylor says that hostilities began about April 24. And in the same report he urges the governor of Texas to recruit four regiments of infantry. It does not appear in this document that he is much alarmed despite the fact that on the day he wrote General Arista came to Matamoros, a Mexican town, with Mexican troops. Some dragoons were sent out to guard the banks of the river above this town, and sixteen of them were killed or wounded when they were surrounded. None of the party returned except one wounded soldier who was sent back on the same morning by a Mexican officer.

It looks as if the people were not altogether satisfied with the present President, and this probably is rooted in the affair with Mexico. It is believed that the Mexican army numbers about ten or twelve thousand men and that a considerable force has proceeded to the left bank of the Rio Grande, twenty-seven miles above Matamoros. The Rio Grande River is the boundary line between Texas and Mexico and the theater of war between the two nations. What the outcome will be, only time will show.

In the President's message to Congress of May 11, it may be noted that the Texan Congress by an act of December 19, 1836, declared the Rio del Norte to be the boundary between Texas and Mexico. And the United States Congress by an act of December 31, 1845, acknowledged the land on the other side of the Nueces as a part of the territory by including it under its customs system and placing customs officers within the boundaries of the district. On January 13 instructions were given the commanding general of the camp on the west bank of the Del Norte — at present the southwestern boundary of Texas. [*Here follows the text of the Army Bill.*]

What is presented above shows how the disturbances began and what action Congress has taken. The President appears to be very Democratic — indeed altogether too much so — as well as the whole party he belongs to, whereas the Whig Party is more peace-loving and wants peace rather than war. If Henry Clay had been in power, the situation would have been quite different from what it is now.

It is reported that Brigadier General W. J. Worth of the Eighth American Infantry on the right bank of the Rio Grande has met the Mexican general R. D. de La Vega. He was sent as a courier by the American commander, General Taylor, guided by his aide-de-camp Lieutenant Smith and Lieutenants Magruder, Deas, and Black, with Lieutenant Knowlton as interpreter. The document that Worth brought with him was first translated into French by Knowlton and then into Spanish by a Mexican. The American general demanded a conference with the consul of the United States, but this was not permitted, though it was requested several times of La Vega. The general said that if armed Mexicans crossed the river, that would be regarded as an act of war. In reply to a question from General La Vega, he said that his forces would remain where they were until further orders from the government. La Vega said further that he was offended at seeing the American flag planted on the Rio Grande, a part of the territory of Mexico. General Worth responded that this might be a debatable question, but that he would continue to be there and that the Army was under orders from its government to occupy its present position. According to reports, the Americans have won two battles and in one of them destroyed the city of Matamoros, the town mentioned above. This we can verify when newspapers are available.

*June 4.* Dr. Theodor Alexander Schytte, who has been staying with us since Johansen's death, left us this forenoon. He is going to a little town on the left bank of Rock River, near Janesville, where he has accepted a position with a druggist, hoping to improve his condition since he has had no luck so far among his fellow countrymen.[2] Yesterday he received a letter from Corneliusen in Madison stating that he was unable to find a position for him there. In the letter Corneliusen said that he hoped I would visit him, a thing I intend to do as soon as possible.

[2] In the original Bache uses the spelling "Jensvil" and in another later entry, "Jensvill."

From letters of General Taylor dated at headquarters, Palo Alto, Texas, May 9, 1846: Near this place, on a march from Point Isabel, he met the Mexican forces, and after a fight of five hours drove them away and took the field. The artillery consisted of two eighteen-pounders and two little batteries. The strength of the enemy was believed to consist of about six thousand men, with seven cannons and eight hundred cavalry. Their losses are estimated to be at least one hundred killed. The American force did not exceed 2,300, and their losses were four men killed and three officers and thirty-seven men wounded, many of the latter fatally. It was believed that the enemy had retreated across the river. This happened the day before [*Taylor's report*].

From another letter, dated the same day, it is learned that there was a clash with the Mexicans on this side of the river about two o'clock in a forest on the way to Matamoros, and the victory was won by the Americans. Eight cannons, a large amount of ammunition, three standards, and several hundred soldiers were captured, among them General La Vega and numbers of other officers. One general had been shot. They also held as booty a large number of mules, abandoned in the Mexican camp. General La Vega and some other officers have been sent to New Orleans. He understands no foreign language and can talk only through an interpreter. He is said to have voiced satisfaction with his situation and reports that he feels himself among old friends.

*June 13.* With bright expectations, humanity peers into the future even though it does not always bring joy and happiness. Days and years pass never to return. Time is like a wind which blows away, we know neither whither nor whence. Somehow everything has its limits — time and space — in ways hidden and incomprehensible to us. All change is bound by time and circumstance. There is a law of growth and decay. Individuals and nations have their time of greatness only to decline. Riches and power are not always granted to the wisest. In all the trials and tribulations of life a man should remain virtuous to the end. Then he will be praised as a model for coming generations. Religion is the basis of all virtue; therefore be virtuous no matter who you are. If you have religion, you also have virtue. They are the opposites of vice and wickedness. Better to be satisfied with a little justly acquired than to have wealth gained through fraud and cunning. The little, honestly earned, will be blessed, while the fruits of fraud will be cursed. Therefore, choose the paths of righteousness rather than the ways of the wicked which lead to ruin. Follow your calling in life, but above all else, be virtuous, because virtue brings no one to shame. Be faithful in big things and small, because truth and honesty will endure when all things else pass away. Embrace virtue and your name shall be blessed and remembered forever.

*June 22.* There was a fist fight here Saturday, eight days ago, and today I was summoned as a witness in the case. The matter was settled amicably before the justice of the peace. The one who started the fight was to pay his victim a barrel of flour and defray all expenses, after which they should be good friends. Since the fellow had no money, I agreed to sign a note for him to the amount of $2.03. As security he gave me a promissory note of $5 made out to him, due October 1. Thus everything was settled without any stir.

The two following days I helped Even Heg move and put up an old house that stood down by the road. He intends to use it as a brewing house in the future.

*June 28.* As I had previously decided to visit Madison, the capital of Wisconsin, I set off from home today. Peder Helgesen accompanied me because he wanted me to act as interpreter for him in looking for some cattle that had strayed. He had heard that they were out on the prairie near Delavan, but when we got there and asked for the cattle no one had seen them. Because we spent several hours scouting about the prairies, it was very late before we came to Delavan.

*June 29.* After breakfast we continued our trip toward Beloit, but in spite of our search we found no trace of the cattle today either. We reached the town about half past two o'clock in the afternoon. I promised Helgesen I would help him search the rest of the afternoon if there was no mail coach leaving for Madison today. I learned, however, that one was leaving in about an hour, so we had to part. At half past four o'clock the coach left Beloit heading north across a plain called Rock Prairie, which proved to be quite extensive. About eight o'clock we reached Janesville, a place I had not seen since November 1839. At that time the town consisted merely of a hotel and seven houses; now it has a thousand inhabitants. Janesville, which is the county seat, is located near the center of the county. It is situated on both banks of the Rock River, the river being spanned by a bridge, while above the town there is a dam that can supply power for factories. Janesville is sixty-five miles from Milwaukee and an equal distance from Racine. I spent the night in the oldest hotel in town. There I became acquainted with a doctor named M. B. Edson, who has lived here nearly two years. Janesville is the trading center for the western part of the Territory. The courthouse, located on a hill, can be seen for a distance of several miles.

*June 30.* At eight o'clock this morning we left Janesville by mail coach for the capital of the Territory, where we arrived about six o'clock in the evening. There were nine of us in the coach when we left, but the number gradually decreased until only five remained when we reached a place some twenty miles from our destination. There, however, we ate dinner and took on two more passengers bound for Madison. In this congenial group we carried on interesting discussions of various matters, but most particularly about public affairs. Along our route we saw much beautiful land consisting mostly of oak-openings, while in other localities the contours were hilly and rolling. As a whole the area was sparsely populated. At times the farmhouses were several miles apart. Much of the land around Madison, to a distance of six miles, is held for speculation. Within this radius hardly a farmhouse is to be seen.

*July 1.* The city of Madison was laid out in 1836, and in December of that year it was by law made the seat of the territorial government, though at that time the "city" consisted of one simple log house. Since there was nothing particularly interesting to see here and as I had decided to spend the Fourth of July in Madison, I said good-by to Corneliusen (whom I had located on my arrival) and set out on foot for the Norwegian settlement on Koshkonong Prairie. About fourteen miles out, on Liberty Prairie, I found Dr. T. A. Schytte, who for the time being is staying with a certain Mons Lasseson from Sogn and his (Lasseson's) two sons-in-law. I spent the night with them.

*July 2.* After breakfast Schytte and I started out to visit some people on Koshkonong Prairie. Having walked about two miles, we came to the West Church (northeast part of Section 14, Township 6, Range 11) which Pastor Dietrichson had been instrumental in building. It was quite large but as plain as any building could be. The surroundings were very beautiful, however. After a brief inspection we left the church and continued our walk. About a mile and a quarter down the way there was a house on our left from which came a terrible stench. We went in and found that it came from some rotten pork which the people there thought would be all right if only the outer parts were cut away. They moved into the house yesterday. Because of this putrid smell we "cleared out" immediately and continued our walk, eventually reaching the other church, which is located in the southwest corner of Section 26, Township 6, Range 12.[3] The door was locked, but I climbed in through a window without much difficulty. More pains had been taken with this church

[3] Pastor Dietrichson arrived in Koshkonong late in August 1844 and "at once proceeded to organize the people into congregations. The so-called East church, in the town of Christiana, was organized October 10, 1844, and the West church, in the town of Pleasant Springs, on October 13, 1844. 'The erection of two houses of worship . . . was begun in the fall of 1844, and

than with the first one, but both of them are poorly constructed and must require much heating in the winter, when the winds sweep in, to save the minister from suffocation in the midst of his mountain sheep. From the church there is a good view over the country toward the south and the west.

Next we went over to visit a man named Gunnul Vindeg from Numedal, who had come across the ocean with me the first time I came to America. We had dinner at his place. Pastor Clausen with his family lives close by. Later in the afternoon we went to see Lars Johansen from Hedemarken. I stayed overnight with him, but there was still enough left of the afternoon for me to visit a couple of families from Stavanger district whom I had learned to know during the winter I spent in Illinois.

*July 3*. After breakfast we started back by the same road as we came. I had dinner at the place where Dr. Schytte stays. These people are filthy like the rest of the mountain folk and so are very unpleasant to associate with. Since I had decided to be back in Madison this evening I left at three o'clock and reached the city very late. Tired out, I went to bed at once and slept soundly.

*July 4*, the American Independence Day, which is loved and celebrated so much. I was awakened at dawn by "cannonading" that continued all day. An anvil was used as cannon since they did not have anything better. The hotelkeeper with whom I stayed, a very young person, was to deliver the main speech of

pushed to completion. The Western church was completed first, and was dedicated December 19, 1844, by Pastor Dietrichson, assisted by his friend, Pastor Clausen, of Muskego. The Eastern church . . . was dedicated January 31, 1845. . . . The Koshkonong churches were both built of logs and were of the same dimensions, 36 feet long and 28 feet wide. In both, movable benches served as seats, a plain table, adorned with a white cloth and a black wooden cross was the altar, a rude desk was the pulpit and the baptismal font was hewn out of an oak log.'" Anderson, *Norwegian Immigration (1821–1840)*, 426. When Løvenskjold visited the two "so-called churches" at Koshkonong in the summer of 1847 he said that "on the outside they resembled barns, but inside they present a neat and tasteful appearance."

the occasion. About half past ten o'clock a band came down to the hotel to lead the speaker with a procession to the platform in the Capitol. They had to wait a few minutes for him, but when he arrived we formed in line and marched to the unpracticed strains of the band. At the Capitol the band formed two lines between which the procession passed up the stairs and into a room to the right. The ceremonies were opened with a brief prayer, after which the Declaration of Independence was read. Then the hotelkeeper delivered his speech, which was very poor. This part of the program ended, we went upstairs to a room on the left where a dinner had been prepared. After dinner the procession quit the building and went to a place in the woods surrounding the Capitol. There we heard several short speeches and some musical numbers, and then the crowd broke up. In the evening rag balls soaked in turpentine were set on fire and thrown into the air. They continued to burn a long time. There was also a procession in the evening. It was not as large as the earlier one, but it followed the same course. The day was very fine, except that a little shower fell while the first procession was under way.[4]

*July 5.* As this was Sunday I attended church both in the morning and evening. The rest of the day I spent quietly with my friend Corneliusen.

*July 6.* About eight o'clock this morning I left Madison, taking a different route than the one by which I came in order to see more new land. There were only three of us in the coach so we had plenty of room. One of my companions told me that he and a group of fifty people spent eighteen days on the road

[4] The Wisconsin *Argus* for July 7, 1846 (vol. 2, no. 46) describes "The Fourth at Madison" in part as follows: "The Day was ushered in by a national salute. At the hour appointed, the procession formed and under the escort of the Madison Brass Band, marched to the Capitol, where the usual exercises were held, the Rev. Mr. Miner officiating as chaplain. The Declaration read by Beriah Brown; the Oration by Wm. Welch; the Singing by the Choir and the Music by the Band. After the exercises were concluded, the procession again formed, marched to the tables where the dinner, prepared by R. W. Lansing, Esq., was discussed in a manner perfectly *free*. . . ."

from Milwaukee to Madison when he made the trip the first time ten years ago. At that time one of the group wrote this inscription on a board: "The great city of Madison, inhabited by one white man and a bunch of Indians."

For a distance sixteen miles out of Madison the land was fairly good, but after that it was very uninviting until we reached a little town called Lake Mills,[5] located by a small body of water. The postmaster there was a tailor by profession. Several miles farther on we came to another little town called Aztalan, which is situated on a branch of the Rock River. After a short stop here we continued our trip and by sundown reached the western edge of Summit. Since this brought me very close to Christopher Aamodt's place, I decided to visit him and arrived there about eleven o'clock in the evening.

*July 8.* Having rested there a day, I continued my trip and by evening came to Elling Helgesen's place in the town of Ottawa where I stayed the following day. This was the warmest day of the year so far.

*July 10.* Around two o'clock in the afternoon I set out again and did not get home until midnight.

Between Rock River and Madison I saw many fine stretches of land still uncultivated, this area being sparsely populated. West of Rock River there is much fine land, but it seems to me that it is too far from market because as yet there are no railways or canals there to ease communications. When a farmer with his team of horses has to spend more than a day on the way to market, transportation becomes too expensive, especially in years like this when the highest price for wheat is fifty cents per bushel while the finest flour brings only three dollars a barrel in Milwaukee. In time, no doubt, transportation will be less of a problem when railways and canals, which are such a blessing to a country, have been constructed.

[5] Bache uses the spelling "Lakemill."

*July 21.* Yesterday Clausen delivered his farewell sermon for he does not expect to come here any more. In the near future he intends to move to the congregation he organized in the Norwegian community some ten miles northwest of Beloit. Since, according to reports, he has also said farewell to several other settlements, it seems as if he plans to devote all his time to this one particular congregation. I am told that he moved people to tears with his sermon, which probably had some political motive.

*August 2.* Judging by the number of Norwegian newcomers who have arrived, it appears that this settlement has regained the reputation it once enjoyed. People are also more anxious to settle here now than they were formerly even though they have to pay more for land than in past years. Our settlers usually ask a very high price for their land. This indicates that they are well satisfied by now, which they have reason to be since they have survived the great hardships of the early years. This season they will harvest a good crop and realize a considerable income in spite of the fact that prices, for the time being, are poor. I have made two trips to the Norwegian settlements west of here this summer, and my observation was that with a few possible exceptions the people there were not any more prosperous than they are in this neighborhood.

*August 24.* The summer has, in part, been very hot and unhealthful. Sickness has already begun its ravages among us. Even Heg's faithful old servant Berthe, who had been confined to bed some time, died in the late afternoon of August 20. She was brought to her last resting place yesterday, quite a number of people from the neighborhood being present at the funeral. All of us in this house have been somewhat indisposed, but now we are getting better.

New Norwegian immigrants reach here daily.

*August 30.* Last Friday afternoon a man named Lars Aaby arrived with his family. For the time being he expects to leave his large family with us while he travels about and inspects the land. He comes from the vicinity of Skien and is a very intelligent and highly respected man. Yesterday evening three wagonloads of people from Hallingdal drove up. They stayed here overnight and then continued on into the West with the exception of two families. One of these families remained because a child was sick with smallpox and died in the forenoon, while the other family stayed because the wife was in labor and gave birth to a baby boy in the evening. Thus today, within a period of six or eight hours, one child died and another child was born in our barn. This was the second child to enter the world in this building. The people are poor and have few means. Several hours this afternoon were spent in devotions. It so happened that a very appropriate sermon for the day was found in the *Book of Homilies*.

*September 8.* Last week Lars Aaby, accompanied by his sons, took a trip of about twenty-five miles north of Milwaukee to inspect the land. Today the children went west towards Galena, not far from the mighty Mississippi, where two of his sons had bought land several years ago. They intend to put up a decent house before moving their parents over. Meanwhile the latter will remain with us. The land they saw on their trip last week did not please them as well as the land hereabouts. Three bachelors who had accompanied the Aabys from their home district in Norway also went along to help with the house since they, too, are carpenters.

For several days now it has been cool and windy, which is a great boon for the many who are sick in bed. There is much illness among the people everywhere.

The two Halling families who have been staying in our barn left today to join their friends west of Beloit.

*October 7.* This forenoon Lars Aaby, with his family, left for Galena to take possession of his sons' land. He stayed here a long time.

The ague has been very bad throughout the Territory this year. I suffered from it a couple of weeks myself, but during the last three weeks I have been quite well.

*December 22.* I had already threshed and winnowed Johansen's wheat, so today I hired a team of horses and a wagon to take it to market in Milwaukee. I arrived there about three o'clock in the afternoon and sold the wheat for a very low price. As I had nothing further to do in town I left about noon the next day and got home in good time.

*December 26.* Two or three days ago a Norwegian from La Salle County, Illinois, came here to solicit subscriptions with the intention of starting a Norwegian newspaper for his countrymen in America. He seemed to be a Whig. A certain Knud Knudsen came at the same time.[6] He is a smith from Drammen and has been in America since 1839. He undertook to gather subscriptions in some of the western settlements. Knudsen is an ardent Democrat who champions his party with tremendous fervor.

[6] Knud Knudsen came to America with Ansten Nattestad aboard the *Emilia* in 1839. At Albany he and Claus Stabäk wrote a letter of thanks to Captain Anchersen in behalf of the passengers. The letter was published in the *New-Yorker Stats-Zeitung*, September 4, 1839, and reprinted in the Drammen paper *Tiden*, December 31, 1839. He also wrote a brief account of his immigrant journey entitled *Beretning om en Reise fra Drammen til New York* (Drammen, 1840; reprinted Minneapolis or Decorah, Iowa, 1926). Together with Clement Torstenson Stabäk he helped found the Rock Run settlement in Stephenson and Winnebago counties, Illinois. Pastor Dietrichson referred to Knudsen as an active member of the congregation he organized in Wiota and as one of the most prosperous Norwegians in that community. *Reise blandt de norske Emigranter,* 80. In 1849 Knudsen joined the California gold rush. In 1852, accompanied by three sons, he again made the overland trip, this time as leader of a large party of Norwegians from Illinois and Wisconsin. Neither trip seems to have been very successful financially. Tosten K. Stabäk, "Beretning om en reise til California," *Numedalslagets Aarbog,* no. 14, 62–85 (1928). An English translation of this article by Einar Haugen is in *Studies and Records,* 4:99–124.

# 14. Launching the Pioneer Norwegian-American Newspaper

*January 2, 1847.* NOW I begin the entries for the year 1847. It is a clear day, and the bright sun, which is already high in the heavens, warms things up so that the weather is fairly mild with a gentle wind blowing from the west. Yesterday, however, was different. Heavy clouds covered the sky and snow fell all day, which, after some traffic, will furnish good sleighing. I ended the old year with sickness, a severe attack of the fever and ague common around here. So far this year I have felt tolerably well, have been able to be up, and have hopes of recovering soon if I take proper care of myself. I hope I will be strong by spring and able to do the things I have planned, circumstances permitting.

This afternoon the hired man whom Johansen and I brought along to America came to pay us a visit. He told us that he had earned a good income as carpenter last summer, which is a fine thing for him.

*January 12.* The last six or seven days have been unusually cold, but today a change for the better has set in. This afternoon an Englishman who was interested in buying land visited us. He was born in Hull, but his last years in England were spent in the great city of London. He came to this Territory four years ago. During our conversation he told me about his family, which consisted of grown sons and daughters. Both the man and the son who accompanied him made a good impression, and I should be able to judge by them what the rest of the group is like.

Yesterday Even Heg's youngest son went to Milwaukee to look for a job in a store.

*January 25.* Today I returned from a walk I had taken to Rock

River, where I spent eight days at Christopher Aamodt's place. When I left home the weather was fairly nice, but the days I spent at Aamodt's were the coldest spell we have had this winter. The cold weather brought on another attack of ague, but it is not as severe as the earlier one. The attack seized me last Friday, and I started for home on Saturday but went by way of some Norwegian friends where I lay abed yesterday, Sunday.

*March 6.* Last month was cold. In fact the whole winter has been severe. But so far this month has had more the appearance of spring.

There has been much discussion lately about starting a Scandinavian weekly. Investigations about founding such a paper and about securing printing equipment are already under way.

It is said that Clausen got married in February after becoming a widower last November. His present wife is from Numedal, a widow with some means left her by the first husband, Hjort of Indiana, whom she married after her arrival from Norway.[1] As a result of this precipitous marriage, people — especially Clausen's closest friends — have lost some of the unlimited faith they previously had in him. An American minister officiated at the wedding. Dietrichson, who was supposed to perform the ceremony, did not appear, and it is rumored that they do not get along so well. It seems as if people in general like Clausen the better of the two. He can mix more easily with them than Dietrichson, who is said to be arrogant and unsociable.

*March 22.* Since there has been much discussion this winter about starting a newspaper among the Norwegians out here, J. D. Reymert [2] and I undertook to visit the settlements farther west to

[1] The Hjort referred to here is probably Hans E. Hjort of Drammen, who is reported to have left Norway in 1825 accompanied by a certain Peder B. Smith. They located near Monticello, White County, Indiana, where they acquired 1100 acres of land and also owned a sawmill which netted them a good profit. Blegen, *Norwegian Migration, 1825–1860*, 49n.

[2] James Denoon Reymert was born in Farsund, Norway, in 1821. He came to America in 1842 after a stay of five years in Scotland, his mother's native land. There he learned English and studied law. In 1844 he settled at Mus-

discover what their attitude would be. Because of the poor sleighing we did not get very far today. The next day [*March 23*] we passed one little settlement and reached another one farther north, called Skubeno [*sic*] where we stayed overnight. We slept on some hay spread out on the floor with no other kind of bedding whatever. Fortunately I had my overcoat along to serve as a quilt. We did not continue our trip until after dinner, reaching Fort Atkinson in the evening, and there we spent the night.

*March 25.* When Johansen and I were in Fort Atkinson more than seven years ago, there was only one log house in the place while now, to the south of that house, a whole little town has sprung up on both sides of the river. After breakfast we continued on toward Koshkonong where we arrived about noon. Later we visited Pastor Dietrichson, who seemed pleased to see us. He told us that he had trouble with his congregation, which contained many undesirable persons who were always bringing suits against one another. Dr. Schytte has been practicing medicine here about a year. Since last fall he has been in company with a certain Paoli[3] and a Swede named Smith. At present they

kego where three years later he became editor of *Nordlyset*, the first Norwegian paper in the Middle West. Soon he launched into politics and was elected a member of the second Wisconsin constitutional convention in 1847 and a member of the first state legislature in 1849. He also held other public trusts but was defeated when he ran for Congress in 1860. During these years he erected sawmills, built plank roads, acquired 3500 acres of land, and tried to found a town named "Denoon," but this venture was frustrated by cholera. In 1861 Reymert opened a law office in New York City and shortly afterward organized the Hercules Mutual Life Assurance Society of the United States. Because of failing health he went to Chili in the early 1870's. He acquired several thousand acres of land there and became manager of a big estate. In 1876, however, he returned to the United States by way of California and settled for a while in Arizona Territory. There he opened a law office, edited the *Pinal Drill*, and organized the Reymert Silver Mines. Later he moved to Alhambra County, California, where he died in 1896. Martin L. Reymert, "James Denoon Reymert and the Norwegian Press," *Studies and Records*, 12:79–90; Blegen, *Norwegian Migration, The American Transition*, 286, 289, 294.

[3] Gerhardt Styhr Christian Hjort Paoli came of a well-known Norwegian family. In 1770 his grandfather, Andreas Essendrop (whose brother was bishop in Oslo), visited Corsica and later, when he had a son, named him

are in Madison trying to collect their inflated fees from the Norwegians. In short, I gather that the Norwegians here have got themselves into a nice mess.[4]

*March 26.* Today we continued our journey and arrived in due time at Madison.

*March 27.* We left about noon and shortly after sundown reached the so-called Blue Mounds, about which I had heard so much. There is nothing remarkable about these hills except that they can be seen from a distance of twenty or twenty-five miles — that's all there is to it.

*March 29.* Today we passed through the little town of Dodgeville lying in three separate parts out on the open prairie. Reymert tried to sell his goods here, but in vain. We met quite a number of Norwegians, however, who intended to subscribe to

Pascal Paoli in honor of the Corsican revolutionary leader. When he grew to manhood, Pascal Paoli Essendrop was thrown into prison. On liberation he dropped the distinguished family name and used Paoli instead. His son, Gerhardt C. Paoli, studied at the University of Oslo from 1839–1844. After failing examinations, he went to Stockholm, where he continued his studies and was licensed to practice medicine. In 1846 he emigrated to America and, after brief stays in Milwaukee and Madison, practiced medicine and took an active part in political life at Springfield, Ohio. He supported the Abolitionist candidate, John H. Hall, in the presidential campaign of 1852. He was much interested in chemistry and invented a process whereby fusel oil could be extracted from alcohol, a discovery which won him a medal at the Crystal Palace exposition in New York in 1853. Soon afterward, Dr. Blaney of Rush Medical College persuaded him to remove to Chicago. There the two formed a company and built a distillery in which the Paoli process was used. Before long the distillery burned, and the company was ruined. When the Republican party was organized Paoli became an active campaigner for its principles and candidates. He was champion of women's rights and was one of the founders of the Women's Medical College in Chicago. He served as city physician of Chicago, was twice president of the Chicago Medical Society, and held honorary memberships in other associations. He died in 1898. See Gjerset and Hektoen, "Health Conditions and the Practice of Medicine among the Early Norwegian Settlers," *Studies and Records,* 1:46–49.

[4] John G. Smith was a Swede who in the early 1840's represented himself as a minister and a doctor in various Norwegian settlements. When he first appeared at Koshkonong in 1841, he claimed not only that he was a Lutheran minister but that he had been the king's chaplain in Stockholm. His tongue and winsome personality are said to have won him the confidence of "the simple-hearted and shepherdless Norwegians." When Pastor Dietrichson

the paper, but at present money is very scarce. In the afternoon we continued our trip and reached Mineral Point at about eight o'clock in the evening. The land around these two towns is very rough and can certainly not be called attractive. The territory between Madison and Mineral Point consists largely of prairies and some areas covered with scraggly woods. The farms are few and far between.

*March 30.* Here at Mineral Point we also met several Norwegians. This town is somewhat larger than Dodgeville, but money is as scarce here as it was there. Reymert tried to auction off his goods here, too, but the sales brought in only four dollars, which was not enough to pay for our stay in town.

There are many lead mines around these towns, and near Mineral Point a copper mine was recently discovered from which I secured a specimen of the mineral extracted. I inspected one of the smelting houses. The arrangements there did not strike me as being very complex. Card playing and drinking are very common in this region.

*March 31.* We decided to travel on, and so we packed our goods and left about noon. Some six miles out we were forced to stop at a house because I had another attack of the ague. There

arrived there in 1844, however, he found Smith's fortunes at low ebb. "He had administered the Lord's holy sacraments among them and performed all the ministerial functions until his numerous and various lies opened the eyes of many people and enabled them to see that he was merely a self-made pastor. When the Norwegians further discovered that he had openly insulted and blasphemed holy baptism by being baptized anew and joining the Baptist sect, in which he is supposed to have some sort of ordination, most of them departed from him." Evidently to reestablish himself in people's confidence, Smith then sought ordination from Dietrichson, and when this request was refused the self-made pastor was suddenly transformed into a self-made doctor, only to find that Dietrichson again put obstacles in his way by warning the Norwegians against allowing him to practice his "quackeries" upon their bodies. Smith's ire was aroused against a man who challenged his authority in every field of endeavor. It is not surprising, therefore, to find him joining other enemies of Dietrichson (see Chapter 9, note 8). After ill fortune both as pastor and as doctor in Wisconsin, Smith removed to Chicago. See Anderson, *Norwegian Immigration (1821–1840)*, 414–15, and Dietrichson, *Reise blandt de norske Emigranter*, 46, 59.

were three American girls there who were dressed exactly alike from top to toe, but they left for home in the evening.

*April 1*. This morning I was well enough to continue our journey. In the afternoon we reached Hamilton's Diggings (Wiota, by another name) where there also are many lead mines.[5] We stayed here several days with Knud Knudsen, the blacksmith, and were well treated. His wife has been very sick the last five or six weeks.

*April 5*. We had decided to leave this morning but rain delayed us until noon, and we got no farther than Monroe in Green County by evening. The road went through oak woods which at times became dense. The country here was more beautiful and also more thickly inhabited.

*April 6*. I was kept in bed most of the day by the ague. Today the people voted whether to accept or reject the new constitution. The majority in this town voted to reject it. I later learned that this was the case everywhere, the majority for the whole Territory being 6,000 according to reports.[6]

*April 7*. Since I felt well today we continued our trip home-

[5] In its early days Wiota was frequently referred to as Hamilton's Diggings in honor of William S. Hamilton, the son of Alexander Hamilton, who became a mining promoter there in 1827. The community developed rapidly during the following years, and many Norwegian immigrants found employment there. Pastor Dietrichson organized a congregation in Wiota in 1844 which numbered about one hundred members. Dietrichson, *Reise blandt de norske Emigranter*, 80.

[6] The enabling act to admit Wisconsin to the Union was approved by President Polk in August 1846. A state constitution drawn up by an "able body of thoroughly representative men" was submitted to popular vote on April 5, 1847, and defeated by a vote of 20,231 to 14,119. The defeat came as a result of majority dissatisfaction with the articles covering the rights of married women, exemptions, banks, the elective judiciary, and the numerical size of the legislature. A second convention drafted another constitution, which was adopted on March 13, 1848, by a vote of 16,799 to 6,394. This constitution was approved by Congress and signed by the President on May 29, 1848. The attitude of the Norwegian immigrants toward these constitutional questions is discussed briefly by Bayrd Still, "Norwegian-Americans and Wisconsin Politics in the Forties," *Studies and Records*, 8:58–64, and Ole Munch Raeder, *America in the Forties: The Letters of Ole Munch Raeder*, 22–28 (Minneapolis, 1929).

ward. We heard many comments on the misfortune which had struck the constitution, but people seemed well satisfied with the result. Awhile before sunset we reached Janesville, and later in the evening we got to Jefferson Prairie, having covered about fifty miles today.

*April 9.* I spent yesterday in bed, so we could not do anything, but this morning I felt well enough to resume traveling. I arrived home about eight o'clock in the evening, but Reymert, who drove oxen, moved along so slowly that he did not get home until the following Sunday. Both of us were glad to have finished this trip, which was made very unpleasant by sickness.

*June 3.* Arrangements having been completed to establish a post office in our newly created township, with Even Heg duly appointed and sworn in as postmaster, the mail from Milwaukee made its first appearance at the house about three o'clock this afternoon. As the pouch contained nothing for this office and we had nothing to put into it, the mailman's burden neither increased nor decreased because of the visit. But when our printing press is set up, I expect he will have enough to do carrying all the papers away from here. Then his pouch will not be as empty as it was today.

*June 27.* Last Friday Even Heg and son, J. D. Reymert, and I went down to Milwaukee to get a printing press which we had ordered from Philadelphia through a book dealer named Hopkins. It had not arrived when we came there in the afternoon. We were not planning to leave town until the following evening, however, and we hoped that it would come by then. But we were disappointed. We got the type, however, and bought paper and other things necessary for the printing establishment.

It is to be hoped that the Scandinavian people out here in the far West will support the new paper *Nordlyset* and so enable it to enlighten them in many fields of knowledge.[7] By supporting

[7] *Nordlyset* (The Northern Light), the first Norwegian paper in the Middle West, was at first financed by Bache and Heg and edited by Reymert.

such a venture they will also rise in the estimation of the country where they now live and where they expect to spend their future.

*July 5.* Today a great convention is being held in Chicago to discuss the future of the harbors on the Great Lakes.[8] Congress had appropriated large sums of money in their behalf, but the

Erik Anderson, formerly with the *Chicago Tribune*, was secured as type-setter. One Ole Carlsen contracted to deliver the paper in Muskego settlement in return for a pair of overalls the first year and thereafter ten dollars annually. The subscription price was two dollars a year, and as no more than two hundred subscribers were ever obtained, the venture proved to be a financial failure. The very first issue (July 29, 1847) emphasized the American spirit of the paper by including a portion of the Declaration of Independence and some remarks by Daniel Webster. "It declared that its purpose was to enlighten the Norwegian immigrants, who could not as yet readily read the American newspapers, concerning the history and government of the country, to present general news of social and religious interest, to purvey information about happenings in the old country, and to do 'everything else that may be appropriate and useful toward the enlightenment and entertainment of our readers and in harmony with the strictest neutrality in political and religious matters, an ideal that we always and most rigidly will attempt to attain.' " The resolution to observe strict political neutrality evidently could not bear the stress of the times because in September 1848 the names of Van Buren and Adams, the Free Soil candidates, appeared at its masthead while the original slogan "Freedom and Equality," gave way to the Free Soil cry, "Free Land, Free Speech, Free Labor, and Free Man." This Free Soil interlude, however, did not last very long, because Reymert soon became an active Democrat, and Knut Langeland, who succeeded him as editor in the fall of 1849, realized that the Free Soil party had failed to gain much support among the Norwegian immigrants. The new editor, therefore, decided to change both the name and the policy of the paper. The last issue under the original name, *Nordlyset*, appeared on May 18, 1850. Under the new name, *Democraten*, the paper ran from June 8, 1850 until October 29, 1851. *Nordlyset* was printed in Heg's log cabin until the summer of 1848 when the press was moved to the village of Rochester. In the fall of 1849 "Heg and Company" sold the establishment to Langeland, who moved it to Racine. A nearly complete file of *Nordlyset* is in the library of Luther College, Decorah, Iowa. For accounts of this editorial venture, see Blegen, *Norwegian Migration, The American Transition*, 289–99; Reymert, "James Denoon Reymert and the Norwegian Press," *Studies and Records*, 12:79–90; Carl Hansen, "Pressen til Borgerkrigens Slutning," *Norsk-Amerikanernes Festskrift, 1914*, 1–40 (Decorah, Iowa, 1914).

[8] The River and Harbor Convention in Chicago in July 1847 grew out of the indignation of the West at Polk's veto on August 3, 1846, of the River and Harbor Bill, which among other things had carried an appropriation of a half million dollars for the improvement of rivers and harbors in the Great Lakes region. The *St. Louis Republican* started the movement for a conven-

President used these sums to help finance the Mexican War. If the appropriations had been used for harbor improvements as intended, the whole interior of the country would have benefited greatly. But this wise policy was sacrificed by the self-willed President who seems bent on extending the sphere of influence of the southern states and on expanding the boundaries of the country to include California and possibly New Mexico, all of which we could very well do without since there already is territory enough to take care of all the immigrants who annually pour in from Europe. The convention is attended by representatives from towns and counties of Wisconsin Territory as well as from eastern and northern states.

Yesterday it was seventy-one years since the thirteen united colonies declared their independence of the British Crown. That day is held in high esteem by the American people.

*July 22.* As I had received a letter from the probate judge, Reymert and I went down there, reaching the town late in the evening.

*July 24.* I took Reymert along this time because I wished him to assume my place as executor of Johansen's will. Since the judge would not allow this, we left Southport at once and went to Racine where we managed to make the desired arrangement.

tion in September 1846, and a preliminary meeting in New York later that month passed a resolution approving the recommendation of the western press and proposing that the meeting be held in Chicago. Some 2,315 enrolled delegates, representing nineteen states, attended the three-day meeting, although *De Bow's Review* in New Orleans said that between five and eight thousand people were present at the convention. Many prominent men were there, such as Horace Greeley, Thurlow Weed, a half dozen governors, and many congressmen. Abraham Lincoln was the delegate from Sangamon County, Illinois. Interest in the meeting was bi-partisan, and letters of support were read from Thomas Hart Benton, Daniel Webster, Henry Clay, Martin Van Buren, Thomas Cass, etc. The speeches and resolutions emphasized the great growth and importance of the commerce on the western lakes and rivers and stressed the need for adequate federal aid. In his letter to the *New York Tribune* on the third and last day, Greeley wrote: "Thus has met, deliberated, harmonized, acted and separated, one of the most important and interesting conventions ever held in this or any other country. . . ."

*July 27.* Having received the proper papers dealing with the sale of Johansen's land, I went up to Prairieville today to put an announcement in the paper.

*July 28.* After breakfast I left for Milwaukee and there ran the announcement in the German and one of the English papers. On my way to Milwaukee I posted notices in three public places in the township where the land is located. About half past four o'clock I left town and got home about ten o'clock, after which I worked in our printing shop until three o'clock in the morning before going to bed.

*August 1.* Just as we had eaten dinner, a carriage drove up to the printing shop. A man came in and told us that he, together with Consul General Løvenskjold and wife, had come to America to visit the Norwegian settlements because of the many rumors and reports concerning them in Norway.[9] Later he told me that he had been sent by the government to study American institutions and that he had been on similar missions in France and England. His name, it seems, is Munch Räder, and he is a native of Trondhjem.[10] He claimed also that he was editor of *Storthings*

[9] Adam Christoffer Løvenskjold (1804–1886) came of a well-known Dano-Norwegian family. He was the first Norwegian to hold important diplomatic positions after the union with Sweden in 1814. At various times he was minister to Berlin, Washington, and The Hague. After leaving the diplomatic service in 1858 he served as "gentleman of the bedchamber" (kammerjunker) at the Norwegian court. At the time when he visited the Norwegian settlements in the West he was consul general in New York. He published an official report of his observations entitled *Beretning om de norske Setlere i Nordamerika* (Bergen, 1848). His report painted rather an unfavorable picture of conditions among the immigrants and aroused considerable resentment on this side of the Atlantic. He summed up his impressions of Muskego as follows: "The settlement has the reputation of being unhealthful, as there are many lakes and large swamps. Some of the settlers live on timber land covering a region of sandy hills. Some government land is found here but few wish to buy it, as it consists chiefly of swamps." See Knut Gjerset's translation of the report, "An Account of the Norwegian Settlers in North America," *Wisconsin Magazine of History,* 8:79 (September 1924).

[10] Ole Munch Raeder, a prominent jurist and former editor of *Storthings Efterretninger*, was commissioned by the Norwegian government to study the jury system in England, the United States, and Canada. He arrived in America in the spring of 1847 and remained until the fall of 1848. His find-

*Efterretninger.* They stayed here only three or four hours, after which they took the road toward Prairieville as they were going to visit the rest of the settlements in the Territory. Before leaving this neighborhood, they also called on Hansen, the gymnastic teacher, whom they had missed on the way out. I suspect that the purpose of their trip was not exactly what they pretended it to be.

ings were published in a three-volume work which helped clear the way for the introduction of the jury system in Norway. Raeder was an intelligent observer who took a keen interest in all aspects of American life. While in this country he wrote a number of letters, many of which were published in various Norwegian newspapers. They contain a wealth of information about American society at the time and give one of the best contemporary accounts of immigrant life in the Middle West. These letters were translated by Gunnar Malmin and published under the title *America in the Forties: The Letters of Ole Munch Raeder.*

# 15. And So Farewell America

*September 17 [1847].* FOR A LONG TIME I have been talking of going to Norway, but difficulties have always arisen making it necessary to postpone the trip. Now, however, the day has finally come. This morning, after many preparations I left with Hans Heg, who took me to Milwaukee. Immediately on my arrival there at about four o'clock in the afternoon, I learned that a steamer bound for Buffalo was expected. I was pleased that I would not have to stay in Milwaukee a long while. During my short wait for the boat I said farewell to a few friends and acquaintances in the city. About nine o'clock I boarded the steamer *Illinois.* There I met three Norwegians from our settlement who were going north to Sheboygan, a distance of about sixty miles, to look for land. The boat left after a brief stay, and the trip across the Great Lakes had begun.

*September 22.* Early this morning we finally arrived at Buffalo, and I made arrangements for continuing my trip. After breakfast I therefore went to the railway station, and the matter was soon taken care of. Then I took a trip to Niagara Falls. Though I had been there once before, the desire to see the Falls again was so strong that I could not resist it, and as the distance is only twenty-two miles it did not take me long to get there. I did not seem to be as profoundly impressed by the Falls and its furious rush of waters now as I was the first time I  saw this unparalleled natural wonder.

The stay at Buffalo was very short. I continued my trip the same day and reached New York on the afternoon of the 24th. I suppose I could say something about this lap of my journey, but I shall refrain from so doing since I would run the risk of repeating much of what I have already related about my trip through this part of New York state in 1842. I followed the same route then as now, passing through the same towns and districts, only that I went by rail a little farther this time than last. Thus we passed through the town of Auburn where a penitentiary is located. Seen from the outside the institution makes a pleasant appearance, but God knows what the life inside must be like with its slavery and bondage.

*September 25.* The weather was very bad today as it rained continuously from morning till evening. The storm began yesterday afternoon while we were on the Hudson and there was no letup. I am glad I was not out on the Atlantic in such weather. Today I have been forced to stay indoors most of the time in spite of the monotony. I did, however, buy an umbrella which enabled me to venture out a little while. I had supper and spent the evening with one of my friends.

*September 26.* Today the weather was as beautiful as it was stormy yesterday. People have been busy attending church. After dinner I went out to visit Chamberlain Løvenskjold and was well received by him and his wife. I was introduced to a certain T. Heierdahl, employed in Løvenskjold's office, and another Norwegian whose name I do not recall. There were two maids in the house, one Norwegian and one American. Evidently realizing that I was unmarried, Løvenskjold very gallantly offered me his Norwegian maid for a wife. At this I scraped and bowed and hemmed and hawed, endeavoring somehow to make my reaction plain. The gentlemen seemed to get the point and accepted it in good humor. I stayed there until some time in the evening when I returned to my hotel.

*September 27.* Today I inquired about passage to Europe and learned that the quickest way to get there was by steamer. This would presumably be the most expensive way of traveling, but the time on the ocean would be reduced, which is an important consideration at this season. Furthermore, I could get passage on a steamer leaving the first of next month. So I went down to D. Brigham, 6 Wall Street, and paid my fare thus settling the question. The *Britannia*, the steamer I am to take, was in dock undergoing repairs as she had sustained some damages. It took ninety-six men four days to repair the ship.

*September 29.* Today I bade my acquaintances farewell, and at parting they gave me something to put in my pocket which I will keep quiet about. I had to go to Boston to board my boat, no one being allowed to embark in New York. Just what was to be gained by this I do not know, nor do I seriously care. Before leaving I became acquainted with a certain Andrew Peterson of Boston, a native of Kongsberg and a tinsmith by profession. If his business in New York had been completed he would have accompanied me to Boston, so he said. At least he did accompany me to the pier where we chatted for about an hour before he left. A little later, about five o'clock, the boat started up Long Island Sound.

*September 30.* About half past five this morning I arrived by train at Boston, having traveled partly by boat and partly by rail. I then took my luggage up to one of the so-called Eating Houses where I had breakfast after which I went out to see the city. It occurred to me that I should go to the Bunker Hill Monument and see this famous place. It stood on a beautifully leveled height encircled by an iron railing, and on the base the monument was erected of cut stone in the form of a column facing north, south, east, and west by virtue of its four sides. When I asked about the height of the monument, one of those present said it was about two hundred and twenty feet — not so small a height! Around it was a black-painted railwork of iron. On one side of the monument was an entrance and inside it a pillar of hewn stone. Between the outer and inner monuments was a stairway of similar material. With the other observers, some five or six in number, I climbed the stairs to the top, where there was a floor and at a convenient height above it four apertures, each with an iron facing and each opening in a different direction. We passed from one to the other opening to look out on the surroundings to a considerable distance. The view would have been more impressive if it had been morning, with sunshine and clear weather, but I had a beautiful outlook upon the city. When we had satisfied our curiosity, we slunk down like thieves, each to his corner. Since I could not stand the lodgings I had taken and would not stay there overnight, I got a man to take my baggage to the *Britannia*, after which I could find a room wherever I pleased and escape the people in the house. When this had been done, I used the rest of the day as I had done the earlier part, and in the evening I found a room in a hotel near the first one.

*October 1*. At eleven o'clock this forenoon I went aboard, and other passengers were embarking all the time. A couple of hours later the boat was ready to leave, and those who had followed friends on board had to go ashore. There was a great waving of handkerchiefs, both from the deck and from the pier, and we joined in shouting a triple hurrah. When the boat had maneuvered a right turn, it fired a double salute. By three o'clock we were already so far out that we dropped our pilot.

*October 3*. This morning as I came on deck I could see the coast of New Brunswick, and before long we were steaming up toward Halifax. The city and its environs pleased me very much. In the background there was a picturesque fortress. We stayed in the harbor some four or five hours, many passengers leaving the boat while others came on. About two o'clock we left the pier, setting our course for Europe — and so farewell America.[1]

---

[1] Since this ends Bache's contact with America, we omit the few remaining pages of the diary. He landed in Liverpool on October 16 and soon left for Hull. Later he spent several days sight-seeing in Edinburgh. On November 1 he sailed from Leith with the Norwegian boat *Dovre*, captain, G. Gulbrandsen, arriving on November 4 in Drammen where, a few days later, he refers to himself as "going about among the other guests like a foreigner and a stranger even though many of them were acquaintances of mine from former days."

# Appendix

At the outset of chapter 4, Bache includes the passenger list of the *Johanna*. This the editor has chosen to reproduce, in translation, as an appendix.

Bache writes, "For the sake of clarity I shall here list all the passengers who in 1843 embarked at Drammen for New York on the sailing vessel *Johanna*, Captain Luider Mensing." Thereupon he presents the list, with several columns giving specific items of information.

The Norwegian-American Historical Association has in its archives a photostat of the official manifest of the *Johanna* as made out by Captain Mensing at the port of New York on July 22, 1843, the date of arrival.

Bache's list, differing in the order of names and in some other details, is as follows:

| Name | Home | Position or Profession | Age | With Board | Without Board |
|---|---|---|---|---|---|
| Mr. Christopher Jagsland............ | Rögen | Saddler | 46 | | 20 specie dollars |
| Mrs. Gunild Torgersdatter........... | Rögen | | 37 | | 20 specie dollars |
| Son Jens Christophersen............ | Rögen | | 12 | | 20 specie dollars |
| Son Hans Christophersen............ | Rögen | | 7 | | 18 specie dollars |
| Son Andreas Christophersen......... | Rögen | | 2 | | 15 specie dollars |
| Daughter Thrine Christophersen..... | Rögen | | 10 | | 18 specie dollars |
| Anne Thoresdatter ................. | Rögen | Servant girl | 59 | | 20 specie dollars |
| Mr. Peder Gaarder ................. | Land | Farmer | 43 | | 20 specie dollars |
| Mrs. Randine Olsdatter ............ | Land | | 33 | | 20 specie dollars |
| Son Hans Pedersen ................. | Land | | 9 | | 17 2 12 |
| Daughter Ingeborg Pedersdatter..... | Land | | 11 | | 17 2 12 |
| Daughter Karen Pedersdatter........ | Land | | 5 | | 17 2 12 |
| Daughter Oline Pedersdatter........ | Land | | 3 | | 17 2 12 |

| Name | Home | Position or Profession | Age | With Board | Without Board |
|---|---|---|---|---|---|
| Anne Mathea Nielsdatter........ | Land | Servant girl | 19 | | 20 specie dollars |
| Søren Olsen................. | Land | Hired man | 20 | | 20 specie dollars |
| Mr. Harald Pedersen Omstad.... | Land | Farmer | 49 | | 20 specie dollars |
| Mrs. Anne Eriksdatter........ | Land | | 62 | | 20 specie dollars |
| Son Hans Haraldsen........... | Land | | 22½ | | 20 specie dollars |
| Son Christian Haraldsen....... | Land | | 20 | | 20 specie dollars |
| Mr. Anders Michelsen......... | Land | Farmer | 38 | | 20 specie dollars |
| Mrs. Ingeborg Pedersdatter..... | Land | | 35 | | 20 specie dollars |
| Son Michel Andersen.......... | Land | | 8 | | 17  2  12 |
| Son Johannes Andersen........ | Land | | 6 | | 17  2  12 |
| Son Peder Andersen........... | Land | | ½ | | 15 specie dollars |
| Bachelor Hellik Olsen......... | Flesberg | Mason | 25 | 28 | |
| Bachelor Guul Guttormsen Illianstad.. | Modum | Farmer | 27 | 28 | |
| Bachelor Truls Rasmussen...... | Drammen | Unskilled laborer | 31 | 28 | |
| Joseph Jonassen ............. | Holmestrand | Hired man | 27 | 28 | |
| Mr. Ole Bogstrand........... | Modum | Farmer | 31 | | 20 specie dollars |
| Mrs. Anne Michelsdatter....... | Modum | | 32 | | 20 specie dollars |
| Bachelor Louis Bernhard Gooyde.. | Modum | Baker | 39 | 28 | |
| Mr. Ole Knudsen Arka........ | Lier | Farmer | 60 | | 20 specie dollars |
| Mrs. Ingeborg Svendsdatter..... | Lier | | 32 | | 20 specie dollars |
| Mr. Peder Helgesen........... | Drammen | Journeyman-Joiner | 28 | | 20 specie dollars |
| Mrs. Anne Karine Helgesen..... | Drammen | | 28 | | 20 specie dollars |
| Mr. Johannes Lie............ | Gudbrandsdalen | Farmer | 45 | 28 | |

| Name | Place | Occupation | | | Amount |
|---|---|---|---|---|---|
| Bachelor Peder Nielsen Brudahl | Gudbrandsdalen | Hired man | 22½ | 28 | |
| Simon Olsen Lilie | Drammen | Carpenter | 23½ | 28 | |
| Mr. Ole Gomperud | Drammen | | 50 | | 20 specie dollars |
| Mrs. Berthe Webjörnsdatter | Drammen | | 46 | | 20 specie dollars |
| Son Engelhart Olsen | Drammen | | 16½ | | 20 specie dollars |
| Gabriel Olsen | Drammen | | 7 | | 17 2 12 |
| Julius Olsen | Drammen | | 3 | | 17 2 12 |
| Daughter Sôrine Olsdatter | Drammen | | 15 | | 20 specie dollars |
| Lene Olsdatter | Drammen | | 11½ | | 17 2 12 |
| Petra Olsdatter | Drammen | | 8½ | | 17 2 12 |
| Mr. Ole Knudsen Siverspladsen | Hallingdal | Farmer | 40 | | 20 specie dollars |
| Mrs. Margith Knudsdatter | Hallingdal | | 37 | | 20 specie dollars |
| Daughter Barbro | Hallingdal | | 7½ | | 17 2 12 |
| Daughter Margith | Hallingdal | | 2½ | | 17 2 12 |
| Kari Anundsdatter Berg | Hallingdal | Servant girl | 22 | | 20 specie dollars |
| Iver Olsen Naerum | Hallingdal | Hired man | 20½ | | 20 specie dollars |
| Mr. Even Olsen Ønska | Hallingdal | Farmer | 35 | | 20 specie dollars |
| Mrs. Siri Kittelsdatter | Hallingdal | | 35½ | | 20 specie dollars |
| Son Ole Evensen | Hallingdal | | 5 | | 17 2 12 |
| Daughter Mari Evensdatter | Hallingdal | | 1½ | | 15 specie dollars |
| Mr. Cleophas Klokkerstuen | Hallingdal | Farmer | 29 | | 20 specie dollars |
| Mrs. Kari Nielsdatter | Hallingdal | | 26 | | 20 specie dollars |
| Son Halvor Kleofassen | Hallingdal | | 1 | | 15 specie dollars |
| Mr. Levor Mile | Hallingdal | | 38 | | 20 specie dollars |
| Mrs. Guri Christiansdatter | Hallingdal | | 37 | | 20 specie dollars |
| Son Herbrand Levorsen | Hallingdal | | 11½ | | 17 2 12 |

| Name | Home | Position or Profession | Age | With Board | Without Board |
|---|---|---|---|---|---|
| Son Christian Levorsen.............. | Hallingdal | | 8 | | 17 2 12 |
| Son Knud Levorsen.............. | Hallingdal | | ½ | | 15 specie dollars |
| Daughter Aase Levorsdatter............. | Hallingdal | | 14 | | 20 specie dollars |
| Daughter Guri Levorsdatter.............. | Hallingdal | | 6 | | 17 2 12 |
| Daughter Ingeborg Levorsdatter.............. | Hallingdal | | 2½ | | 17 2 12 |
| Karen Olsdatter ............. | Røgen | Servant girl | 22½ | 28 | |
| Mrs. Marthe Skougen............. | Rygge | | 57 | 28 | |
| Son Marthin Christiansen............. | Rygge | | 22 | 28 | |
| Bachelor Søren Bache............. | Lier | Farmer | 29 | 60 Cabin | |
| Andreas Larsen ............. | Hedemarken | Hired boy | 15 | 28 | |
| Berthe Olsdatter ............. | Drammen | Servant girl | 23 | 28 | |
| Bachelor Christopher Aamodt............. | Modum | Freeholder's son | 23 | 28 | |
| Bachelor Peder Aamodt............. | Modum | | 19 | 28 | |
| Ingeborg Sørine Jensdatter............. | Drammen | Servant girl | 22 | 28 | |
| Mr. Lars Houkelien............. | Røgen | Farmer | 31 | | 20 specie dollars |
| Mrs. Berthe Hansdatter............. | Røgen | | 32 | | 20 specie dollars |
| Daughter Anne Mathea Larsdatter............. | Røgen | | 7 | | 17 2 12 |
| Daughter Caroline Larsdatter ............. | Røgen | | 5 | | 17 2 12 |
| Son Hans Peter Larsen............. | Røgen | | 2½ | | 17 2 12 |
| Hanna Axelsen ............. | Drammen | Servant girl | 21½ | 28 | |
| Mr. Anders Brynildsen............. | Drammen | Cabinet maker | 36 | 50 Cabin | |
| Mrs. Anne Brynildsen............. | Drammen | | 40 | 50 Cabin | |

| Name | Place | Occupation | | | |
|---|---|---|---|---|---|
| Peder Jensen ............... | Lier | Hired man | 25 | 28 | |
| Niels Sørensen ............ | Drammen | | 30 | 28 | 20 specie dollars |
| Mr. Krogh ................. | Drammen | Gunsmith | 30 | | 20 specie dollars |
| Mrs. Catharina Krogh....... | Drammen | | 34 | | 20 specie dollars |
| Daughter Nicoline Andrea Krogh. | Drammen | | 4½ | | 17 2 12 |
| Son Bernhard Julius Krogh.... | Drammen | | 3 | | 17 2 12 |
| Son Peder Gustav Krogh...... | Drammen | | ¼ | | 15 specie dollars |
| Hans Petter Johansen ........ | Drammen | Hired man | 25 | | 20 specie dollars |
| Lars Jørgen Hansen ......... | Drammen | Hired man | 23 | | 20 specie dollars |
| Josephine Eriksen .......... | Drammen | Servant girl | 14 | | 20 specie dollars |
| Bachelor John Christensen.... | Drammen | Blacksmith | 28 | 28 | |
| Mr. C. L. Clausen........... | Denmark | Teacher | 23 | 50 Cabin | |
| Mrs. Martha Clausen......... | Denmark | | 27 | 50 Cabin | |
| Bachelor Hans Jacob Hansen... | Drammen | Shoemaker | 26 | | 20 specie dollars |
| Bachelor Jens Hellum........ | Modum | Farmer | 34 | 28 | |
| Mr. Jens Strøm............. | Ringerige | Farmer | 40 | 28 | |
| Mrs. Randi Amundsdatter .... | Ringerige | | 41 | 28 | |
| Son Hans Andrias Jensen .... | Ringerige | | 2½ | 24 | |
| Knud Olsen Asdørdalen ...... | Lier | Hired man | 23 | | 20 specie dollars |
| Bachelor Amund Aamot....... | Modum | Farmer | 33 | 28 | |
| Mr. Peder Nielsen Søløs ..... | Eger | Farmer | 32 | | 20 specie dollars |
| Bachelor Ole H. Øvern....... | Ringerige | Farmer | 30 | | 20 specie dollars |
| Bachelor Colbjørn H. Øvern... | Ringerige | | 27 | | 20 specie dollars |
| Marie Clemetsdatter ........ | Ringerige | Servant girl | 22 | | 20 specie dollars |
| Simon Hansen Østre Lie...... | Gudbrandsdalen | | 18 | 28 | |
| Bachelor Torger Solem....... | Ringerige | Farmer | 26 | 28 | |

| Name | Home | Position or Profession | Age | With Board | Without Board |
|---|---|---|---|---|---|
| Mr. John Helgesen .......... | Drammen | Merchant | 42 | | 20 specie dollars |
| Mrs. Anne Louise (Died Sept. 2) .... | Drammen | | 45 | | 20 specie dollars |
| Son Hans Helgesen.......... | Drammen | | 14 | | 20 specie dollars |
| Son Edvard Helgesen.......... | Drammen | | 12 | | 20 specie dollars |
| Daughter Anne Margrethe .......... | Drammen | | 10 | | 17 2 12 |
| Daughter Gunnild Marie .......... | Drammen | | 7 | | 17 2 12 |
| Bachelor Gunder Evensen Jahren.......... | Modum | Farmer | 25 | 28 | |
| Widower Christopher O. Svendsen.......... | Ringerige | Farmer | 52 | 28 | |
| Son Ole Christophersen.......... | Ringerige | Farmer | 23 | 28 | |
| Daughter Caroline Christophersdatter.......... | Ringerige | | 7½ | 25 2 12 | |
| Daughter Gunnild Christophersdatter.......... | Ringerige | | 4 | 25 2 12 | |
| Mr. Hans Ulen.......... | Modum | Farmer | 50 | 28 | |
| Mrs. Bolethe Thorsdatter .......... | Modum | | 34 | 28 | |
| | | | | 1203— | 1596 specie dollars |

5 Cabin passengers

34 Steerage passengers with board .......... 260 specie dollars

943 specie dollars

84 Steerage passengers without board .......... 1586 specie dollars

Total 123 passengers .......... Total 2789 specie dollars

232

Drammen, May 22, 1843
L. MENSING
*Captain*

# Index

Aaby, Lars, immigrant, 209
Aadland, Mons Knudsen, pioneer, described, 121–22
Aamodt, Christopher Olsen, 80, 207; marriage, 97; home, 106–107, 108, 128–29, 130–31, 145, 172
Agriculture on the frontier, 20, 36, 37–38, 155, 177, 191, 202, 207; sheep, 132
America, described, 7, 8–9; settlement of, 118–19, 142
"America fever," ix, 3
*Argus* (Wisconsin), quoted, 206
Arista, Mariano, Mexican general, 199
Auburn penitentiary, 223

Bache, Marie, daughter of Søren, vii, 33 n. 2; quoted, xix
Bache, Niels, Søren's brother, xi, 70, 124, 144
Bache, Søren, writings evaluated, v, vi, xiv; travels, vi, 3–26, 28–40, 46–68, 74–86, 110–16, 175, 179–81, 195, 222–25; character, xi–xii, xiv, xix, 25; attitudes, xii, 100, 103, 138–40, 157, 202; fight against "papistry," xiv, 133–38; businessman, vi, xiv–xv, xviii, 39–40, 179–80, 182–84, 187–88, 194–95, 197–98, 210, 219–20; marriage, xviii; homes, xviii–xix, 40, 42–43, 44, 99; illness, 157, 208, 211, 212, 215, 216
Bache, Tollef O., father of Søren Bache, 70, 83 n. 4, 144; Haugean activities, ix–xi
Baltimore, Maryland, described, 57
Beaver Creek settlement, described, 11–12
Bellerud, Sheriff, 105–106, 126–27, 145
Beloit, Wisconsin, growth of, 186
*Book of Homilies*, 155, 209
Boston, Massachusetts, described, 53–54

Breck, James Lloyd, frontier pastor, 149
Brooklyn, New York, described, 51–52
Brownsboro, Texas, settlement, 96 n. 4
Brynildsen, Anne, 69, 102, 109–10
Budde, Jan Adolph, Norwegian educator, xvii–xviii
Buffalo Synod, 89 n.
Bunker Hill Monument, 224–25

Canada, 47–48
Chicago, unhealthful, 12; described, 30–31, 34; growth of, 34, 117; Norwegian settlement in, xii n. 6, 34 n. 3, 104 n. 3
Christensen, John, blacksmith, 183, 187–88
Churches on the frontier, described, 148 n. 2, 204–205 n. 3
Clausen, C. L., Pastor, xiii, xiv, 83 n. 4, 84, 85–86, 121; ordination, 89–95, 152–54; described, 90–91, 92, 138; innovations, 96, 97; charity work, 103; home life, 109; his report on his work, 133–36; Romanism, xiv, 133–38, 162, 164–65; Muskego dedication, 150–52; dispute over church, 152–54, 155, 164–65, 167–71; business dealings, 183–84; farewell sermon, 208; marriage (second), 212
Congress, session described, 59
*Constitutionen*, Norwegian steamship, 67 n. 3
Coos, Henry A., clerk of court, 95
Corneliusen, Carl, immigrant, 54–55, 61–62

Danielsen, Gitle, 97, Mormon convert, 140
Danish immigrants, 10, 12, 56, 89, 122–23, 127